THE CONCEPT OF CARE IN CURRICULUM STUDIES

"The link that the author explicitly makes between self-care and the care for the other in the context of Korean education and cross-cultural experiences makes important contributions to reexamining the relationship between self and other in autobiography, cross-cultural settings, and curriculum studies."
     Hongyu Wang, Oklahoma State University—Tulsa, USA

"Jung-Hoon Jung connects various inquiry domains such as curriculum studies, problems of modern schooling, moral education, and curriculum methods. Relating the *currere* method to caring philosophy is clearly a practical approach to deal with/solve personal, psychological, and interpersonal problems which present educators and students are faced with under competition and standards-based curriculum reform in the U.S. and other countries."
     Young Chun Kim, Chinju National University of Education, South Korea

The question at the heart of the book is what might an education with self-care and care-for-others look like? Juxtaposing self-understanding through the method of *currere* and the historical character of *hakbeolism* (a concept indigenous to Korea referring to a kind of social status people achieve based on a shared academic background), this book articulates how subjective reconstruction of self in conjunction with historical study can be transformative, and how this can be extended to social change. Articulating how having one's own standard can be a way of making one's life a work of art, the author looks at how Korean schooling exercises coercive care, disconfirmation, and the "whip of love" for the children's own good. Emphasis is given to the internalized status of these practices in both students and teachers and to teachers' and parents' culpability not only in exercising but also in reproducing these practices through themselves.

Going beyond describing and analyzing the educational problem of academic (intellectual) achievement-oriented education based on aggressive competition, this book suggests ways to address these issues through autobiography (using the method of *currere* to reconstruct one's subjectivity) and an ethic of care.

Jung-Hoon Jung holds a Ph.D. from the University of British Columbia, Canada.

STUDIES IN CURRICULUM THEORY
William F. Pinar, Series Editor

Sandlin/Maudlin (Eds.)	**Disney, Culture, and Curriculum**
Jung-Hoon Jung	**The Concept of Care in Curriculum Studies: Juxtaposing** *Currere* **and** *Hakbeolism*
Nohl/Somel	**Education and Social Dynamics: A Multilevel Analysis of Curriculum Change in Turkey**
Ng-A-Fook/Ibrahim/Reis (Eds.)	**Provoking Curriculum Studies: Strong Poetry and the Arts of the Possible in Education**
Tröhler/Lenz (Eds.)	**Trajectories in the Development of Modern School Systems: Between the National and the Global**
Popkewitz (Ed.)	**The "Reason" of Schooling: Historicizing Curriculum Studies, Pedagogy, and Teacher Education**
Henderson (Ed.)	**Reconceptualizing Curriculum Development: Inspiring and Informing Action**
Magrini	**Social Efficiency and Instrumentalism in Education: Critical Essays in Ontology, Phenomenology, and Philosophical Hermeneutics**
Wang	**Nonviolence and Education: Cross-Cultural Pathways**
Hurren/Hasebe-Ludt (Eds.)	**Contemplating Curriculum: Genealogies/Times/Places**
Pinar (Ed.)	**International Handbook of Curriculum Research, Second Edition**
Latta	**Curricular Conversations: Play is the (Missing) Thing**
Doll	**Pragmatism, Post-Modernism, and Complexity Theory: The "Fascinating Imaginative Realm" of William E. Doll, Jr. Edited by Donna Trueit**

Carlson	The Education of Eros: A History of Education and the Problem of Adolescent Sexuality Since 1950
Taubman	Disavowed Knowledge: Psychoanalysis, Education, and Teaching
Pinar	What Is Curriculum Theory? Second Edition
Tröhler	Languages of Education: Protestant Legacies, National Identities, and Global Aspirations
Hendry	Engendering Curriculum History
Handa	What Does Understanding Mathematics Mean for Teachers? Relationship as a Metaphor for Knowing
Joseph (Ed.)	Cultures of Curriculum, Second Edition
Sandlin/Schultz/Burdick (Eds.)	Handbook of Public Pedagogy: Education and Learning Beyond Schooling
Malewski (Ed.)	Curriculum Studies Handbook—The Next Moment
Pinar	The Wordliness of a Cosmopolitan Education: Passionate Lives in Public Service
Taubman	Teaching By Numbers: Deconstructing the Discourse of Standards and Accountability in Education
Appelbaum	Children's Books for Grown-Up Teachers: Reading and Writing Curriculum Theory
Eppert/Wang (Eds.)	Cross-Cultural Studies in Curriculum: Eastern Thought, Educational Insights
Jardine/Friesen/Clifford	Curriculum in Abundance
Autio	Subjectivity, Curriculum, and Society: Between and Beyond German Didaktik and Anglo-American Curriculum Studies
Brantlinger (Ed.)	Who Benefits from Special Education?: Remediating (Fixing) Other People's Children

Pinar/Irwin (Eds.)	**Curriculum in a New Key: The Collected Works of Ted T. Aoki**
Reynolds/Webber (Eds.)	**Expanding Curriculum Theory: Dis/Positions and Lines of Flight**
McKnight	**Schooling, The Puritan Imperative, and the Molding of an American National Identity: Education's "Errand Into the Wilderness"**
Pinar (Ed.)	**International Handbook of Curriculum Research**
Morris	**Curriculum and the Holocaust: Competing Sites of Memory and Representation**
Doll	**Like Letters In Running Water: A Mythopoetics of Curriculum**
Westbury/Hopmann/Riquarts (Eds.)	**Teaching as a Reflective Practice: The German Didaktic Tradition**
Reid	**Curriculum as Institution and Practice: Essays in the Deliberative Tradition**
Pinar (Ed.)	**Queer Theory in Education**
Huebner	**The Lure of the Transcendent: Collected Essays by Dwayne E. Huebner. Edited by Vikki Hillis. Collected and Introduced by William F. Pinar**

For additional information on titles in the Studies in Curriculum Theory series, visit **www.routledge.com/education**.

THE CONCEPT OF CARE IN CURRICULUM STUDIES

Juxtaposing *Currere* and *Hakbeolism*

Jung-Hoon Jung

LONDON AND NEW YORK

First published 2016
by Routledge

2 Park Square, Milton Park, Abingdon, Oxfordshire OX14 4RN
52 Vanderbilt Avenue, New York, NY 10017

Routledge is an imprint of the Taylor & Francis Group, an informa business

First issued in paperback 2018

Copyright © 2016 Taylor & Francis

The right of Jung-Hoon Jung to be identified as author of this work has been asserted by him in accordance with sections 77 and 78 of the Copyright, Designs and Patents Act 1988.

All rights reserved. No part of this book may be reprinted or reproduced or utilised in any form or by any electronic, mechanical, or other means, now known or hereafter invented, including photocopying and recording, or in any information storage or retrieval system, without permission in writing from the publishers.

Notice:
Product or corporate names may be trademarks or registered trademarks, and are used only for identification and explanation without intent to infringe.

Library of Congress Cataloguing in Publication Data
Names: Jung, Jung-Hoon, author.
Title: The concept of care in curriculum studies : juxtaposing currere and hakbeolism / by Jung-Hoon Jung.
Description: New York, NY : Routledge, 2016. | Series: Studies in curriculum theory | Includes bibliographical references.
Identifiers: LCCN 2015032535 | ISBN 9781138935044 (hbk) | ISBN 9781315676258 (ebk)
Subjects: LCSH: Education—Social aspects—Korea (South) | Education—Moral and ethical aspects—Korea (South) | Self (Philosophy)
Classification: LCC LC191.8.K6 J86 2016 | DDC 370.95195—dc23
LC record available at http://lccn.loc.gov/2015032535

ISBN: 978-1-138-93504-4 (hbk)
ISBN: 978-1-138-34182-1 (pbk)

Typeset in Bembo
by Apex CoVantage, LLC

Dedicated to my wife, Se Jin Lee

CONTENTS

Foreword by William E. Doll, Jr.   xi
Acknowledgments   xv

Introduction   1
Lamenting   1
Subjectivity in Danger   3
An Arduous Step   4
Overview of the Chapters   6

1 Hakbeolism   9
What Is Hakbeolism?   9
The Birth of Hakbeolism   12
The Growth of Hakbeolism   12
The Dire Consequences of Hakbeolism   15
Conclusion   20

2 The Reciprocity of *Currere*, a Reconstruction of Self, and Autobiographical Theory   25
Introduction   25
Currere and Its Philosophical and Theoretical Groundings   27
Circumstances of the Study   29
Breakdown and the Arrested Self   31
Understanding: Recognizing the Distance Phenomenon and Witnessing Signals   32
Understanding: Anxiety and Paradox   35

	Incorporation	37
	The Dialectic of Anxiety	39
	The Reciprocity of *Currere*	41
3	**An Ethic of Care**	**44**
	Introduction	44
	Roots of the Ethic of Care	46
	An Ethic of Care and Ethics of Justice	59
	Coercive Caring	61
	Reciprocity and Inclusion	63
	Conclusion	64
4	**Self-Care and Self-Understanding**	**68**
	Introduction	68
	Self-Care	68
	Self-Understanding Through Autobiographical Study As a Form of Self-Care	73
	Having One's Own Standard	76
	Conclusion	78
5	**Care-For-Others**	**80**
	Introduction	80
	The King's Speech: A Jungian Take	82
	Disconfirmation, Love, and Anomaly	89
	Semantic Environment and Speech	91
	Compliance of Others in Disavowing a Student's Inner Voice	94
	Implications of *The King's Speech* on the Self–Other Relationship	96
	Conclusion	99
6	**Self-Care and Care-For-Others**	**102**
	Introduction	102
	Distance Between Ethics and Repressive Structures	105
	Understanding Love	108
	Discernment and Distance	113
	Conclusion	116

Conclusion	*119*
References	*129*
Index	*139*

FOREWORD

William E. Doll, Jr.

> "Can we care for others, if we are not caring for ourselves?"
> *Carl Leggo (2011, p. 77)*

This quotation illuminates the thread running through the six chapters of Jung-Hoon Jung's *The Concept of Care in Curriculum Studies*. The first three chapters, personal in their expression, form a triad that Jung-Hoon revisits in the final three chapters. In this way lived experience is intertwined with scholarly analysis, producing a multilayered book, one worthy of many visits.

Jung-Hoon begins his book with a poem he wrote expressing his feelings of grief, angst, and sorrow that flowed over him when he realized that a boy he knew was no longer on the elevator they took from their respective apartments on the way to school. The teenager had thrown himself off a railing in the high-rise apartment he lived, saying in a note to his mother: "Mom, I cannot endure this pain any more. My brain nibbles my heart. I am sorry." This young man had indeed lost his soul, his being, his subjectivity. Jung-Hoon then delves historically into Korea's culture of Hakbeolism—thousands of years old—and its current disastrous effect on Korea's educational system. Here one is defined not in terms of self but in terms of test scores and other external standards. One is trapped in an inauthentic relationship with one's self. Suicide in Korea is sometimes seen as the only way out.

Jung-Hoon's way out is through a deep study of William Pinar's *currere*. To say that Jung-Hoon's analysis of *currere* is brilliant is hardly to do it justice. Much, mostly academic, has been written about *currere*, but in Jung-Hoon's hands it acquires a soul, a spirit, a process with vitality. *Currere* allows Jung-Hoon to claim his own existence, to escape the cultural devastation of Hakbeolism.

In his struggle with finding his own voice, his subjectivity—something no one can do for another—Jung Hoon realizes that this struggle is an ethical one: personal, political, psychological. Here he turns to Nel Noddings and her study of ethics in its various forms. Noddings takes what many call a "maternal view" of ethics: one based not on a traditional (Kantian) ethics, with its strict rules and procedures, but one based on a *feeling* of compassion for the other. Noddings's work forms a foundation for Jung-Hoon's feelings of compassion for those who chose suicide and for his own reconstructed subjectivity utilizing *currere*.

In the final three chapters, Jung-Hoon engages two huge issues, each vitally important to him, but also of value to anyone wishing to develop his or her own subjectivity (own sense of Being). These issues are self-care, care-for-others, and the association between them. His first chapter in this new triad (Chapter 4) is personal, as is his first chapter in the beginning triad. His work on self-care is illuminating; drawing on Socrates, "Haewol" (Si-Hyung Choi), and Michel Foucault, he delves into the concept of self-care. For Jung-Hoon, self-care is a form of self-development, the ability to free ourselves of the social constraints that bind us and thereby to create our own standards, our own ways of being. This creating of one's own standards is, and is meant to be, challenging. It is not though random. For Jung-Hoon it is part of the process of *currere* that undergirds it.

Defining self-care as "building a creative relationship with one's self," Jung-Hoon, in Chapter 5, explores the transformation of Bertie's (King George VI) self from an inauthentic one, dominated by others, to an authentic one, where his subjectivity comes forth. Bertie's struggle with his stammering is really in overcoming the powerful external constraints placed upon him in his childhood. The scene when Bertie explains, "I am a man; I have a Voice," is indeed dramatic. Bertie praises his therapist, Lionel. Lionel, though, insists that it is Bertie who did the work of creative transformation; Lionel could only encourage and give a bit of aid. Turning to the relation of student (Bertie) and teacher (Lionel), the teacher cannot give and the student take; rather a mutual, trustful relation between student and teacher needs to be created to allow the student's own potential (his or her spirit) to come forth. Regretfully, Korean education is not built on this caring premise. Nor, following Foucault, as does Jung-Hoon, are many institutions. An alternative to the discipline and punish model so prevalent is one of the challenges Jung-Hoon puts forth for us as educators (or parents).

The final chapter of the book is in some ways the most fascinating, especially following a reader's close and reflective engagement with the preceding five chapters. In this last chapter, Jung-Hoon presents his analysis of the book: his hopes, fears, struggles, and the insights he has acquired during the process of writing under *currere*. Here he draws on Foucault, Noddings, and Pinar as he works to associate the inseparable and complementary relation between self-care and care-for-others. This relational association I have earlier called entwined; I now realize this is too simple a description. Complementary or creative association or tension would be better. Drawing on Hongyu Wang, Jung-Hoon talks of turning away from others in order to cultivate one's own space, as well as having simultaneous relationships with others. This relationship should be interesting to complexity theorists and of help to curricularists wishing to design a nonlinear alternative to the dominant educational paradigm prevalent not only in Korea but worldwide.

Continuing with insights worthy of reflection, Jung-Hoon brings forth a gem from Deborah Britzman. He quotes her as saying "*To act ethically . . . is already to place the act in question; learning must begin with a question that places the ego in question*" (Britzman, 1998, p. 43; emphasis added). Indeed, this is a challenge for all of us who teach.

In this short Foreword, I have tried to do justice to the multilayers of richness found in Jung-Hoon's book. A relook at the Leggo quotation with which I began will show, I hope, the sense of relations that run throughout the book. Again, a book worthy of multiple visits.

ACKNOWLEDGMENTS

This book is a revised version of my Ph.D. dissertation. I would like to thank, first and foremost, my Ph.D. supervisor, Dr. William F. Pinar, and committee members, Drs. William E. Doll, Jr. and Anne M. Phelan, for supporting me on the journey of my study at UBC. I am grateful to Dr. Pinar for the opportunity to learn from him. This study would not have been possible had he not accepted me as his student. It is his scholarship in curriculum theory that has been the greatest influence on my research, as indicated here. From the day I met Dr. Doll, he has been one of my greatest teachers and mentors. This book has emerged from his course, which was co-taught with Dr. Donna Trueit, an invaluable mentor and supporter. After taking their course I have had the privilege of being their teaching assistant for three consecutive years. From Dr. Doll, not only did I learn various curriculum theories, but also I experienced an amazing enactment of teaching. Dr. Doll's unfailing generosity and care strongly supported my journey. I must thank Dr. Anne Phelan strongly as well. It was her course Storying Teacher's Lives through which my autobiographical study started to emerge. Since then, she has provided invaluable comments concerning my work. I feel greatly fortunate to have studied at UBC.

I could not have dreamt of pursuing a Ph.D. in Canada without the help and support of Dr. Young Chun Kim, my lifelong mentor from my undergraduate program at Chinju National University of Education in South Korea. I had the privilege of learning from and working with him through various projects. His knowledge in curriculum theories and qualitative research prepared me to pursue my Ph.D. in Canada. He is a remarkable mentor and teacher.

I am in deep gratitude to my family for their emotional and financial support throughout this journey. My wife, Se Jin Lee, has been the strongest supporter over the journey. Her insights and comments on my chapters are invaluable; her voice as a mother, wife, and female teacher especially has provided me with a different perspective. The presence of my children, my son, Hee Woo, and my daughter, Ha Young, has always been a strong energy source, and the stories they have told me have been invaluable sources for theoretical and pedagogical contemplation. Without the help of my family I would not have finished this journey.

A version of the Introduction and Chapter 1 has been published previously:

Jung, J. H. (2014). *Hakbeolism*: A historical and curricular consideration of Korean test-focused education. *Transnational Curriculum Inquiry: The Journal of the International Association for the Advancement of Curriculum Studies, 11*(2), 48–66.

INTRODUCTION

Lamenting

Screaming

He screams a desperate scream
Holding his head which is tearing his heart

Screaming, not heard only echoed

Wailing
Belated wailing, always
Wailing soon disappears

Screaming and wailing swallow one another
Again and again

Screaming is prisoned in his flying body
A body that suffers from the loss of its soul

My poem laments the death of a sixteen-year-old boy who threw himself off his apartment balcony on March 28, 2013. He left the message, "Mom, I cannot endure this pain any more. My brain nibbles my heart. I am sorry."

My deepest sympathies are aroused by his memory and extend to other children who have found the pressures of their lives to be unbearable.

The tragedy of these children killing themselves came home to me, personally and dramatically, in 2006. In the elevator of the apartment building where I lived, every day I met a high school student. One day he was not on the elevator—he had jumped off the balcony of his fifteenth-story apartment. The investigating officer said such an event was not unusual: pressure, from parents, teachers, and classmates to do well on academic tests, was the culprit. This kind of tragedy affects not only secondary students, however: in 2002, a fifth-grade student jumped off his balcony, leaving this note behind: "I do not understand why I have to study 28 hours and rest 20 hours whereas dad works for 20 hours and rests for 28 hours in two days."

The Korean educational system is internationally renowned for its students' high test scores—Koreans scored fifth in the world in reading, math, and science (Organization for Economic Co-operation and Development [OECD], 2014). Many Korean educators take great pride in these results; while the scores have dropped a little from the previous years, Korean students still do pretty well. But less well known is the high suicide rate among Korean adolescents (Ang & Huan, 2006; Lee & Jang, 2011), and the least number of students among OECD countries responded to surveys that they are happy at schools (OECD, 2014). While research, mostly in sociology, has shown a strong correlation between this suicide rate and Korean adolescents' academic stress—pressure related to knowledge transmission and the acquisition of test-taking skills (Juon, Nam, & Ensminger, 1994; Kim, 2008)—the reason that both academic stress and suicide rates continue to increase in tandem is a topic that has received little attention.

The core of this problem, I argue, is Koreans' strong societal tendency to make obtaining credentials from highly ranked universities their top educational priority. To that end, scoring well on university entrance examinations is the main, if not only, purpose of education and study for almost all Koreans. People perceive that excelling on tests, especially university entrance exams, determines their success throughout life because university credentials are decisive determiners of social status in their socially stratified society. Arguably, fear of failure on these university entrance exams is the *hamartia*[1] for some students that relates to their depression and thus to their suicide (Ang & Huan, 2006; Lee & Jang, 2011; Lee, 2011). Nevertheless, with the help of their parents and teachers, Korean students continue to focus all their efforts on improving their test scores in order to enter top universities.

Tenth-century Korea provides a clue to this malaise, called hakbeolism.[2] As elaborated in Chapter 1, hakbeolism is a uniquely Korean concept of "symbolic capital" (Bourdieu, 1986) based on hierarchical status or on the reputation of the school a person graduates from (Lee, 2003). Those graduating from the same educational institution gain social capital while also helping and relying on each other. *Hakbeol* is obtainable, for many, via high test scores on university entrance examinations, and thus getting a good score on the university entrance examination is their main, if not only, purpose for studying. Education has been structurally, culturally, and indeed psychologically conformed to instrumental rationality.

Instrumental rationality, in Martin Heidegger's critique, is the greatest danger to modern humans. It often focuses on the most efficient and effective ways to achieve a given end without reflecting on the value of the end, and humans are deployed in work places only to improve efficiency. Many of us become exploited workers and at the same time naïve consumers of goods and information. Instrumental rationality is also the greatest danger to current Korean education. Students are evaluated on the efficiency of their learning; teachers are rewarded, or blamed, on the efficiency of their teaching. Thus learning has become mere absorption of externally imposed information and skills, and its efficiency is measured only by tests, with no reflection on the value of the preordained goal of education and the subjective experiences in it. At the center of the politics of scapegoating teachers is the confusion between information and knowledge. "Information," Pinar (2006a) tells us, "is not knowledge" (p. 110). The age of information void of ethical judgment and intellectual critique by students and teachers about what they study constitutes an "Age of Ignorance" (Pinar, 2006a, p. 110). The root of this danger in today's Korean education lies in the ignorance about subjectivity.[3]

Subjectivity in Danger

The subjectivity of both teachers and students is in danger in Korean education. Subjectivity is an essential and fundamental source of learning and teaching and thus of education. Information and skill practices should be carefully chosen, organized, and provided in ways that benefit students. Without the consideration of subjectivity, teaching is reduced to procedural and systematized implementation, and learning is a dead act of mimicking whatever teachers or subject specialists choose for students; there is only intellectual submission and the substitution of numbers for subjectivity, which is a camouflaged form of political and psychological oppression.

Coupled with the productivity of 20th-century industrialization and consolidation for the sake of nationalism and anticommunism after the Korean War, the obsession with tests has increased rather than diminished in South Korea. Suffering from the influence of history, culture, and politics in schools, "[t]eachers may become increasingly identified with their professionalized role as educators, less attentive to educating and to learning" (Pinar, 1976, p. 57). The teacher, Pinar continues, gives up "his or her own voice, and nearly exclusively relies on others . . . [and] judges severely the artless attempts by students [to express themselves in their own voices]" (Pinar, 1976, p. 57). In the almost entirely institutionalized status of the teacher's role, there is no need for the teacher's voice; their entire reliance is on the national curriculum and institutional mandates; the emphasis is on others' judgment. Teachers have been forced to do the "dirty work" (Pinar, 1981, p. 164; see also pp. 164–171) and have hardly been considered "reflective practitioners" (Phelan, 2005, p. 354; see also Schön, 1991, p. 132). One possible explanation for the current situation is "repression, unconscious role-identified behaviour, [and] intellectual and psychological arrest" (Pinar, 1976, p. 57).

What renders dormant the status of subjectivity in Korean education can be better understood by studying the strong societal tendency to put obtaining credentials from a highly ranked university at the top of the educational goal. What one gets from having certain university credentials is "hakbeol." Hakbeolism is the prevalent belief that academic performance, especially on the university entrance exam, shapes one's entire life because it most powerfully influences one's social status. It has led to "the worst stratification in Korean society" (Kim, 2004, p. 47; T. H. Kim, 2011).

The harmonized political oppression and cultural malady of hakbeolism, I argue, strengthens the psychological trap in teaching and learning. The frozen structure of education (the national curriculum and the censoring of textbooks and school performance, for example) and the deep embeddedness of the cultural tendency for people to care much more about others' objectifications than about themselves and to care more about test results than about any other aspects of learning make it difficult for people to recognize that they are in those traps, as in my experience (see Chapter 2). What is most dangerous is that those from this background lose their sensitivity to their subjectivity.[4]

It is my belief that our urgent task is to recover our sensitivity to and the agency of our subjectivity and in turn to cultivate our ability to reconstruct our educational experiences and thus our society. This task for us as teachers means on the one hand proclaiming our independence from politicians and including our voices in making educational decisions and on the other hand awakening in ourselves and our students the dulled, or numbed, awareness of our ability to negotiate, deconstruct, and reconstruct our educational experience and thereby our society. Teachers face a political trap, as Chapter 1 explains, in that the national curriculum in Korea functions as a way to control the information sets[5] and censor educational activities through tests and in various other ways with the help of highly developed technologies. Students face psychological arrest, as Chapter 2 testifies, in that their subjectivity remains dormant.

An Arduous Step

> Changing consciousness toward liberating activity can be effected by focusing upon school persons' ideas and perspectives, personal growth, subject matter, and upon the preference and constitutive rules, with the intent of bringing to bear our analysis upon the quality of the living relationships that exist in our school lives.
>
> The avenues and aspects will be manifold, but essentially any change in consciousness or practice that moves one step closer to freeing ourselves from arbitrary domination by social structures or other persons (past or present) may be counted as a legitimate step toward liberation.
> —*James Macdonald (1981, p. 170)*

> Unless he or she attends to the character of that work [understanding the dialectic relation of the knower to the known], its symbolic function of his or her life and for the culture, it is likely that this work functions

> to maintain stasis. Unfortunately, this knowledge is available only once the initial and arduous step is taken. . . . Advice can be given; invitations issued. Nothing more. "More" is political oppression.
> —*William Pinar (1976, p. 41)*

If subjectivity is in danger in Korean education, what kind of project are we, Korean educators, taking on? Since rescuing subjectivity is a political and psychological project, it requires collective as well as private endeavors. Although changes in structures and in individuals are not entirely exclusive of one another, change in humans, change in one's consciousness, which is aware of the external world and of oneself, is "necessary and [a] precondition of a later political change" (Macdonald, 1981, p. 157). Structural changes without individual awareness function as still another form of political control or oppression, as seen in the many "school deforms" (Pinar, 2004, p. xiii [emphasis omitted]; see also Pinar, 2006b, p. 118) that have failed in "reforming" Korean education. As Chapter 1 makes clear, I argue that a "real" attempt at educational reform in Korea, in my experience, has never been tried.

To change one's consciousness necessitates self-understanding. Pinar argues for the primacy of self-understanding:

> The self-knowing may well choose a life of social service, but it is also true that often those who take upon themselves a calling to intrude in the lives of others are precisely those who have failed to intrude in, or study, their own lives. Such people are the psychic equivalents of untrained surgeons. At the same time it must be acknowledged that for many it is work with others that is a medium through which they work with themselves.
> *(Pinar, 1976, p. 53)*

Self-understanding inevitably requires understanding both one's lived experience and one's ongoing engagement with the world, always changing and unchanging and simultaneously constituting one another. Through self-understanding we are able to free ourselves from the political and psychological trap, to which my *currere* work in Chapter 2 and the case of King George VI in Chapter 5 testify.

When one's ego is arrested through "arbitrary domination by social structures or other persons (past or present)" (Macdonald, 1981, p. 170), one is identified only by external standards, often those of significant others, and then one develops an inauthentic relationship with oneself, possibly masking one's identity, as we see in Chapter 4. Once the external standards subordinate one's own standards, one always seeks ways to meet the standards externally imposed and then fails to find one's own voice. The internalization of objectification makes one's self–self relationship inauthentic (see Chapters 2 and 5). Thus self-understanding is a way to rehabilitate an authentic self–self relationship, which can be, I believe, a form of self-care.

Changing our consciousness for our self-understanding and thus forming an authentic self–self relationship is not easy. Nobody can do it for anybody else. The task is always singular but occurs through proper engagement with others: one's inability to access one's subjectivity affects, and in turn can be affected by, one's relationships with one's self and with others. Through my *currere* work and my study of *The King's Speech*, I found that, although the contexts are different, the self–self relationship and the self–other relationships are inextricably intertwined.

Therefore, to rescue one's subjectivity is to create an authentic relationship with one's self, which requires us to study the self–self relationship, the self–other relationship, and the association between them. I argue that this is an ethical project. The "ethical" part is twofold: expressed in the Foucauldian sense of one's creative relationship with one's life and in Noddings's sense of one's way of caring for others.

Overview of the Chapters

In this introduction, I have labored to contextualize and rationalize this study, asserting the importance of subjectivity and its status in Korean education, and suggesting the primacy of the self-understanding that may be achieved through self-care and care-for-others.[6] These themes are expanded in the chapters as summarized below.

Chapter 1: Hakbeolism provides a historical and cultural understanding of Korean test-focused education through the indigenous Korean concept of hakbeolism from its birth and growth to its current state. I then discuss the dire consequences of hakbeolism from political, psychological, and metaphysical points of view. This chapter concludes with a discussion of the essence of the problem and the general suggestion that the political and intellectual freedom of teachers and students in their study is primary.

Chapter 2: The Reciprocity of Currere, *a Reconstruction of Self, and Autobiographical Theory* offers an example of self-understanding through *currere*. More specifically, it explicates how I was "trapped" in Korean education, how I have come to understand what learning has meant to me, and how I reconstruct(ed) my subjectivity through *currere*. Understanding that anxiety expresses the unforeseeable, indefinable, and paradoxical character of my existence has helped me create an authentic relationship with myself. This chapter not only indicates the primacy of the subjective endeavor for self-understanding but also discusses the significance of others' contributions to the process. Furthermore I suggest considering certain modes of reciprocity in autobiographical inquiry.

Chapter 3: An Ethic of Care focuses on Nel Noddings's ethic of care. I first discuss the roots of an ethic of care from ontological, philosophical, and theoretical points of view. I point out that three aspects of an ethic of care are 1) its difference from ethics of justice, 2) coercive caring, and 3) reciprocity and inclusion in an ethic of care in consideration of education. I conclude by emphasizing the importance of self-understanding in an ethic of care.

My aspirations to study the topics in the first three chapters emerged almost simultaneously. They are driven by my intellectual interest, biographical need, and reflection on my educational experiences. When the three topics are juxtaposed, I see certain overarching themes—self-understanding and care and the association between them—which constitute the topics of the next three chapters.

Chapter 4: Self-Care and Self-Understanding articulates how self-understanding can be a form of self-care. I first discuss what I mean by self-care, building a creative relationship with oneself, which necessarily requires learning and then unlearning the self that may have been objectified, or arrested, by imposed constraints (political, cultural, and psychological). I argue that through self-understanding, which is never complete or definite but always in progress, we can better care for ourselves by making our own standards and not resorting to, or not being subordinated by, the constraints. This work should be done in solitude but for many might also need relationships with others. Thus I move to the next chapter.

Chapter 5: Care-For-Others discusses how others, and one's relationship with others, might contribute to the journey of self-understanding. Focusing on the movie *The King's Speech* for my analysis of one's relationship with others, I discuss the themes of voice and speech, which symbolically express one's subjectivity and one's ability to work with it. This analysis is followed by an example of how one's stammering voice can be cured through the concept of the semantic environment, disconfirmation, love, and anomaly. I also discuss the role of speech therapists in the process of curing stammering, that is, recovery of subjectivity and the self–self relationship. The chapter concludes with the implications of the movie for care-for-others in education.

Chapter 6: Self-Care and Care-For-Others focuses on how the two are associated with one another. The relationship between self-care and care-for-others is inextricable, complementary, and mutually constitutive of the other. Given the challenges in/between self-care and care-for-others, I argue for cultivating a certain distance or noncoincidence between self and the world, our ethics and oppressive structures, and our preferences and reality so that we may be able to make better decisions for the well-being of self and others. I also suggest that discernment might help us achieve a balance in the difficulties or challenges emerging from the activities of self-care and care-for-others. Finally, I argue that through discernment one can both connect and separate one's relationships with oneself and with others.

Notes

1. *Hamartia*, an ancient Greek word, is a tragedy that has occurred by a mistake or error in judgment. On the day following the 2002 SAT in Korea, a terribly ironic tragedy involving Korea's test-focused system occurred. A girl committed suicide after hearing through the media that that year's exam had been easier than the previous year's, so the

mean score would be 10–20 points higher than usual. Her provisional mark, however, was 20 points lower than what she had hoped it would be. On the day after her death, the media and the SAT institution announced that it had made an error: the mean score would be *lowered* rather than raised because the test had been more difficult than the previous year's test, not easier.
2. The *Korean Standard Unabridged Dictionary* defines *hakbeol* as "a group of people who are from the same school and who help and rely on each other in strengthening their social capital. Hakbeol is formed based on one's school." Essentially, it is "a group of people under the concept of alumni based on the 'societal status or reputation of schools'" (Lee, 2003, p. 20).
3. I take the term "subjectivity" from Pinar (2009); he uses it to mean:

> the inner life, the lived sense of "self"—however non-unitary, dispersed, and fragmented—that is associated with what has been given and what one has chosen, those circumstances of everyday life, those residues of trauma and of fantasy, from which one reconstructs a life. (p. 3)

4. The effect of an outer-directed culture and the difficulty of recognizing the traps are discussed in Chapter 2 through my *currere* work.
5. I deliberately use "information," which is not knowledge and lacks ethical and intellectual interpretation and judgment.
6. One may see the binary between self and other in this work. I admit that there is a binary between them in my thinking. The binary, however, seems to be blurry given that self and other—and self and the world—are co-constitutive of one another. Self-care is associated with how self treats one's subjectivity, which is what makes one unique and irreplaceable. Education helps individuals cultivate their distinctiveness.

1
HAKBEOLISM

The problems with standardized tests are universal educational concerns. In Korea, these problems have unique elements that require historical interrogation. Tenth-century Korea provides a clue to this emphasis on testing: hakbeolism, a uniquely Korean concept of symbolic capital based on hierarchical status or on the reputation of the school a person graduates from. Those graduating from the same educational institution gain social capital while also helping and relying on each other. Hakbeol is thus obtainable, for many, via high test scores on university entrance examinations. This chapter analyzes the test-focused nature of Korean education and its links to the historical, cultural, and political issues that are closely related to hakbeolism.

What Is Hakbeolism?

Hakbeolism is a concept that is indigenous to Korea. *Hakbeol* is a kind of social status people achieve based on a shared academic background. It is also "a group of people who help and rely on each other, who are from the same school" (Hakbeol, 2015). That is, it is a group of alumni who share the "societal status or reputation of their school" (J. K. Lee, 2003, p. 21). Strictly speaking, their university's reputation rather than their ability or knowledge thus determines how they are judged by others.

While hakbeolism is similar to credentialism—in both, people place value on others' credentials—these phenomena are different. In-sook Nahm's (2011) differentiation is helpful for readers in the West:

> In the transition from a status society to a credential society, credentials become the most reliable criteria by which to evaluate others' abilities. A

credential society is a society in which credentialism functions as a predominant ideology. . . . Credentials are social products and achieving them is an effective way to be successful in the society. This phenomenon functions as a major impetus for the movement in American social status. America is a "functional credential society" since it is focused on the functional attributes and abilities of the credentials, whereas Korea is a "symbolic credential society" in that it values the particular schools from which people graduate (Kim, 1995). . . . To be successful in Korean society, a person must put symbolic credentials above functional credentials.

(p. 105, personal translation)[1]

In its emphasis on symbolic credentials as essential to better, higher status and more social opportunities—indeed, to success in life—hakbeolism cannot be conceived of as the same as Western credentialism. This may not be convincing enough for those who have not experienced hakbeolism. Thus, I provide three aspects of hakbeolism that might help the readers in the West to understand hakbeolism.

What makes hakbeolism an indigenous concept specific to Korea? First of all, the origin of hakbeolism makes it unique; the succeeding section provides the historical details. Secondly, hakbeolism carries positive association with social stratification and discrimination (Kim, 1995; Kim, 2004; Kim, 2007; T. H. Kim, 2011; J. K. Lee, 2003). Lastly, while credentialism is a more general and broad concept in a way that it can be achieved from various schools and institutions, which confer certificates, hakbeolism is strongly associated with formal educational institutions such as elementary, middle, and high schools, and universities. Interestingly enough, in terms of hakbeolism, graduate schools do not count as much as undergraduate schools. For example, one who graduates from an undergraduate program at Seoul University holds better capital than others who graduate only from graduate programs at the university. I think that this shows the acknowledgement of the society for passing exams (the university entrance examinations in this case, because the exam to enter graduate schools at the university is not as difficult as entering into its undergraduate programs).

Koreans tend to believe that belonging to a better hakbeol by earning a diploma from a highly ranked university will provide them with greater social capital. And it does. In his problematization of the cultural function of hakbeolism as social capital in Korean society, Young Chun Kim (2010) argues that hakbeolism has become "one of the most powerful [forms of] social capital in South Korea" (p. 543) because of its influence on individuals' social success. Children from upper socioeconomic families, Kim posits, are more likely than others to enter good universities and obtain hakbeol. Sang Bong Kim (2004) states this argument more strongly: "The society of Korea is not stratified into upper class, middle class, and working class; rather, it is stratified by hakbeol, with that of Seoul University as the royalty, the hakbeol of Yonsei and Korea University as the nobility, and the rest of the subgroups as the plebeians" (p. 30). Without factoring in hakbeol, Sang Bong Kim argues, there is no explanation for the social authority and capital enjoyed by those belonging to certain hakbeols.

In a 2004 study produced by the Korean Women's Development Institute (KWDI; see Park, Jung, Kim, & Park, 2004), 21.5% of respondents identified hakbeolism as the strongest source of discrimination in Korea, well ahead of other reasons for discrimination.[2] Only seven years later, Tae Hong Kim (2011), a researcher at KWDI, surveyed 948 adults and found that 29.6% felt credentials or hakbeol was the strongest source of social discrimination. These surveys indicate not only that hakbeolism is pervasive, but that it is a growing social problem. In fact, 46.5% of respondents in Chong-Hyun Lee's (2007) study feel intimidated in their daily lives by people who belong to a more prestigious hakbeol. What interests me about these studies is not the actuality of hakbeol—even though its strong impact on society clearly matters—but rather, people's perception of it. The hakbeol phenomenon has been acknowledged and criticized in Korea, but ironically, it is also desired and pursued by many, perhaps in the same way that people criticize capitalism but want to have more money.

The predominant criticism of hakbeolism, which is mostly from a sociological perspective, focuses on social inequity issues in terms of educational experiences and the centralization of social power. These studies provide highly detailed information about how deeply hakbeolism affects social structures and people's psyches. In his *Hakbeol Society* (2004), for example, Sang Bong Kim takes a sociological and psychological stance in critiquing hakbeol, arguing that it is a kind of "corruptive collective subjectivity fallen into the bottomless pit of inauthenticity" (p. 193).[3] According to Kim, authentic collective subjectivity has its rationale when both my subjectivity and yours remain alive and are actualized within our collective identity. In my view, however, subjectivity influenced by hakbeolism loses its vitality, since hakbeol is established at the expense of individual subjectivities. Within a hakbeol collective, individuals surrender their power of subjectivity to the collective.

Why is hakbeolism at odds with subjectivity? Hakbeols are an extended form of family, modernized clans. Historically, Korean society was a clan society, but the notion of clans significantly weakened during the Japanese colonial period, the Korean War, and the subsequent dictatorships (Kim, 2004, pp. 179–183). This modernization process, Kim (2004) argues, transformed the traditional form of family: "People who moved to cities in order to work lost their connections, the clans that used to link them to each other and to their society" (p. 183). Not surprisingly, a person who feels anxious about this process may try to become part of a clan-based community to replace that loss of family (Kim, 2004). Hakbeols thus help to reduce what Kim calls the common "regressive phenomenon" (p. 193) that Koreans affected by modernization have felt as their family ties have weakened. Kim's (2004) point is that hakbeolism assuages a kind of social and individual immaturity by submerging individual subjectivities in the "corruptive collective subjectivity" (p. 193) in which subjectivities conform to the collective subjectivity.[4] The root issue here, from my perspective, is simply the loss of people's awareness of their individual subjectivity, a problem that I turn to in the following sections.

The Birth of Hakbeolism

Jung Kyu Lee (2003), another Korean sociologist studying hakbeolism, traces its origins to 958 AD, near the beginning of Korea's Goryeo Dynasty (918–1392). This date marks the implementation of the *gwageo*, the highest-level state examination used to recruit high-ranking officials.[5] The relationship between examiner and examinee, one that would last for the rest of their lives, was considered as important as that between father and son (Korean Studies Promotion Service, 2015). Thus, for example, when the examiner (father) became successful, the son shared in that success. The gwageo was in that sense also a way to build political parties. In different areas and forms and to varying degrees, this phenomenon lasted almost 1000 years, until the Gabo Reform in 1894.

While the social effects of this system are important, J. K. Lee (2003) points out that the gwageo was not the only way that officials were recruited. There were other systems: the *umso* (蔭敍), a "protected appointment system" (p. 48) used during the Goryo and Chosun dynasties to select persons from high-ranking families whose ancestors had made contributions to the country in founding the dynasty, and the *chungeo* (薦擧), the system by which officials could recommend a certain number of people for certain official positions. Because of the political struggles between kings and powerful families throughout the dynasties, the umso and chungeo were used by families to pass on their family power, whereas the gwageo was used by the king to reduce the power of these families. Thus, we should not attribute hakbeolism to the gwageo alone; rather, all three systems contributed to the growth of hakbeolism because they all privileged a few not according to merit but to personal connections. Nevertheless, although the gwageo was abolished more than a century ago, its basis for selection most clearly contributes to today's hakbeolism.

The Growth of Hakbeolism

The End of the Chosun Dynasty and the Japanese Colonial Period

The turbulent twentieth century greatly strengthened hakbeolism in Korea. Toward the end of the Chosun Dynasty (1392–1910), "commoners' discontent with the exclusive social status formation increased" (J. K. Lee, 2003, p. 91). By this point, it had become possible for commoners to achieve nobility through success on the gwageo, so common people increasingly sought to obtain higher social status through education. This growing reason to pursue education was strengthened when the Japanese colonial period (1910–1945) opened up educational opportunities to all (J.K. Lee, 2003; Son, 1993). Educational background rather than one's social status started to be critical to finding work and establishing social status. Japanese educational policy during this period was intended to make education a way for Koreans to achieve power: the "appropriate educational background was prerequisite to getting jobs and the Japanese colonial government had complete control over education, which their test system made possible" (Son, 2007, pp. 41–42).

Some sociologists, such as Jong-Hyun Son (2007), ascribe today's educational fever and test competitiveness in Korea to this Japanese educational policy, because the Korean education system was modernized and institutionalized during this era. Although Son's argument seems plausible to me as far as it goes, the much older gwageo and other selection systems discussed previously had already established the cultural norms of hakbeolism—the employment of entrance exams and textbooks, and the administrative role of the government in various exams—that these twentieth-century changes entrenched.

Centralization and Efficiency in Education After the Korean War

Notions of centralization and efficiency marked the Korean educational system after the Korean War (1950–1953). Trampled by powerful countries and socially and economically devastated during these years, Korea had to emphasize centralization, nationalism, and universalism in order to revive the nation. Unity in language, in the educational system, and even in ways of thinking was therefore highly valued. Political universalism, aimed at binding all Koreans into one collective, was considered "the only way to break through the national crisis"(Kim, 2008, pp. 148–149).[6] Solidarity was promoted as indispensable, regardless of the government in power; and given the country's strong centralization, "anyone who thought differently or wanted a different kind of education was excluded" (Kim, 2008, p. 149). Justified by the Miracle on the Han River,[7] for instance, this approach saw the achievement of remarkable economic development within a relatively short period of time, a result that commended this approach to many.

To advance national solidarity, Jung Hee Park's military government (1961–1979) pledged to pursue two policies: anticommunism and economic development. The combination was intended to ensure that the Korean people had clear evidence of the enemy outside of the country and that economic development would legitimize the government's power. In the name of economic development, then, efficiency in conjunction with political solidarity became Korea's most important social and educational value. While this solidarity and nationalism certainly were valuable in overcoming the national crisis after the Korean War, they discounted the people's subjectivities and discouraged educational diversity: variety, differences, and discussions were rejected as inefficient (Y. Lee, 2003). These approaches also hampered the development of democracy itself, because political diversity is a prerequisite for democracy.

For the sake of efficiency in education, in the 1960s and early 70s the national Ministry of Education implemented Bloom's taxonomy, Mager's concept of behavioral objectives, Skinner's behavioral psychology, and McClelland's achievement motive theory, all approaches intended to "improve" educational efficiency by optimizing the transfer of knowledge and skills from teachers to students. Also in the 1970s the Ministry of Education introduced Jerome Bruner's (1959) "theory of the structure of knowledge," deciding that "Bruner's theory corresponded to Piaget's psychological schema" (Y. Lee, 2003, p. 547). Along with the already well-established Tyler-Bloom-Mager rationale that saw curriculum as a means to an end, the Korean government's relatively narrow understanding and use of both theories[8] effectively ensured that within the Korean test-focused system, curriculum was extrinsically imposed. The notion of "curriculum development," rather than "curriculum understanding," continues to prevail in the understanding of the people about what education is or should be.

In the frame of curriculum development, university entrance examinations are still seen as efficiently summarizing students' previous education; therefore, most educational experiences in and out of school continue to focus on test preparation. Of course Korean students do engage in other activities such as art, the playing of musical instruments, sports, or elocution that are not closely related to tests. But as students progress through schooling, these activities become secondary and eventually tend either to be sacrificed to improving academic achievement or to become test-driven themselves, components that may enhance university applications.[9]

In Korea, the last three decades have produced some ostensibly democratic changes to improve education, including reduced school hours, additional alternative curricular activities, integrated subjects, the concept of a local curriculum, and a teachers' union that argues for the implementation of the democratic and progressive educational policies legalized during Dae Jung Kim's administration in 1991. Even earlier, beginning in the 1980s, some curriculum scholars in Korea started to question the Ministry's reliance on Tyler, Bloom, and Mager (Y. Lee, 2003, p. 548) and to demand an alternative understanding of curriculum. They were interested in alternatives that were based on such notions as Michael Apple's social reproduction theory and William Pinar's *currere*—respectively, a new understanding of curriculum and a mode of understanding one's own educational subjectivity. Over the last decade, these positive steps have brought several different perspectives to the previously unified field of curriculum studies in Korea. However, these changes in curriculum studies, Kim (2010) states, mostly involved new research methodologies and research contexts rather than fundamentally questioning the purpose or raison d'être of education. One promising aspect of the situation, nevertheless, is that some curriculum scholars have turned their attention from "developing curriculum" to "understanding curriculum" (Kim, 2010, p. 546). Yet curriculum is still under the shade of curriculum development in Korea.

However, despite these indications of some change in the field of curriculum in Korea, the 1979 collapse of Jung Hee Park's military dictatorship and the 1988 installation of the country's first civilian president, Dae Jung Kim, had little effect on Korea's strong procedural and scientific curriculum formula, the so-called "Tyler rationale." According to that frame, education is an externally imposed means to a socially engineered end. Today, supported by highly developed internet-based technology, governmental surveillance of the performance of students, teachers, and schools has actually increased.[10]

I want to point out three legacies of the twentieth-century growth of hakbeolism that still affect education in Korea: first, the Education Law decrees that "subjects of schools, colleges of education, and informal schools except for colleges shall be prescribed by a Presidential decree, and courses of study and class hours of those by a regulation of the Ministry" (Educational Act Compilation Committee, 2015, article 155); second, the Ministry of Education still publishes, examines, and approves all textbooks, so all curriculum reforms have been inescapably bound by the government's control of publication. This textbook screening is now challenged as "unconstitutional" (Kim & Yoon, 2009)[11]; and third, university entrance examinations continue to be perceived as the culmination of students' efforts to that point. While official elementary- and secondary-school entrance exams were abolished in the 1970s, the ongoing emphasis on unification continues to justify "individual needs and differences being subjugated to the preorganized uniform curriculum" (Y. Lee, 2003, p. 546).

These educational legacies can be summarized as a continuation of governmental control through the policies exercised through post–Korean War centralization and efficiency. Together, these three crucial consequences continue to support the fallacy that education provides little more than the training that can help students prove their achievements on tests. Thus, people who suffer from "education fever" have little curiosity about what students are learning; instead, they are interested only in how students can learn more, and more efficiently, compared to their peers.

The Dire Consequences of Hakbeolism

Hakbeolism's negative effects can be discussed from societal, curricular, and personal perspectives. First, some argue that hakbeolism is the source of the predominant social discrimination and monopoly of power. The research on hakbeolism by Tae Hong Kim (2011) explores the concept's negative impact on Korean society and education and concludes with the statement that Koreans see hakbeolism as the predominant source of social discrimination. Sang Bong Kim (2004) provides detailed information about hakbeolism's role in Korea's power monopolies. People belonging to the hakbeol of Seoul University dominate positions in parliament and the highest government offices: from the Korean War to 2003, 283 departmental ministers (43% of all such ministers) had graduated from Seoul University, while only 7% came from Koryo University and just 4% from Yonsei University. Seoul University's monopoly far surpasses the comparable figures in Japan and the U.S. for top officials having graduated from prestigious universities: in Japan, just 18.5% of government officials graduate from Tokyo University, while in America, no single American university supplies more than 5% of the country's senators (Kim, 2004, pp. 65–66). Korea's private sector is not exempt from the effects of hakbeolism either.[12]

Some might argue that the people from Seoul University are perhaps better qualified for their high-ranking positions, since they likely know more or are smarter. If indeed these people are better qualified and have made more contribution to the society, people can hardly object to their appointment: greater contributions deserve greater recognition and reward.[13] If socially elite people are *not* better qualified, however, their status is a serious problem. Unfortunately, hakbeolism indicates little about the contributions to society that one has made or one's ability to contribute. Rather, it is a kind of internalized value system that merely rationalizes social stratification on the basis of prior academic achievement.[14]

Hakbeolism, I suspect, is a perverted form of "meritocracy" (Macdonald, 1981, p. 168). The rationalization using goals and efficiency as "a tyranny of knowledge and basic skills" (Macdonald, 1981, p. 169) has "the effect of replicating the social structure in terms of meritocracy" by convincing "the winners and the losers that they deserve the status they achieve" (Macdonald, 1981, p. 168). Khen Lampert (2012) argues that an "educational meritocracy" is based on the ideology of "aggressive competition and social Darwinism" (p. 50). Lampert explains the winner–loser trap that Macdonald criticizes:

> [An] educational meritocracy, which focuses on cultivating the excellent and the talented, is a manifestation of the social ideology that education could on some level be egalitarian, but is ultimately meant to groom the "excellent" for positions of influence, scientific development, decision-making, and leadership.
>
> *(Lampert, 2012, p. 51)*

Lampert (2012) points out that an educational meritocracy is ostensibly based on an egalitarian viewpoint. While not forgetting to mention individual students' backgrounds (family, cultural, and financial), Lampert (2012) criticizes "its underpinning argument that 'anyone can' as long as they work hard" (p. 51). What an educational meritocracy undergirds is the thesis that educational success is a matter of each student's effort since all students have so-called equal opportunity. Not to mention the differences of students' backgrounds, the corollary of this ideology blames academic failure or students' difficulties on their lack of effort and hard work. Of course this ignores the issues of economic hierarchy and social reproduction. The essential problem of this proposition is that it obfuscates the key curricular question, *what knowledge is of most worth?* (Pinar, 1978, 2009, 2012), the answer to which is highly individual, and always historically, culturally, and politically contextual. Educational meritocracy serves only a few at the expense of many others.

The state of hakbeolism today boils down to an "obsession with tests" because students cannot enter a highly ranked university in Korea unless they achieve good university entrance examination results. When such standardized high-stakes tests become the ultimate purpose or culmination of study, schools turn into cramming institutions and teachers become workers exploited only for "banking education" (Freire, 1970, pp. 71; see also pp. 71–73). Immediately obvious in the literature is the fact that this situation in Korea has caused test corruption to become pervasive—student cheating, score manipulation by teachers and administrators, and leaking questions and answers of examinations by those who made the questions are all problems that have been well documented (Ang & Huan, 2006; Hong & Youngs, 2008; Jung & Lee, 2003; Juon et al., 1994; Kandel, Raveis, & Davies, 1991; Kang, 2011; C. W. Kim, 2011; Lee & Jang, 2011; Son, 2007).

A second negative effect, from my curricular perspective besides the societal one I have discussed, is that hakbeolism has shaped and strengthened the test-focused system based on the assumption that educational content can be/should be provided, transmitted, and assessed for the purpose that the providers intend. Thus, it is necessary to point out the problems of standardized tests. I raise the following questions. What kind of knowledge do these tests evaluate? That is, knowledge that tests measure is not free of gender, ideology, politics, ethnicity, race, sexual orientation, and other issues. How well do tests actually measure what they intend to measure?[15] Are the current tests fair to students?[16]

Content outside subjectivity such as "humanity, culture, and the world" (Pinar, 2011, p. 66) is that through the study of which we achieve "self-determination and freedom of thought and action" (p. 66). Of course, tests may be useful on certain occasions, but tests should be no more than a tool that may be used in education, rather than education being merely a means of improving test scores. When the tests that are used to achieve one's hakbeol by demonstrating certain knowledge and skills become central to education, these tests are almost certainly unlikely to raise the fundamental question that Pinar urges us to ask repeatedly: *what knowledge is of most worth?* This question necessarily requires one's self-determination, intellectual and political freedom, autonomy, responsibility, and independence. Instead, tests like these focus students' and educators' attention on the "mandated knowledge" that Doll (1972) calls "predetermined and externally imposed [educational] ends" (p. 309). Twentieth-century education, not only in Korea but also in the West, has experienced countless so-called failures of students, teachers, and education in general, as judged by traditional, scientific, and neo-liberal perspectives and that the phrase "intellectual banking education" might summarize well. Empirically speaking—the way that is preferred by those who want to quantify educational outcomes—isn't it enough to say that these failures "prove" or "argue" that "intellectual banking education" is a poor system? In scientific research, the assumptions that are made initially can be modified as the research progresses. Why can the assumption that educational content is given not be modified similarly according to the demonstrable failures of "banking education"?

In my view, the "failure" to accept that knowledge cannot be given is the reason, as Pinar (2006a) suggests, that "intellectual education does not speak to many children, and, in failing to engage children's interests, alienates them, leaving many child behind" (p. 118). The failure of banking education as a means to an end, as Gert Biesta (2013) elegantly puts it in *The Beautiful Risk of Education*, might not actually be a failure but rather a kind of "beautiful risk" (p. 1): a possibility, not a weakness. The risk is there, Biesta continues, "because education is not about filling a bucket but about lighting a fire.... Education is not an interaction between robots but an encounter between human beings" (p. 1). Biesta's point is, on the one hand, an ontological one about the nature of our being and the unpredictability of our existence: there are educational outcomes, which cannot be predictable, measurable, quantifiable, or standardizable. On the other hand, Biesta's point is that there is no necessary connection between "inputs" and "outcomes." "Any connections between teaching and what its effects are," Biesta (2013) contends, are *weak*, which is established "through interpretation rather than through causation" (p. 120). The causation takes away the interpretations of teachers and students in their study and "overrule[s] [the] professional judgment [of teachers]" (Biesta, 2013, p. 120).

Blame for the fallacy that educational content should be provided by subject specialists or curriculum developers lies not only with instrumental rationality itself, but also with our educators' "culpability for their faith in instrumentalism [that has] ... provided a green light for applied social science with its emphasis upon measuring outcomes quantitatively" (Pinar, 2006a, p. 118). I agree with Pinar that we teachers are caught within an "intellectual and political trap" (p. 120): an intellectual trap because students depend on their teachers in order to learn, and a political trap because responsibility for learning falls on teachers rather than on their students.[17]

The third negative effect, the stultifying effects of test-focused education on educators and students are multi-dimensional, political, psychological, and metaphysical, which I try to understand through reading Pinar's (1976) "The Trial," in which he analyzes Joseph K.'s situation in Kafka's *The Trial*. Politically speaking, in this kind of system students are told what to study, and teachers are told by their prescribed curriculum what, how, and when to teach. Testing inspects how well both students and teachers have met these externally prescribed standards. In the meantime, an "omnipresent bureaucracy which exercises a political control as mystifying as it feels complete" (Pinar, 1976, p. 38) censors the whole process. Having been raised in this kind of outer-directed culture, I feel and recognize how tests signified and intensified others' objectifications of me.[18]

From a psychological viewpoint, students in such a system are always being evaluated by that system and their teachers and compared to other students. Not recognizing their subjectivity, those involved in the educational system—that is, teachers and students—become "nearly exclusively social" (Pinar, 1976, p. 38). As Pinar explains,

> The ego [specifically, the nearly exclusively socialized ego] is incongruent with its unconscious to the extent it is primarily social in nature, a construction of social conditioning. It limits severely the information it can assimilate, just as it limits what it can externalize. Such an ego is always beleaguered, always "accused" in some sense; it is arrested.
>
> *(1976, pp. 38–39)*

The ego that is concerned primarily with external factors most likely fails to listen to, recognize, or reflect on its inner forces. This failure may be caused by fear of a looming test (and thus be related to studying), by shame from their family or self (and thus be related to pride), or by anxiety (and thus be related to a conscious or unconscious belief that one's value is always measured by others). A student's fear, shame, or anxiety might be linked not only to test results but sometimes also to a fear of study itself, arising from the tendency to decipher experience through exterior filters—others' objectification. To maintain its psychological stability, the ego thus arrested must rely on outer evaluation, and consequently work continuously to satisfy perceived examiners or judges. This psychological stasis is an "intra-psychic corollary of political arrest, of social authoritarianism" (Pinar, 1976, pp. 39).

From a metaphysical viewpoint, the problem with the ego being in this immature stage is the failure to ask metaphysical questions properly. In "The Trial," Joseph K. asks himself, "What is the nature of this case [this life]?" and "What are the means of absolution, if any?" Pinar would say that here the character is directing his questions the wrong way, outward instead of inward, because Joseph K. thinks that only the outer world—not himself—can answer these questions. The problem for people in highly outer-directed cultures—and my problem, as a student and an educator in such a culture—is not only the *presence* of these questions, but also the *absence* of curiosity. To raise the questions properly and to be conscious of being trapped in this situation is hard for those whose psychological development has been stopped. I wonder if this dilemma explains why, even though Koreans realize it is problematic, hakbeolism continues to grip Korean education and society. When I was in the system that I am harshly criticizing here, I was almost completely unaware of these issues; instead, I found that the system's clarity of direction provided a certain comfort, what Pinar (1976) terms an "intra-psychic corollary of arrest, of social authoritarianism" (p. 39). Because escape from this system might feel uncomfortable, those within it are highly vulnerable to stress, related both to their own uncertainty about their personal aims and to their unexpected experiences. In other words, their "arrest is signified by [their] exclusive attention to the social world, [and their] denial and ignorance of the 'lived world'" (p. 52).

The evaluation frame within hakbeolism, I argue, functions as arbitrary social conditioning and psychological constraints that should not be reflected in our educational activities. The test-focused system in Korea is, as Macdonald (1981) might describe it, a "tyranny of cognitive knowledge and skills in our schools" (p. 169).

Conclusion

> Study is the site of education. While one's truths cannot be taught, they can be acquired through the struggle of study, for which every individual has the capacity, but not necessarily the will or the circumstances.
> —*William F. Pinar (2006a, p. 120)*

To solve or at least reduce the problems associated with hakbeolism, critics have suggested structural or institutional changes: the "abolition of Seoul University" (Hong, 2004) has been much discussed, as well as the abolition of university entrance examinations and the establishment of more democratic university entrance processes, such as a lottery system. Certainly the hierarchical prestige of universities is a problem, but I doubt if these suggestions would work or are even possible, because while they might succeed in addressing the current problematic situation, they would fail to address the fundamental educational issues discussed above.

Unfortunately, even if Koreans understand its nature, history, and consequences, hakbeolism will not likely disappear any time soon, given its complex and deep embeddedness in Korean society. Institutional changes certainly need to be investigated, but if we continue to allow students and teachers to assume that prescribed education should be unquestioningly accepted, such changes will most likely fail. Teachers and students will remain caught in hakbeolism's political and intellectual trap, and education will continue to be a process in which "parents and politicians exploit their anxieties over their children's future" (Pinar, 2006a, p. 120).

What can we—*must* we—do as educators to prevent the *hamartia* suffered by the students who gave rise to my poem, to spring them from the test-based trap, and to fight against the governmentalization of education? How can Koreans come to understand the relationship between their educational lives and the fallacies of hakbeolism? What educational questions should we educators raise? The answers to these questions lie in Pinar's entreaty that we teachers rehabilitate education by forcing "the teaching genie back into the bottle" (2006a, p. 120), by throwing away the mythic belief that only what we teach our students matters: we have to break the unnecessary causation between "inputs" and "outcomes."

John Dewey (1916) tells us that "no matter how true what is learned [is] to those who found it out and in whose experience it functioned, there is nothing which makes it knowledge to the pupils" (p. 378). In other words, the knowledge that tests evaluate is possibly always secondary and instrumental to a person's own act of thinking. Knowledge is not definite, stable, fixed, and value- and context-free. Rather, it is in a state of flux, ongoing, changing, challenged, converted, and modified, as students live with it, reflect on it, deconstruct, and reconstruct it. Knowledge that simply satisfies tests cannot be the end of learning. It should, Dewey (1916) tells us, fructify in individual students' own lives (p. 378).

As teachers, we must remember that what a teacher brings into a classroom conversation is no more important than what a student brings. We provide educational experiences, and students benefit from them if they want to, no more, since *more* would be political oppression. Accepting the limitations of our responsibilities and of our abilities to support our students in their studies, while at the same time keeping in mind that what we teachers do with our intellectual and practical wisdom and judgments does have value, might provide us with a way to demystify the educationally destructive assumptions that have dominated in Korea since the birth of hakbeolism. The consequences, I imagine, might free the soul of the boy in my poem. Macdonald argues that "essentially any change in consciousness or practice that moves one step closer to freeing ourselves from arbitrary domination by social structures or other persons (past or present) may be counted as a legitimate step toward liberation" (1981, p. 170). Changes in consciousness or practice for liberation can be manifold. One of the ways for teachers, I suggest, is self-understanding through autobiographical inquiry, which I articulate in the next chapter.

Notes

1. All works originally in Korean have been translated by the author.
2. Other bases for discrimination that respondents identified as socially dominant were homosexuality (16.0%), people's physical appearance (11.7%), disabilities (6.8%), nationality (6.2%), and being an unmarried mother (6.0%), along with ethnicity and skin color (6%).
3. The phrase "collective subjectivity" sounds a bit problematic to me since I don't see how subjectivity can also be collective. I think that "collective subjectivity" might be better termed "identity." But the use of terminology is not my point in this paper.
4. In what way can hakbeol be an alternative to a clan? Kim (2004) explains that "the immutability, exclusiveness, and class homogeneity of hakbeol, which are the innate qualities of clans, are what make hakbeol an alternative for a clan" (p. 185). However, there is a difference between family and hakbeol. While the raison d'être of a family is the existence of the members, and it does not change, the raison d'être of hakbeol is distorted: hakbeol is a group from the same school whose raison d'être is studying

and building communities for study. It has nothing to do with the raison d'être of its origin.
5. The gwageo was a concept that came from China. In 958 AD, the fourth king of the Goryeo Dynasty (918–1392), Gwang Jong (光宗), inaugurated it by accepting the recommendation of Ssanggi (雙冀), a Chinese scholar who had become a Korean citizen. The gwageo was the dominant selection system used by the government throughout this and the following dynasty, the Chosun (1392–1910) (retrieved from http://chang256.new21.net/board/board.php?db=536&no=683 on September 10, 2013).
6. In *Symbolic Violence and Pre-Modern Academic Clique Society*, Suk-Soo Kim (2008) traces governmental unification policies in Korea after the Korean War.
7. The "Miracle on the Han River" refers to South Korea's highly accelerated export-fueled economic growth, including rapid industrialization, technological achievement, the country's education boom, the exponential rise in living standards, rapid urbanization, the "skyscraper boom," modernization, the successful hosting of the 1988 Summer Olympics and the 2002 FIFA World Cup, rapid democratization, and globalization, all of which seemed to miraculously transform the country from the ashes of the Korean war to the wealthy and highly developed country it is today (Cumings, 1999).
8. The application of Bruner's theory of the structure of knowledge and Piaget's psychological schema is more than mere misunderstanding, given the complex and powerful legacy it has left. These scholars and their theories were combined extremely effectively along with the theories of Tyler, Bloom, and Mager. The fallacy is not exclusive to Korea, however: Deweyan pragmatism, the basis for the work done by Bruner and Piaget, among others, has been misunderstood in America also, as William Doll (1986) observes in *Prigogine: A New Sense of Order, a New Curriculum:*

> American educators and psychologists have been able to focus on the correlational aspects of stages—the measured age aspects. But the heart of Piaget is the process of internal, transformatory development. "Life is essentially auto regulation." The measured curriculum has no place for autoregulatory systems.... Both Dewey's notion of experience and Piaget's notion of development have a sense of internality and duration; both are progressive and transformational, coming out of themselves and leading back into themselves, but always at higher, qualitatively different planes. (p. 12)

Identifying Newton's scientific stance as a closed-system paradigm and Prigogine's as an open-system one, Doll (1986) further argues that Piaget's and Bruner's ideas, along with Dewey's educational model "would be a transformative curriculum, with the individual and his or her structures or levels of understanding being transformed" (p. 14). Dewey is not a positivist, as he was understood by many to be because of his positive perspective on the scientific method. Rather, Doll continues, Dewey's philosophy constitutes a way to overcome the limitations of rationality while at the same time questioning the predetermined ends of experience. For Dewey, as Biesta (2013) insists, "rationality is about intelligent human action and human cooperation, ultimately motivated by an attempt to restore rationality, agency, and responsibility to the sphere of human action" (p. 22). Duration, internality, and transformativity are in this regard central to Dewey's philosophy.
9. On this, see Young Chun Kim's (2007) *Secrets of Academic Success of Korean Students: Stories of Hakwon*. Hakwon are private educational institutes, so-called cram schools or "shadow education." Kim's research probes the nature of hakwon and reveals its mechanisms for improving academic achievement: its emphases on learning by repetition, tracking systems, continuous assessment, and sharing ideas and information regarding students' progress between hakwon and parents.

10. There is a very powerful technological surveillance system at work in Korea today, the National Education Information System (http://www.neis.go.kr/pas_mms_nv99_001.do), which continually asks teachers to do "computer stuff." The purpose of the system is to collect complete information about information (individual and collective) on students and what happens in schools (not only curricular information but also information for parents, as well as fiscal information) according to MOE's policies, all of which require the involvement and responsible work of teachers. I can argue from my 10 years of experience, observation, and conversations with colleagues that most of the work that needs to be provided on the system is not necessary for students' study.
11. In their study, *A Constitutional Review on the Official Approval/Certification System of Textbooks in Korea: Focused on Educational System and Rights*, Kim and Yoon (2009) argue that the Official Approval/Certification System of Textbook is "unconstitutional according to education system ordained by law (article 31, section 6) and independence, professionalism, and political neutrality of the education (article 31, section 4)" (p. 228). It also, they further argue, "infringes on a right to teach or right to receive an education (Article 31 Section 1)" (Kim & Yoon, 2009, p. 228).
12. For detailed relevant data, see Jung Kyu Lee's *Korean Credentials and Hakbeolism in Korean Society* (2003) and Sang Bong Kim's *Hakbeol Society* (2004). According to a survey conducted by hakbooki.com in July of 2013, 39.5% of CEOs in the top 1,000 companies in Korea graduated from three universities: Seoul (20.4 %), Koryu (9.8 %), and Yonsei (9.3%) universities. Retrieved from http://weekly.hankooki.com/lpage/sisa/201307/wk20130711092514121210.htm on August 25, 2013.
13. To show their similar superiority—in their case, their greater sacrifices for the empire—heroes in ancient Rome wore mesh clothing that revealed the sword scars on their bodies.
14. Those with an impressive hakbeol are, I think, unlikely to retain what they have learned, and of course their achievements during their long years of education are also questionable. Nichols and Berliner (2007) observe that the current overemphasis on testing is causing corruption as well as waste. "Not only is there more student cheating but there are also more cases of cheating by sympathetic teachers and desperate administrators" (Noddings, 2007, p. 71). There were many cases of test corruption during the Goryeo Dynasty (918–1392) and the Chosun Dynasty (1392–1910). Nam Hee Lee (2008) explains in her study on the shadow of gwageo that often "the only reason that students learned was to pass the exam. Practices such as cheating, the exchanging of answer sheets, and payments further corrupted the exam results" (pp. 130–131). This kind of corruption, seen nowadays also in test-paper theft and inappropriate testing practices, is not limited to schools in Korea, however. An instructor in a private American SAT preparation institution, for instance, was accused of leaking SAT test papers and answers (Retrieved from http://news.naver.com/main/read.nhn?mode=LSD&mid=sec&sid1=102&oid=003&aid=0004308250 on August 12, 2014).
15. In his study of whether the standardized test in New York State measures what it is intended to measure, Reich (2013) argues, "The content tested by an item is not always obvious at first glance, and selecting the correct or incorrect answer does not necessarily mean that a test-taker knew, or did not know, the material" (pp. 9–10)—a conclusion suggesting that the results tended to over-estimate test-takers' knowledge.
16. The 500 total points on the university entrance examination in 2013 broke down as follows: 100 for Korean; 100 for math; 100 for English; 50 each for social studies, science, and vocation; 50 in total for a second foreign language and Chinese characters. Each year, this test is made, organized, and supervised by the Korean Institute for Curriculum and Evaluation. Retrieved from www.kice.re.kr/contents.do?contentsNo=29&menuNo=215 on August 26, 2013. Although the inauguration of the admissions officer system is bringing some changes in the university student

selection system, the results of the SAT are important criteria. Thus the problems that I mentioned in Note 14 still exist.
17. Perhaps more importantly, however, the more students work at storing the knowledge deposited with them, the less they can develop the critical consciousness that could lead to their making positive contributions to their world, because in the control frame, students are conceived of as objects of intervention, not as subjects of encounters. To voluntarily and ethically engage in the matters of society, individuals need to develop their own agency and ability to conceive, understand, critique, or reject what happens around them. When students are always treated as objects that do not have agency or subjectivity, they are more likely to be unable to exercise their agency. In other words, the dependency is strengthened, and agency is weakened by objectification.
18. I explain how this happened to me in Chapter 2.

2

THE RECIPROCITY OF *CURRERE*, A RECONSTRUCTION OF SELF, AND AUTOBIOGRAPHICAL THEORY

This chapter has two foci: to depict the reconstruction of my subjectivity, and to detail the reciprocity among the circumstances of the study, my experiences, my academic interests, and my process of *currere*. I first share my subjective reconstruction through *currere*. I discuss my breakdown and the paradoxical elements of existence, the dialectic of anxiety, and the dialectical relationship between the world and myself. In this process I acknowledge how others have contributed to my process of *currere* and to the reconstruction of my subjectivity; although the reconstruction of subjectivity must be done essentially *in solitude*, the influence of others is undeniable in the circumstances of my work, subjective issues, my academic interests, and my *currere* work. Paying attention in this way to the reciprocity in play among these elements suggests how autobiographical work may not only benefit one's own development, but also contribute to autobiographical theory and method generally.

Introduction

> Autobiographical theories, at this historical juncture, need to evoke fractured, fragmented subjectivities as well as provoke discontinuity, displacement, and even estrangement in self-referential forms of curriculum inquiry to highlight how (self) knowledge can only ever be tentative, contingent, situated, and constantly re-situated in momentary yet swift streams of global mobilities.
> —*Janet L. Miller (2010, p. 65)*

> *Currere* is a method that produces a self in relationship to others.
> —*Nicolas Ng-A-Fook (2005, p. 55)*

Autobiographical theories of curriculum and the reconceptualization of the field of curriculum that occurred in the 1970s were pioneered by William Pinar's *Currere: Toward Reconceptualization* (1975a) and *The Method of Currere* (Pinar, 1975c) and Pinar and Madeleine Grumet's *Toward a Poor Curriculum* (2006 [1976]). With their phenomenological and existential approaches, autobiographical theories have challenged American curriculum studies by suggesting a shift in focus "from external, behaviorally oriented learning objectives and predetermined subject matter content to the interrogation of students' and teachers' inner experiences and perceptions" (Miller, 2010, p. 62). The decade-long challenge was, Pinar (2005) recalls, "simultaneously intellectual, political, and personal" (p. ix). By directly challenging the dominant mechanistic and technologized construction of curriculum, *currere*, as both a concept of curriculum and a form of inquiry, has "dramatically changed the nature of curriculum theorizing" (Miller, 2010, p. 62).

What *currere* seeks is "an architecture of self, a self we create and embody as we read, write, speak and listen" (Pinar, 1985, p. 220), and through which we can "reconnect the minimalized [and arrested], psychological self to the public, political sphere as it de-commodifies interpersonal relations" (p. 219). Felman notes that "one goal of autobiography is to create, use, and explore readings and writings of autobiography that recognize their own social construction and cultural conditioning" (quoted in Miller, 2005, p. 53). Similarly, Megill understands autobiography as "the task of self formation, deformation, learning, and unlearning. . . . Writing, and in particular, the craft of autobiography, can soar, and from the heights, discern new landscapes, new configurations, especially those excluded by proclamations of Government, State and School" (quoted in Pinar, 1994, p. 217). The potential for autobiographical work to reveal to us how we have been conditioned by culture, discourse, and history shows that it can be used for more than just the "telling of teachers' stories" (Miller, 2005, p. 53). At the same time, "interpretations [of autobiography are] always incomplete, always interminable" (Felman, quoted in Miller, 2005, p. 53) since the constantly expanding self "incorporates what it fears and resists as well as what it desires" (Pinar, 1985, p. 220). While for this reason we must accept that we can never completely understand the self, through autobiographical work we can perceive and reconstruct our subjectivity and our subjective sensitivity to the biographic and educational significance of our lived experiences. Autobiographical theories have provided me with a way to have a more authentic relationship with myself and to be most fully myself.

Despite criticisms of autobiographical theories,[1] *currere* continues to be a valuable method for studying one's subjectivity: for example, Ng-A-Fook (2005) found that *currere* offered "a migratory practice, and a place without an originary departure or final return" (p. 55); Wang (2010) used it to point out "the fundamental role of temporality in transformative education" (p. 275); Chien, Davis, Slattery, Keeney-Kennicutt, and Hammer (2013) attempted to combine it and the Second Life virtual world to make what they called a "virtual *currere* process"

(p. 215). In the range of issues they were investigating, as well as in the variety of ways in which they made use of *currere*, these researchers have suggested how wide its usefulness is as a method of study.

In my own work, I have seen how *currere* has contributed uniquely to my subjective reconstruction, to my relationships with others during that process, and to my present academic focus. I see a certain kind of reciprocity among these three *currere*-influenced aspects of my life. In the first section of this paper I discuss *currere* as both a concept and a method and briefly introduce its philosophical and theoretical groundings. The second section explains the circumstance of how this study began and proceeded. In the following section I share my endeavors to reconstruct my subjectivity through my attempts to draw on Kierkegaard's concept of anxiety. I close this chapter with the suggestion that those who engage in *currere* pay attention to the reciprocal relationships that exist between the circumstances of their work and their subjective issues, academic interests, desires and fears, and methods of using *currere*. It is my hope that this study exemplifies not only these reciprocal relations but also the fact that the reconstruction of subjectivity occurs both *in solitude* and *with others*.

Currere and Its Philosophical and Theoretical Groundings

There are two major contributions *currere* has made, in my judgment, to the field of curriculum studies: first, it provided a reconceptualized understanding of "curriculum" that rescued that term from its historical legacy best represented by so-called Tyler rationale; it provided a research method to the field of curriculum studies. Until *currere* appeared, methods in curriculum studies had relied heavily on the sociological and psychological theories prevalent in Tyler's time. These two historical legacies, the curriculum development model and adaptation of methods from other fields, have not yet altogether vanished from this field, either in the U.S. or in Korea.

In 1975, William Pinar proposed *currere*, from the same Latin root as that of curriculum—"to run the course," or "the running of the course"—as an alternative to the prevailing understanding of curriculum as the designing, planning, and development of materials and instructional strategies. Like others, including Heubner, Macdonald, and Greene, Pinar was troubled by the accepted view that curriculum exclusively concerned the observable, the external, and the public. The problem with such outer-directedness and with the resulting submerging of the self was, as Pinar (1975b) observed, that "we are not integrated, and further that many of us have forgotten that we are not integrated" (p. 388). In his essay titled "The Trial," Pinar (1976) powerfully describes the "arrested" character of modern life that causes us to become less attuned to our "inner world." This is the world that Jung would describe as comprising the "preconscious and unconscious layers" of our waking lives, and that Husserl and Heidegger would call *lebenswelt*: "the world of lived experience, the preconceptual experiential realm that is usually beyond our perceptual field" (Pinar, 1975b, p. 389). Because modern life causes us to forget we *have* inner worlds, our inner world seems obfuscated and even absent. In our educational lives, we lose our awareness of our subjectivity: that sense of inner life, "the lived sense of 'self'—however nonunitary, dispersed, and fragmented [—that is associated with the] . . . circumstances of everyday life, those residues of trauma and of fantasy, from which one reconstructs a life" (Pinar, 2006b, p. 3). *Currere* seeks to incorporate our inner lives into curriculum.

Until the early 1970s, those in curriculum studies had no method for studying their inner lives. To turn their attention inward, Pinar along with Madeleine Grumet devised a method—also called *currere*—to study individual educational experiences. *Currere* gives us a way to approach our inner world, which is present but more often than not hidden from us. It is a method according to which "students of curriculum [can] sketch the relations among school knowledge, life history, and intellectual development in ways that might function self-transformatively" (Pinar et al., 1995, p. 515). This method is, Pinar (1975b) acknowledged, grounded in "existentialism, phenomenology, Jungian psychoanalysis, the radical psychiatry of Cooper and Laing, and aspects of literary and educational theory" (p. 423).[2]

Although each of the above philosophical and theoretical approaches contributes uniquely to *currere*, they converge at three points: identifying the disintegration of the self; seeking a way to reverse this process through connecting the preconscious or inner world with the conscious self; and, most importantly, I argue, emphasizing the importance and primacy of an individual's awareness and capacity to engage in the integration process. Essentially, *currere* recognizes the existential human freedom that always accompanies existential human responsibility. Thus, "I" can and should do *currere* work. While advice certainly may be given, if I am solely responsible for how I do that work and the decision to do it, then the process might function self-transformatively for me. For more understanding about *currere*, let us turn to its groundings.

Psychoanalysis is a method of "systemic self-reflection" (Pinar, 1994, p. 195) that can reveal what one does not know, what one is silent about or even unaware of, or who one was and perhaps no longer is. One of its fundamental elements is Jung's concept of individuation, the psychological process of integrating the conscious with the unconscious so that a person has opportunities for better self-understanding. Jung considered individuation to be the central process in human development. Through the psychoanalytic technique of free association, a person can turn his or her attention inward, toward preconscious or unconscious layers of experience. Then that person may access fragments of the past that comment on the nature of individual experience and thus perhaps on present biographical and/or intellectual issues.

Existentialism gives priority to ontology before epistemology and seeks to understand the nature of the existence within which one inquires. In seeking the ontological meaning of educational experiences, Pinar (1975a) incorporates the contributions of existentialists, most notably Heidegger but also Greene, in understanding the role of the imagination or "wish" in one's determination of what the present contains (p. 423). A phenomenological method is incorporated for existential understanding. In Husserl's notion, phenomenological reduction, often called *bracketing*, is a suspension, as far as possible, of all interpretation and judgment on fragments one recalls or imagines. Bracketing is a prerequisite to phenomenological practice, a method of recording what appears when one uses *currere*. What does one put within these brackets? It is not our preunderstanding of our past, future, and present experiences: if that were the case, meaning or essence would also be absent—in *currere* writing, one's understanding of what emerges, which might be useful for later study, emerges intermittently. Rather, by bracketing we set aside our definitive judgments about what we have written in order to remain open to any possible, initially implicit, meanings that might not otherwise be observed.

The process of *currere* is hermeneutic and interpretive rather than descriptive and conclusive. Pinar (1985) explains that psychoanalysis "is a theory of knowing that takes creation more seriously than discovery" (p. 205). This emphasis on creation is essentially a rejection of the linear and goal-oriented act of discovery. The knowledge that can be obtained from *currere* is one's own knowledge: "while its roots are elsewhere, its plant and flower are its own; it is another species, a discipline of its own" (Pinar, 1975a, p. 402). The hope that Pinar (1975a) had four decades ago for the knowledge arising from *currere* was that it would "surpass these roots and [become] an area in its own right, with its own boundaries, content, and research method" (p. 423). For me, it has indeed become such knowledge.

Circumstances of the Study

This study arose as the consequence of several events. First, I experienced a breakdown[3] at the beginning of 2012, after months of frustration with myself. Second, during that time I was taking Professors William Doll and Donna Trueit's course, one of the special topics courses in curriculum theory offered by the Department of Curriculum and Pedagogy at the University of British Columbia. The conversations in the seminar were open-ended and allowed me to gain insight into my particular biographical and educational concerns. Third, in the spring of 2012 I audited Professor Anne Phelan's teachers' narrative course, for which I did some autobiographical writing on my own; and finally, I translated William F. Pinar's *Autobiography, Politics, and Sexuality* into Korean over that summer, a project through which I gained an in-depth understanding of *currere*. At the end of that translation project, I decided to do my own *currere* project for one of my comprehensive examination papers, which became the source for this chapter.

In that writing process of *regressive* (*re*: back; *gradi*: to step, go) and *progressive* (*pro*: before; *gradi*: to step, go), I freely associated with my past and future as I sat *in solitude*, a necessary condition in these phases of *currere*. I sat in a comfortable chair, leaning back and rocking a bit, in the dim light of a pleasant room. During the regressive step, I closed my eyes and recalled my past educational experiences, while during the progressive step, I imagined how my life might be a few years in the future. I tried to suspend my judgment and my inclination to interpret what came to mind during these steps, although doing so was not easy. Whenever reflections and interpretations arose, I put them in separated sections.

In the *analytic* (*ana*: up, throughout; *lysis*: a loosening) phase, I reflected on my biographical present, exclusive of the past and future: *What is my present? What are my academic interests? What is my emotional stance? What do I find compelling?* Then I compared these three pictures of my life—my past, future, and present—asking myself *Are there any issues, themes, or ideas flowing between them?* During this analytic phase I discerned themes, among them punishment, oppression, resistance, objectification, anxiety, love, fear, shame, and voice. I tried to ensure that my interpretation did not subordinate my lived present to the thematic abstractions, although the process was challenging since the abundant data and my analysis of it were complicated by my intellectual and emotional stances. When I read a piece of regressive writing that I had titled "love," for instance, I recalled that when I had written it for a previous course, I had thought of it as describing shame. My original interpretation of shame was now juxtaposed with a new interpretation of love. Yet I had to try not to revisit my original interpretation in light of my later emotional and intellectual perspective.

Once a person engaged in *currere* understands his or her subjectivity through the interpretation of these three life snapshots, a reconstruction of reality begins. This final phase of the *currere* process, the *synthetical* (*syn*: "together," and *tithenai*: "to place"), occurs when the person tries to find connections between the issues and themes that have been identified during the process. Unlike the coding used in grounded theory (a systematic methodology involving the discovery of theory through the analysis of qualitative data), the synthetical phase of *currere* does not aim to involve all the themes or issues that have been recognized in the analytic phase. One's intellect, emotions, and physical condition, all appendages of the self, the "I," are related to each other in complex ways. Central to this phase is to understand the self, which thus requires struggling with these complexities and which may involve misunderstanding. To understand is not only to attempt to make things clear and linear but also to engage with the nature of the problem or question; as a result, understanding is often not a one-time event but a continual and recursive process.[4] At this point in my *currere* project, I asked myself *Who is this "me" who is doing this work? What does the present mean to me, and how meaningful is this work to me? What point am I making in this phase? What issues and concerns am I disregarding if I decide to focus on my breakdown?* These questions indicated that I had chosen to study the biographical as well as the intellectual meaning of my breakdown. This synthetical interpretation of my subjectivity not only summarized the work I had done in my *currere* process but was itself a constituent of my biographic present.

In addition to presenting my solitary endeavor of *currere*, this chapter explores the importance to *currere* of one's relationships with others. When I realized the significance of these relationships to my process of self-understanding, in fact, I revised this whole chapter. I provide below my own journey of *currere*, which is a complex and ongoing project.

Breakdown and the Arrested Self

> Only via destruction of false self can the buried, authentic self be revealed. Laing (1960) understood that breakdown, even madness, can represent necessary means to sanity in some cases.
> —*William F. Pinar (1994, p. 212)*

One gloomy day in February of 2012, feeling extremely low, disappointed with myself for doing nothing, knowing nothing, not even why or from where such a seemingly endlessly deep gloominess came, I walked down to Wreck Beach—a nude beach I had never been to before, near the building that holds the desk and chair that have held me for almost two years. I felt that I had to escape from that building in which I had been stuck. I no longer knew what had brought me to that building. A meeting with Dr. Anne Phelan was scheduled in the afternoon. But I did not know what I would say. Was my depression due to this inability to speak? I realized that I had felt this way for at least a couple of months.

I felt a severe loneliness, though nobody could hear my silent, painful exclamation. The breakdown that had slowly been overtaking me broke through on that day. I wanted to flee from my despair or cure it, but I did not know how. Nor did I realize that this painful experience was the beginning of the destruction of my taken-for-granted ego, a release of my oppressed emotion and thus of arrested subjectivity.

Coming from an outer-directed culture and a test-focused educational system, and having been a full-time graduate student for two years, I eventually realized that I was struggling with the question of what I should think and study. Strangely, the very issue of finding my voice left me silent. And *nobody was there to tell me what I had to do*. I felt abandoned. Like Joseph K. in "The Trial" (Pinar, 1976, pp. 29–62), I was asking myself *Where is this feeling coming from?*

K. is a banker buried in his work, a "socialized, conditioned being" (p. 30). At work he has access to the law, but he does not at home; thus, it is not the bank where "he is arrested; it is at home" (Pinar, 1976, p. 31) because here he is stymied "intellectually, psychologically, and socially" (p. 33). While this blockage does not prevent him from carrying out his necessary tasks, K. is locked out of himself. His private life is almost entirely overshadowed by his social life. Because K.'s persona as a banker becomes his entire identity, he seeks solutions to problems in all aspects of his life the way he does at the bank. He therefore fails to direct his question appropriately. Similarly, in my own struggle it was my error of habitually seeking answers and solutions from outside rather than from within myself that had obstructed my access to my inner self.

For me, as for most people, the *habitual* was public and outer-directed, and "the force of habit is probably positively correlated with unconsciousness and captured by the past" (Pinar, 1994, p. 22). Both my questions and their directions were habitual. Janet Miller (2005) urges a person struggling in this kind of situation to break "the taken-for-grantedness of one's 'self' or of one's world" (p. 49). However, to break free of the force of habit, even to assess whether one is submerged in the taken-for-granted, is a challenge, especially for one who is psychologically arrested. My advisor asked me, "Why are you feeling that breakdown? Have you been comparing yourself with others?" "Yes," I replied without hesitation, "always." Saturated by my outer-directed culture, feeling that I was always being evaluated by others and more concerned with their objectification of me than with my self-reflective relationship with myself, I confessed that I felt left behind because several members of my doctoral cohort were already taking their comprehensive examinations, and some were even collecting data for their dissertations. I was reminded of Earle's assertion that, as Pinar (1994) put it, "In relative, everyday terms, others' objectification of oneself often does take precedence over one's first-person subjectivity. In an outer-directed culture, children are socialized from early on to care very much about others' objectifications" (pp. 105–106).

Becoming through this process aware of my arrested state, though still not clear about its cause, I tried to change what I was asking myself: *How can I better understand the nature of this breakdown?* Yet at the same time I had to suppress the strong desire of my arrested ego to satisfy my advisor with this paper, to realize my hope of hearing, "Oh, this is a really good piece." Without such reassurance I knew I would fall into fear, hesitation, and doubt about the quality of my work. This almost totally objectified aspect of my ego was something that I had to reconstruct: of course what others—especially my advisor and committee members—thought of my work was important, but what *I* thought of it was even more important. Cultivating the primacy of this relationship with the self is what Earle (1972) calls an "ontological autobiography with no particular emphasis upon its 'graphical' or recorded character; it is a question of a form of consciousness rather than of literature" (p. 10). For me, doing autobiographical work to free my arrested self thus required that I find what Jung called one's own voice, the voice of the self.

Understanding: Recognizing the Distance Phenomenon and Witnessing Signals

I was in the midst of a breakdown. I was lost, had lost my comfortable certainty, that stable, fixed home place. I was no longer sure if "here" was where I should be; I didn't want to return to the site of my previous arrest. I felt that rather than being stuck, I was in a psychological state akin to floating where my balance was challenged, where I was both uncomfortable about the uncertainty of that new state and relieved to be released from stasis. How could I understand these perceptions?

So I asked myself related questions: *What caused this change? What is the nature of these feelings?* The sense of "floating" might be invoked by a "distance phenomenon," a "juxtaposition of difference that create[d] distance and dissonance and that [would enable] me to rethink myself and the issues about which I [was] concerned" (Pinar, personal communication, Nov. 25, 2010). The "exile and estrangement" (Wang, 2004, p. 3) I had experienced by leaving South Korea to study in Canada might have initiated this distance phenomenon. For many, such distance seems necessary to understanding the self. A leading thinker, writer, and commentator on the Korean Buddhist tradition, Wonhyo (617–686 AD), tells this story:

> Wonhyo decided to travel to China, where he hoped to deepen his Buddhism. When he and his colleagues arrived at Dangjugye on a stormy day, darkness had fallen, so they took shelter in a cave that had been hollowed out of the earth. During the night Wonhyo was overcome with thirst, and reached out and grasped what he perceived to be a gourd, and drinking from it he was refreshed with a draught of cool water. Upon waking the next morning, however, his companions discovered much to their amazement that their shelter was actually an ancient tomb littered with human skulls, and the vessel from which Wonhyo had drunk was in fact a human skull full of brackish rainwater.
>
> *(Park, 2007)*

Moved by the experience of mistaking a gruesome site for a comfortable haven and a skull filled with stale water for a refreshing drink, Wonhyo was astonished at the power of the human mind to transform reality. Wonhyo realized that enlightenment consists of understanding that *everything is in your mind*. The story illustrates not only this famous Buddhist maxim but also the links between geographical and psychological journeys.

Can a journey beyond a familiar place trigger a journey into one's unknown self? Hongyu Wang (2004) suggests that a physical journey might actually give rise to a third space, "a space of creating one's own subjectivity among and through the multiple [layers of the self]" (p. 9). For Wang (2004), entering that third space is "enabled by 'the complicated conversation' (Pinar et al., 1995) that is curriculum among multiple layers of the conflicting double" (p. 9), which requires interaction, whether or not with other people. For example, the fact that international students bring their culture, language, and epistemology—that is, their particular realities—with them "transforms, as by magic, the physical environment labeled *office* into a *human situation*" (Aoki, 1981, p. 221): the physical environment becomes a human situation in which "conversation" arises between human beings. Aoki's notion of conversation is "open conversation, although not empty conversation. Authentic conversation is one in which the participants in the conversation engage in a reciprocity of perspectives" (Aoki, 1981, p. 228). The geographical distance from one's own country, along with encounters with others, allows for the possibility of new understanding and, evidently, of breakdown. Breakdown may not be a prerequisite to understanding, but understanding *is* a prerequisite to the reconstruction of one's subjectivity—in my case, comprising my escape from a state of arrest and my rebuilding of my subjectivity. In short, the phenomenon of geographical distance assisted my entry into this third space, where I could meet my unrecognized self.

Sometimes this distance phenomenon involves rigorous or painful attempts to recognize one's unrecognized self, especially for one who is arrested and therefore *insensitive* to the signals that could initiate self-understanding, as I was. I had previously written a commentary titled "An Inner Conflict Between *Kimchi* and *Starbucks*" to try to articulate how my geographical distance from Korea was affecting my understanding of myself. Pinar told me that geographical distance could help me overcome parochialism or provincialism, saying, "Distance is a prerequisite for understanding. Nothing has helped me [Pinar, American by birth] understand the USA more than working in Canada" (Pinar, personal communication, Dec. 10, 2011). After the course, I forgot his comment, as if its value had expired. When I revisited this comment after experiencing my breakdown, however, I felt its value. I suspected that I had forgotten about its biographical meaning because of my habitual approach to academic work: get the assignment done, get the grade, and then forget it, unless I need to use it for a later test. Did I miss the chance to reconstruct my arrested self when I wrote the commentary? Not forever, fortunately, since I did eventually recall the paper during my process of *currere*, and doing so helped me find other ways to understand my experiences.

Another kind of signal, a resistance to the memorization-oriented education, appeared in my *regressive* writing. Despite my customary conformity to authority, exams, and punishment, I exploded once during high school:

> *In my vocational high school, most subjects required memorization, which I hated. For one test, I had to memorize which amounts of elements (carbon, manganese, nickel, and silicon, among many) were present in each of the numerous types of steel (high-, low-, or middle-carbon steel, spring steel, aluminum, and so on). One question asked how much nickel was in spring steel, and I had to remember the exact percentage or guess one of the multiple choices. I thought the question was ridiculous. Why not provide students with a table that showed the types of steel and their constituent elements? Eventually I gave up, and I received a score of 25 or 30 out of 100. Although I began high school in the top fifteen percent of students, when I finished I was among the bottom ten percent.*

Failing meant that I gave up on excelling as a student and decided to be a "punk." In retrospect, I see this decision as an effort at resistance; I was exercising agency. What I am interested in here, however, is not only the signals themselves but also my changed response to them. This fragment of my educational experience might have remained dormant if I had not undertaken this *currere* project.

What awoke my sensitivity to signals that I had to resist the educational authorities in my life? First, the geographical and cultural distance from my home country and its educational system might have been at least partly responsible; as the physical distance and the different culture in academia increasingly became psychological, I came to see those parts of myself that had been arrested. Second, as I was gaining access to these previously unrecognized parts of myself through the distance phenomenon, my relationships with others were also contributing to the process. After I had talked about my breakdown with Dr. Anne Phelan, whose teachers' narrative course I was auditing, she and I recognized punishment, memorization, love, competition, fear, oppression, subjectivity, and resistance in my autobiographical writings; we then discussed how I might use these emotions as themes in my studies. At the same time, I was taking Dr. William Doll and Dr. Donna Trueit's curriculum theory seminar. Their approach was for me as surprising as it was successful. Thanks to the idea of subjectivity suggested by Dr. Phelan and "the art of listening" (Taubman, 2012, p. 24) demonstrated by Dr. Doll and Dr. Trueit, the great wall between my inner self and my academic work began to crumble. They met with me not to talk to me but rather to listen, their focus being to help me in my development: to help me "grow and actualize" myself (Noddings, 2002b, p. 19). That is "care."

Rather than being the passive acceptance of information, this kind of listening is powerfully constructive, the active encouragement of the other's revelation through support and respect. The atmosphere thus created ignites thinking, not the sort that is the "heritage of the scientization of contemporary thought" but rather the "passionate thinking with which Heidegger was concerned, . . . meditative rather than calculative" (Pinar, 1994, p. 211). Encouraged by supportive listening, such thinking has great ability to transform "misery into existential angst" (Britzman, quoted in Taubman, 2012, p. 24), as the next section of this chapter reveals.

Understanding: Anxiety and Paradox

To understand my breakdown, *such a seemingly endlessly deep gloominess*, I wanted to think about a statement I had found in my regressive writing: *disappointed with myself for doing nothing, knowing nothing. Nobody told me what I had to do.* Why was I disappointed with myself for knowing that I did not know what to do? Why was I waiting to be told what to do by somebody else, probably by my teachers? My inability to listen to myself, to discover my academic interests, was probably my biggest challenge in the early stages of my graduate studies. Recognizing this inability may have caused my disappointment with myself. While I realized that that anxiety could be in part attributed to my outer-directed cultural background, I wanted to study my anxiety itself.

The notion of angst, meaning *anxiety* or *dread*, is derived from Kierkegaard's notion of *Begrebet angst*. To explain angst, Kierkegaard described a man standing on the edge of a tall building or cliff. The man experiences a fear of falling, but at the same time he is terrified by his impulse to throw himself off the edge. The freedom to decide what to do precipitates anxiety or dread, what Kierkegaard termed our "dizziness of freedom" (Park, 1999, p. 197). For me, Wreck Beach was, I think, equivalent to Kierkegaard's cliff or mountain; according to Kierkegaard, angst informs us of our choices, our self-awareness, and our personal responsibility. It is such anxiety that brings us from a state of unselfconscious immediacy to self-conscious reflection, whereby we recognize our potential and our inevitable responsibility for our decisions. Thus, anxiety is not always detrimental.

According to Chunkik Park (1999), "Kierkegaard acknowledges that learning anxiety well or truly is the best learning. When one does not know how to do 'anxiety,' one loses his or her self because of not having the experience of anxiety or merely falling into anxiety" (p. 201). Park (1999) explained the significance of anxiety in understanding human existence:

> A mood of anxiety that in fact pushes one into questioning one's own existence is truly a mood that makes a human being a truly human being. Anxiety is not a mere feeling but rather a signifier of a fundamental element of human existence. Once anxiety sweeps over one, one can flee from his or her naïve peacefulness, as Kierkegaard says.
>
> *(p. 215)*

For Heidegger, anxiety is an appropriate response to the open-ended nature of human existence. Therefore, in relation to my own process of *currere*, I asked myself, *Does my breakdown reflect the anxiety that precedes or coexists with freedom? Can anxiety move me to the practice of freedom?* I think that I was struggling with these questions. Although I could not explain my psychological state definitively, I saw ways in which I could convert my distress into an opportunity to further my intellectual and biographical development. Paradoxically, my experience made me aware of both my arrest and my existential freedom, of my outer-directedness and of the possibility of breaking from the familiar comfort of following instructions by moving into the anxiety of experiencing freedom. Should these opposites be resolved, or reconciled? If so, how could I do it? Or might the paradox in itself constitute an opening for understanding, since "paradoxes provide opportunities for denaturalizing what appears as natural" (Derrida, quoted in Wang, 2010, p. 282)? Grumet (2006) explains that the paradoxical nature of our being "preclude[s] certainty, [which is] an understandably attractive feature of any rationale that may be employed to guide actions and decisions (p. 35). Then, perhaps the problem was my difficulty in tolerating "uncertainty, resistance, and the unknown" (Britzman, 2003, p. 15). Grumet (2006) elaborated on Hampden-Turner's (1971) identification of tolerance for "paradox and dialectic as a requirement of full psycho-social development" (p. 72):

> The test of a first rate intelligence is the ability to hold two opposed ideas in the mind at the same time and still retain the ability to function. . . . We cannot talk about education without talking about the dialectic between man and his world, a dialectic that holds all the mysteries and ironies of paradox. The apparent polarities of subjectivity and objectivity, immanence and transcendence, particularization and generalization, essence and existence dissolve into reciprocity, each constituting the other.
>
> *(p. 36)*

In light of Grumet's ideas, the paradox of my being, and the dialectic between myself and the world,[5] I realized that I might be able to understand my experience as my entry into the anxiety of freedom. That perspective made me willing to tolerate the paradox; even if my angst was painful, it was the pain of renewal or rebirth. However, at that point a familiar concern arose: that I was falling into another arrest by uncritically accepting Grumet's and Hampden-Turner's ideas. I decided that although that may be the case, at least I knew the risk and I would just have to move through another stasis if I had to. In fact, I would probably move constantly, since my study of anxiety functioned biographically "to provoke movement and release from arrest, a phenomenon recognizable enough to hint at a dramatic word such as *liberation*" (Pinar, 1994, p. 48).

Incorporation

Every morning, I found myself sitting with my laptop in my study, surrounded by books and by notes pinned to the walls. I imagined what would happen to me when I finished this program. I imagined my committee complimenting me on this paper and feeling proud of myself. At that moment, however, my fantasy was replaced by a strong concern (sometimes this seemed to be fear; other times, hesitation): my interest in the committee's response was foremost in my mind, before my own relationship with what I was writing. The by-product of learning had become more important than learning itself. With that, I lost my confidence and desire to study—I was frozen and arrested again. Then I took a moment to catch my breath. I reminded myself of how significant this work was to me, and how the relationship between my work and myself mattered. I suppressed my outer-directed self.

My underlying intention in this study is to gain a deeper understanding of my subjectivity. To that end, every day since I first became aware of my angst I consider my changing feelings and my states of mind, my hope and despair. At the same time, I know that I remain who I was the previous day, with the same feelings, fears, and aspirations. I am surprised at how complex my feelings are and how they increasingly complicate my subjectivity. The thought that I may be falling into narcissism or nihilism at first made me disappointed, discouraged, and uncertain. Pinar (2011) acknowledges the complexity of the effort to understand "I":

> "The more we think about the 'I,'" George Grant (1966 [1959], p. 69) reminds us, "the more mysterious this subjectivity will appear to us." Knowing oneself is, then, no simple matter of paying attention to what happened—although it depends on that—as it requires retrieving what has happened already and remains only as residue and sometimes [is] not readily accessible. The ongoing sense of mystery in fact impels self-study and haunts the formation of the subject.
>
> *(p. 8)*

Thus, understanding my "I" is as mysterious as it is complicated. The process still takes my breath away. At times I decided that I would stay away from this work for a time. And I would think that maybe these reactions relate to that ongoing sense of mystery that impels self-study. Certainly, I welcome the time when my self "constantly expands to incorporate what it fears and resists as well as what it desires" (Pinar, 1994, p. 220). The verb *incorporate* is important here: I have been struggling to rid myself of the uncomfortable, unfamiliar feelings of fear and resistance that I have been experiencing. But *should* I be trying to dispel them? Is doing so even possible? Or should I live with them? And can I?

These questions seem to complicate my situation more than they clarify it.[6] Nevertheless, I will try to answer them, however tentatively. My first question at this point should be "Can I rid myself of my fear and resistance?" because the answer will determine which questions follow. This question presumes that fear is detrimental, negative, or at least does me no good. However, is that necessarily so? For Kierkegaard, the seemingly negative feelings resulting from anxiety were neither negative nor permanently eradicable:

> Despair is a qualification of spirit, in that it is related to the eternal in man. But the eternal he cannot get rid of, no, not to all eternity; he cannot cast it from him[self] once [and] for all, nothing is more impossible; every instant he does not possess it he must have cast it or be casting it from him[self]— but it comes back, every instant he is in despair he contracts despair. For despair is not a result of the disrelationship but of the relation which relates itself to itself. And the relation to himself a man cannot get rid of, any more than he can get rid of himself, which moreover is one and the same thing, since the self is the relationship to oneself.
>
> *(Kierkegaard, 1941, pp. 23–24)*

If Kierkegaard is right, then I cannot cast my despair away, and despair is not necessarily undesirable. I suspect that I had assumed that it came to me from outside myself, so I had to expel it. However, it may be a part of myself that I cannot get rid of unless I get rid of myself (perhaps this is why some people *do* get rid of themselves). I see that I can't "get rid" of anything; rather, I have to work with what causes me pain, treat it like clay and make something else of it.

How can I incorporate my ambivalence about myself? Incorporating these feelings might mean letting them be, accepting who I was and who I am, simultaneously different and the same, aware of this ambivalence, of my paradoxical attachment to certainty and my aspiration for openness, and of my arrested ego and my liberated self.

The Dialectic of Anxiety

Studying my educational life has yielded moments of self-understanding, although as an ongoing task, that knowledge is inherently incomplete. Since I now see that my breakdown was a form of anxiety, I have found Stephen N. Dunning's (1985) understanding of Kierkegaard's systemic analysis of anxiety to be pertinent to my process of understanding and incorporating my experience. Dunning (1985) asserted:

> The three moments of the dialectic of anxiety [anxiety-in-itself, anxiety-for-itself, anxiety-in-and-for-itself] can be analyzed as follows: an initial, abstract unity in which the self has not yet consciously distinguished itself from its external world; a negative dialectic of opposition between the self as inner and an external power that determines it; and the self that finds in faith the culmination and fulfillment of its dialectical education by anxiety.
>
> *(pp. 31–32)*

In the first moment of the dialectic of anxiety, anxiety-in-itself, the self is exclusively socialized, and arrested, by social roles. But is living immersed in one's job, for instance, always problematic? It becomes so when the social role subjugates the private life. When a teacher, for instance, sees his or her self as being defined only by the government or institutions, that person is unlikely to exercise personal agency. He or she is arrested.

The second moment in the dialectic, anxiety-for-itself, is a state of negative opposition between the inner self and the external power that defines it. An arrested self constantly finds external solutions to the problems of being. The arrested self is not aware that the anxiety is a constituent of the self. Thus, for a time I looked to others for help or advice in working through my breakdown. Indeed, psychological consultation might have helped somewhat, and simply talking about my experience with people to whom I was close was usually helpful to some degree—but only temporarily. Without understanding that my anxiety came from within, my efforts to expel it with the help of others could provide no lasting solution.

Dunning (1985) describes the third phase of the dialectic as a final reconciliation in which a person recognizes and appropriates the power of self-determination. To that end, I wanted to accept the fear, resistance, and anxiety within my subjectivity that I might earlier have disavowed or ignored. In perceiving such ignored but present parts of the self, one also perceives that although others can assist in the process of understanding the self, one's subjectivity is, ultimately, one's own responsibility.

Although I feel that I have moved through these three stages, several dilemmas nevertheless remain unresolved for me. While I have glimpsed the nature and characteristics of my experience, I doubt that I am ready to embrace "the dizziness of freedom": I still feel more alienated than liberated or "at home within the world" (Pinar, 1994, p. 211). Perhaps more accurately, I feel *both* alienated and liberated: certainly the phases of anxiety are dialectical rather than linear. I continue to struggle with them all, perhaps because my sense of myself is constantly moving. As Pinar (1994) points out, "As one becomes conscious of one level of arrest, and through a self-reflexive understanding of that level, one moves to another level, that [level] will someday become experienced as static. To remain on any one level means arrest" (p. 40). That arrest is, Pinar (1994) argues, "death" (p. 40). When I was psychologically static and anchored by strong certainties, I was comfortable and felt no danger or risk. Once I began to move, danger and risk arose, but so did possibility and vitality. I see now that I have the right to choose and to be responsible for my choices, and that "liberation is a process and one which has gradations of realization" (Pinar, 1994, p. 102); it is never final or complete. I feel that the misery of my breakdown has turned into existential angst. While this psychological and intellectual change might not entirely change my "self," it has given me the capacity to reconstruct my arrested self.

The reconstruction of self requires rigorous intellectual and psychological contemplation. This labor can take various modes, including academic study, conversation with others, or "meditative inquiry" (Kumar, 2011, 2013). Whatever form it takes, the purpose of this labor is to build the "autobiographical consciousness" (Pinar, 1976, p. 42) that enables us to understand, deconstruct, and/or reconstruct our subjectivity. Through this work I have come to understand how, as a student and a teacher, I have been conditioned by my educational experiences in South Korea; what my breakdown meant to me; and what I want to do with it. I have begun to understand the complexities and paradox of my being-in-the-world, an awareness that may signify what Pinar calls the "ontological shift from outer to inner" (Pinar, 1974, p. 15). In the unstable freedom of angst, one should neither entirely deny the remnants of the arrested self nor subordinate the self to any form of authority.

Autobiographical inquiry, *currere* in my case, aims to improve one's relationship with one's self. I see my process as resembling a dance with my arrested self in which "[I] hold my damaged ego like a father tenderly holding his son" (Pinar, personal communication, Jun. 3, 2012). I aspire to become aware of my physical, emotional, and intellectual states; for me, this possibility of resensitizing my subjectivity and revealing its biographical and educational meanings is an important function of *currere*.[7] However, the consequences of this work are implicit rather than explicit; complicated rather than simple; recursive rather than linear; descriptive rather than prescriptive. Although this work has not given me a clearly defined way to act in the future, it has provided me with a better relationship with my self, a better understanding of my educational experiences.

The Reciprocity of *Currere*

The reciprocity of *currere* is multidimensional. First, there is reciprocity between the modes of study: in my case, between being *in solitude* and being *with others*. Private endeavor is, of course, necessary to self-understanding; however, as Pinar (1994) points out, for many people "work with others . . . is a medium through which they work with themselves" (p. 53). The agency of self and the self's relationship with others contribute to self-understanding. A Chinese four-character idiom (啐啄同時; mutual pecking out and pecking in) is pertinent here. It describes the pecking of the chick (啐), the pecking of the hen (啄), and their mutual relationship (同時) as the shell is broken and the chick hatches. The hen never leads the process; rather, she observes, listens, and responds to the chick as necessary. For me, "the others" were my professors and the authors whose thoughts I brought to this work.

The process of acquiring self-understanding offers the opportunity to reconstruct one's reality. Although the only one who can do that reconstruction is "I," that reconstruction can occur only if "I" works reciprocally with others. These relationships with others may occur through in-person conversations or other means, including close engagement with texts and dialectical relationships between the knower and the known. Both of these ways of fostering relationships answer the criticisms of *currere* and autobiographical theories (see Note 1, this chapter).

Reciprocity also resides between the mode of study and the issues that are studied. The roles of other people in my *currere* work resonate with my current academic interest, the association between self-understanding and the notion of care (Noddings, 1984, 2005, 2007, 2010d). That I have become attuned to others' roles in my *currere* may be either the cause or the result of my interest in the notion of care and its emphasis on reciprocity. Whichever one gave rise to the other, however, there certainly now seems to be a reciprocal relation between these interests.

The psychological shift "from outer to inner" may be an ontological form of reciprocity. I have learned that I was, am, and at times will be arrested. At the same time, while I know that I want to be free from that stasis, I also know that from time to time, I will be pulled back by its strong gravity. One might say that my take on Kierkegaard, Grumet, and Pinar is another form of my habitual outer-directedness. But that state of arrest is different from the state that caused my breakdown, because I am aware that this academic mode of being might be a form of conformity or submission. I go forward and backward between the old and new, but without a final destination. This may be why Ng-A-Fook calls his *currere* work "migratory practice" (2005, p. 55).

Reciprocity addresses the uniqueness of one's autobiographical study in that it encourages one to appropriate, or revise, the theories or methods one employs. If I share the method of *currere* with colleagues and my students, I certainly also share my experience of that process, and specifically the roles of others in person and in texts, since for me the contributions of others were vital to what I gained through *currere*. However, I would not suggest that everybody should prioritize the contributions of others over other necessary elements of *currere* work, such as study through reading; rather, I am proposing that one of our autobiographical tasks should be to reflect upon our application of autobiographical theories or methods, perhaps asking ourselves such questions as *Why choose this method over that one? How are my biographic situation and intellectual interests associated with various methods or theories? How are my academic interests and my way of doing currere associated with each another? If I feel the need to revise the method I am using, how and why do I want to do so?* By paying attention to the reciprocity between the circumstances of the work, subjective issues, academic interests, and autobiographical theory and method, we may each find a method for doing autobiographical work that not only benefits our personal development but also contributes to autobiographical theory and method. Thus, this study does not claim to provide the most effective way of doing autobiographical study; rather, it emphasizes the importance of reciprocity in the paths we choose for our autobiographical journeys.

Notes

1. The application of autobiographical theory is not without criticism. Critics have argued that it amounts to "mystical alchemy" (Tanner & Tanner, 1995), that it is "narcissistic and solipsistic and purely personal" (Gibson, 1991, p. 498), and that it is only a "superficial affirmation of (re)interpreted lived experiences" (Rodriguez, 2005, p. 119). Janet Miller (2010) also warned that there are "(mis)appropriations of *currere* as autobiographical method" (p. 63). The (mis)appropriations Miller identifies are the assumptions [beliefs?] that autobiographical theory is no more than the swapping of life stories and that by drawing on a wealth of data, the teller and the listener might be able to discover a way to change education. Responding to the first concern, Miller (2010) argues that autobiographical theories are actually neither the "telling [of a] . . . story that repeats or reinscribes already normalized identity categories" (p. 64), nor a "means of arriving at solutions and answers to pedagogical and curricular issues and problems" (p. 63). Rather, autobiographical theories, Miller (2010) argues, "address inquiries into dislocated and destabilized versions of selves, of nations, cultures, and languages, as well as of multiple and competing transnational discourses that now frame and constitute any iterations of identities and subjectivities" (p. 65).

   Currere has also been attacked by Hlebowitsh (1992), who argued that it is interesting but "appears to come at the expense of the collective-encounter so obviously valued

by Dewey [which is the civic mission of the school for democracy]" (p. 76). "*Currere* may seem solitary work. Indeed it must be, at least occasionally" (Pinar, Reynolds, Slattery, & Taubman, 1995, p. 523). But *currere* by no means ignores the culture, discourse, history, and politics of the society in which the one doing the work dwells; these factors are/should be involved in understanding the self.
2. Pinar details this method through the four essays in his edited book *Curriculum Theorizing: The Reconceptualists* (Pinar, 1975b) and in his collection of essays, *Autobiography, Politics, and Sexuality* (1994). Pinar's acknowledgement of the influence of Laing's and Cooper's work should be noted, given that both were important figures in the antipsychiatry movement.
3. I use the word "breakdown" literally here to describe the breaking down of the arrested self. This term does not imply mental illness or the need for medical intervention; rather, it signifies my experience of subjective disintegration.
4. Recursion, which William E. Doll (1993) discussed as one of his "4 Rs," is a "looping back," a self-reflection, that allows one to "[create] one's own conscious self—the highest expression of human awareness" (p. 289).
5. For a discussion of phenomenology's emphasis on the reciprocity of subjectivity and objectivity and of existentialism's emphasis on the dialectical relationship of people and their situations, Grumet's (1975) paper *Existential and Phenomenological Foundations of Currere: Self-report in Curriculum Inquiry* is helpful.
6. "Complicating" is a significant function of the autobiography of self; as Pinar (1994) argues, "Autobiography is interesting when its telling enlarges and complicates the telling subject, and the listening subject. We are not the stories we tell as much as we are the modes of relation to others our stories imply, modes of relation implied by what we delete as much as by what we include" (p. 218).
7. I do not imagine that those in an arrested state will attain complete "acquittal" by engaging in *currere* or other autobiographical work; however, that process may provide them with moments of insight into the "complexities, sources, and the depth of [their] . . . internalized oppression" (Miller, 2005, p. 73). The self-reflective understanding I was hoping to achieve with my *currere* project concerned "the nature of my arrest" at that specific historical, biographical moment, though that understanding was complicated and obscure because it was multidimensional and deeply embedded within me. This kind of understanding, Pinar (2012) argued, "automatically leads to change; more exactly, understanding, itself, is change. Without understanding, there is only spectacle, fascism in our time" (p. 214). For Miller, autobiographical engagements also might become "modes of action" (Miller, 2005, p. 73).

3
AN ETHIC OF CARE

In Chapter 1, I argue that what is suffocated under the tyranny of information and skills in Korean history and culture is the subjectivities of students as well as those of teachers. Chapter 2 testifies to the consequences of the tyranny, the arrested self, and shares my (unending) journey to reconstruct my educational experiences through the method of *currere*, a journey of self-care through self-understanding. In this chapter I discuss Nel Noddings's ethic of care, which provides me with the foundation of my understanding of care-for-others. I first discuss the roots of an ethic of care from ontological, philosophical, and theoretical angles. I then discuss three aspects of an ethic of care that I think important for curriculum studies specifically as well as for education in general: its difference from ethics of justice, coercive caring, and reciprocity and inclusion. I conclude with an emphasis on the importance of self-understanding in an ethic of care.

Introduction

> The living other is more important than any theory.
> —*Nel Noddings (2005, p. xix)*

> Whilst Carol Gilligan's *In a Different Voice* (1982) introduced the ethic of care into academic and public discourse, it is Noddings who has done most to outline a specific feminist position on moral education.
> —*Bernard E. McClellan (1999, p. 104)*

As soon as I read *An Ethic of Caring and Its Implications for Instructional Arrangement* (Noddings, 1988), I was captivated by Nel Noddings and her theory. From reading her books and articles, I have learned how Noddings's private life has informed her academic aspirations. Her educational philosophy, professional collegiality, and private life are all welded together, as the collection of letters *Dear Nel* (Lake, 2012) demonstrates. For this chapter's discussion of her philosophical contributions to the field, I therefore begin with a short biography of Noddings and then turn to the roots of her ethic of care (relations, philosophy, and the feminine perspective) and the themes in her work that are fundamental to my research: an ethic of care *vs.* ethics of justice, coercive caring, and reciprocity and inclusion.

Nel Noddings was born January 19, 1929 and grew up in a working-class family in northern New Jersey. Now she lives on what is known as "the Jersey shore" in the mid-Atlantic coast of the United States. Recalling how her school life became her real life, she says:

> It is a peculiar history. . . . Somewhere around age of seven my whole sort of psychological orientation changed and school became my real home. . . . My mother was reasonably supportive. But for some reason or another I made that psychological change.
>
> *(Noddings, 2010b)*

Noddings described the school she attended as a progressive public school: "There was a lot of art, music, drama and no homework, so it must have been progressive!" (Noddings, 2010b). Although many students are terrified if not traumatized by their school lives,[1] Noddings's unusual psychological change signifies the source of her aspiration for education.

She met her future husband, Jim, in high school when they both were fourteen. They have ten children, five biological and five adopted. When asked about the influence of her children, Noddings explained, "I am so grateful for that experience [having ten children] because I learned so much from those kids. . . . I suspect if I hadn't had all those kids, I might have become an intellectual snob. . . . I have been rescued from that" (2010b). No one would doubt that being a mother of ten children would affect one's thinking about education and vice versa.

Lynda Stone (2006) also emphasizes the significance of Noddings's early life and of where she lived and now resides:

> This place [the New Jersey shore area] fostered her many personal interests, greatly influencing an early desire to become a teacher and writer. From the second grade on, she wanted to be a teacher. Lifetime loves of history and literature were initiated in that school just as lifelong loves of gardening, canning and cooking were germinated in the fertile coastal soil.
>
> *(p. 17)*

Noddings's experiences in gardening, canning, and cooking, domestic tasks traditionally considered as women's work, in fact "contributed to her general conception of education and to specific views about schools" (Stone, 2006, p. 17).

In an interview with Joan Montgomery Halford (1999), however, Noddings reported that her first three years of teaching—throughout which time she taught the same class of students—"colored her life more than anything else" (p. 39). After graduating from Montclair State College, where she trained as a high-school math teacher, she was unable to find a teaching job, so she decided to teach a class of sixth-grade students. The first year went well; meanwhile, the school found that the junior-high classes were extremely crowded. Noddings therefore asked the school if her students could stay with her for another year, given consent from their parents. At the end of that second year, because the junior-high classes were still crowded the students stayed with Noddings for a third year. Noddings taught them all of the subjects in the curriculum, and was especially proud that her students not only achieved almost exactly the same academic levels as students taught by specialists, but were "head and shoulders over all the other kids in that they were more polite, happier and nicer to each other in an affective review" (Noddings, 1995). This extraordinary combination of events in her life as a student, mother, and teacher seems to have strongly informed Noddings's ethic of care.

Noddings went on to earn a bachelor's degree in mathematics and physical science from Montclair State College, a master's degree in mathematics from Rutgers University, and a doctorate in the philosophy of education from Stanford University. Starting in 1949, she worked for seventeen years in elementary, secondary, and post-secondary institutions, serving not only as a mathematics teacher but also school administrator, department chair, assistant principal, curriculum supervisor, curriculum developer, and university instructor.

After earning her Ph.D. in 1973, Noddings took faculty positions first at Pennsylvania State University and then the University of Chicago, returning in 1977 as a faculty member to Stanford University. Her career at Stanford included the posts of the Lee L. Jacks Professor of Child Education in 1992, associate dean of academic affairs, and acting dean in 1990 and 1992. Leaving Stanford in 1998 as a professor emerita, she accepted positions at Teachers College, Columbia University, Colgate University, the University of Southern Maine, and Eastern Michigan University (Stone, 2006, pp. 14–15). She has held memberships in the Philosophy of Education Society and the John Dewey Society (Coleman, Depp, & O'Rourke, 2011). To date, Noddings has authored 18 books as well as numerous articles, book chapters, and contributions to conference proceedings. Her works have been translated into 12 languages, and she has reviewed and served on the editorial boards of over 30 journals. Her 1998 retirement from Stanford did not signal the end of her academic contributions.

Roots of the Ethic of Care

> Only the individual can be truly called to ethical behavior, and the individual can never give way to encapsulated moral guides, although she [or he] may safely accept them in ordinary, untroubled times.
>
> —*Nel Noddings (1984, p. 103)*

As a scholar of educational philosophy, feminism, and pragmatism, Noddings is in the forefront of educational philosophers and theorists in North America today (Bergman, 2004, p. 149; Stone, 2006). The ethic of care that Noddings has developed over three decades outlines "a specific feminist position on moral theory" (McClellan, 1999, p. 104) and on educational practice (Bergman, 2004, p. 149). For Noddings, caring is relational, not a principle or form of ethical deliberation nor a virtue in the sense of a list of personal qualities. It is in direct contrast to traditional ethics—such as "principled Kantian ethics" (Stone, 2006, p. 31), which are based on justice and principles—that are often "shortsighted and arrogant [approaches to] . . . what it means to be moral" (Noddings, 1988, p. 218). Noddings's ethic of care has its roots in both relational feminine and pragmatic naturalism (Noddings, 1995, p. 137). In the following section, I discuss the three roots of her ethic of care: relations as ontology, pragmatism, and the feminine perspective.

Relation, Obligation, and Autonomy

> Relation is ontologically basic and the caring relation morally basic. We become individuals only within relations.
> —*Nel Noddings (2010d, p. 101)*

In Noddings's (2003) view, "Before individuals, communities, or sub-cultures come into existence, there is a relation—encounter and response" (p. iv); that is, ontologically we are dependent upon one another in a society; when we are born we are existentially already in the world. She elaborates: "We are recognizable individuals as separate physical entities, but the attributes that we exhibit as individuals are products of the relations into which we are cast" (Noddings, 2010d, p. 101). The argument can be found in its negative form in the example of feral children.

Noddings (2002b, pp. 91–117) further argues that an individual is a "relational self," the self continuously growing through its encounters and their effects, a dual process that creates the self. In effect, the complex concept of self is a co-constructed entity that "directs and interprets the activities of the organism" (p. 117). Thus, *self* constantly constructs, reconstructs, and expands in nature, having neither "the essential freedom . . . to construct itself" nor being "entirely shaped by the environment" (Noddings, 2002b, p. 117).

While this concept seems relatively easy to accept—who would argue for a completely pure self—Noddings also puts forward a controversial view on *obligation*: there are moments when our inclination to care-for-others "naturally arises, as a feeling, an inner voice saying 'I must do something'. . . . No ethical effort is required and there is no demand to care" (1984, p. 81). Noddings calls this inclination *natural caring*. She extends that idea in the following rather radical statement:

> We cannot demand that one have this impulse ["I must"], but we shrink from one who never has it. One who never feels the pain of another, who

> never confesses the internal "I must" that is so familiar to most of us, is beyond our normal pattern of understanding. Her case is pathological, and we avoid her.
>
> *(1984, p. 81)*

The pathological case that Noddings is referring to is that of a mother who neglects or abuses her child until that child dies, asserting that such a mother is "often considered sick rather than immoral" (Noddings, 1984, p. 83). Thus we can say that, other than pathological cases, most humans have the "I must" impulse. In this passage Noddings expresses no requirement that carers act for reasons of obligation; she is discussing feelings here rather than principles and action. Certainly I agree with her, in that there are moments when we each *feel* "I must."

Nevertheless, a critical question arises: does the fact that we are always in relationships with others obligate us to *feel* obligated by summoning the feeling "I must"? Noddings would answer *yes*: "We are obligated to accept, and even to call forth, the feeling, 'I must'" (1984, p. 84). She makes clear that caring is not unconditional and does not imply uncritical acceptance—she discusses how critical thinking in conjunction with autonomy interacts with caring, as I explore later. At this point I have two further concerns. First, how can we generate the feeling "I must" if we do not already feel that impulse? Second, how can we prevent "I must" from quickly becoming an excessive inclination, one that might cause coercion or pathological caring? The latter problem I discuss in the section that follows on "coercive caring."

In regard to the question of how the "I must" feeling arises, Noddings recognizes that there are moments when that inclination of obligation to the other fails or is resisted, conflicted, or denied. In that case, "we must call upon our capacity for ethical caring" (Noddings, 1984, p. 81), the capacity that many of us experienced in our intimate experiences with our mothers. Noddings (1984) argues that when the spontaneous sense of obligation fails in a caring relationship, in addition to *natural caring*,

> [the] second sentiment is required if I am to behave as one-caring [one who cares for another]. I care about myself as one-caring and, although I do not care naturally for the person who has asked something of me—at least not at this moment—I feel the genuine moral sentiment, the "I ought," that sensibility to which I have committed myself.
>
> *(p. 82)*

While pointing out that "we are not compelled by this impulse: that is, we have choice; we may accept or reject what we feel" (Noddings, 1984, p. 83), Noddings also asserts that "if we have a strong desire to be moral we will not reject it" (p. 83). This desire to act morally, she explains, can be cultivated from the fundamental and natural desire to be and to remain related to others. In other words, what Noddings emphasizes is not that we are all obliged to take action as carers, although it is encouraged, but that *we have the ability to choose our response to our initial impulse of "I must," or even call forth that feeling if it does not arise on its own.* Noddings is boldly advocating that we preserve and utilize our deepest and most tender human feeling, that of "a caring mother for her child, of human adult for human infant, which elicits the tenderest feelings in most of us" (Noddings, 1984, p. 87).

By arguing that the feeling of "I must" can indeed be summoned, Noddings wants to breach the wall between emotion and logic. My initial reaction to her idea was to wonder whether "I must" *can* be summoned. That is, given that "I must" is a feeling, as Noddings defined it, can logic summon that impulse? Regarding this question, Noddings, agreeing with Hume, starts with the assumption that

> human beings have a natural tendency toward benevolence—to be pained by another's pain, troubled by another's predicament, pleased by another's pleasure. Hume (probably an atheist) does not claim, however, that people are born good, . . . For Hume, sympathy is the universal human emotion that links us together as individuals in particular circumstances and as human beings in a universal moral world.
>
> *(1984, p. 160)*

What about people like Taliban extremists, one might ask. They may lack benevolence, not be pained by others' pain. But when we think about the idea of benevolence within the family—between father and son for Taliban—I think we can agree that most people feel the benevolence and sympathy that Hume described.

Through her discussion of sympathy, Noddings (1984) emphasizes the characteristics that a carer should develop: engrossment (thinking about somebody to understand him or her, being in a burdened mental state of solicitude about someone or something), commitment (acting on behalf of the cared-for, thus showing a continuing interest in the other), and motivational shift (the carer's energy flowing toward the other without the carer relinquishing her own soul). Later, in *The Maternal Factor: Two Paths to Morality*, Noddings renamed "motivational shift," calling it "attention," to clarify that the carer's "motive energy is directed (temporarily) away from her own projects and towards those of the cared-for" (Noddings, 2012, p. 53). While motivational shift is not entirely an emotional attribute, which means that it can be triggered by our intention or desire, Noddings (2012) identifies it as a component that is characteristic of and appropriate to caring. Through this logical argument, Noddings tries to indicate how we can indeed summon the feeling of "I must." Noddings thus keeps alive in her thinking both feeling and logic, as Pinar (1999, p. 58) and Mayer (2012, p. 15) applaud.

Noddings's ideas about obligation have, however, raised criticism. One objection is that Noddings's ethic of care "underestimates the significance of personal agency" (Alexander, 2013, p. 493); a related criticism is that Noddings's emphasis on relationality "undermines women's autonomy" (Davion, 1993, p. 161; Hassan, 2008; Keller, 1997). Keller, for example, complained that Noddings's ethic of care is not suitable for feminism. Care interrupts autonomy by interrupting the development of a woman's ethics and thinking for herself (Hassan, 2008, p. 160). Keller concludes that "under the obligation to care, the ability of a woman to choose her relationships is diminished" (1997, p. 161). Essentially, these critics think that Noddings's theory is "not beneficial to feminism because it . . . hinders a woman's ability to become autonomous, and [thus] reinforces traditional gender roles" (Hassan, 2008, p. 159).

These criticisms raise an important point about human autonomy. An ethic of care challenges individual autonomy at its roots by its emphasis on the relational nature of human existence. Noddings argues that "it is clear that human beings are not autonomous (free to choose) in many of the categories governing our lives" (Noddings, 2010d, p. 112), such as being parents and belonging to particular cultures, language groups, historical eras, and so on. Of course one can leave any institutional affiliations or original associations, such as family, if one chooses to, as Noddings (2010d, p. 112) acknowledges, but it is not easy to do so. The issue of autonomy is often in conflict with "self-sacrifice" and "self-denial," and "pathological forms of caring, forms characterized by continual self-denial" (Noddings, 2005, p. 105).

"Limited autonomy" (Noddings, 2010d, p. 113) by no means requires self-denial or self-sacrifice in an extreme sense. A person, Noddings quotes Ruddick, "who counts herself as nothing lacks the confidence needed to suspend her own being to receive another's" (2010d, p. 122). If a carer's emptiness is involuntary and often frightening, Ruddick continued, "she searches in her child to find the self she has sacrificed" (quoted in Noddings, 2005, p. 105). Ruddick (1989) agrees that "to court self-denial for its own sake perverts rather than expresses attentive love" (p. 122). Since mothers are rewarded for self-sacrifice and daughters learn this behavior from their mothers, women are "especially prone to this perversion" and always therefore face "the danger of denying their own needs only to find they have projected them onto their children" (Ruddick, 1989, p. 122).

Noddings and Ruddick therefore reject the idea that caring should involve the total loss or perversion of self, instead arguing for the caring soul that can empty itself *without* losing itself, "a soul that already has known, respected, albeit ever-developing self to return to when the moment of attention has passed" (Ruddick, 1989, p. 122). How then can we empty our souls without losing them, so as to prevent our caring from becoming servitude or self-denial? The answer to this question can be found in critical thinking, which Noddings emphasizes (2002a, 2006, 2010d) as integral in developing autonomy and in exercising ethical caring.

Noddings (2010d) argues that "no other moral approach has greater need for critical thinking [than caring], and it must be exercised in every facet of life" (p. 119). Rather than blindly complying with another's demands, Noddings asserts that carers should evaluate their own responses to those encounters:

> I think about whether I should feel the way I do about various encounters. Past encounters become the objects of new encounters. The self at previous moments becomes another object of encounter, affect, and evaluation. I approve of certain ways of being in the world and reject others. Further, some are approved or rejected unreflectively (without this second layer of evaluation, on the basis of mere feelings), some become habitual (evaluated once and for all), and others are objects of continual scrutiny. This highly complex relation, the self, will continue to all encounter-pairs in which one element is its present self or its associated organism, others in which self and past or future self (imagined) compose the pair. In this elementary and highly abstract start I have asserted that the self *is* a relation, that it is dynamic, in continual flux, and that it is a center of affect and meaning.
>
> *(Noddings, 2002b, p. 99; emphasis in original)*

In Noddings's view, caring thus requires analysis of circumstances; understanding the people, both carer and cared for, involved in those circumstances and their needs; one's values; the resources available; and—possibly most importantly—self-reflection. Self-reflection in turn requires continual scrutiny of past experiences with the awareness of the complicated, dynamic, and unending formation and reformation of self. This self-reflective mode of being connected to others is what Noddings calls "intelligent heteronomy" (Noddings, 2010d, p. 30) or "relational autonomy" (Noddings, 2010d, p. 111). Caring strongly requires us to activate agency and self-reflection, although acting according to an ethic of caring may often involve risk, sometimes extreme, as in the example of a woman who killed her husband because he had severely abused her child (see Noddings 1984, pp. 98–103). Sometimes too, acts of caring are refused or fail. Nevertheless, Noddings argues that we need to commit ourselves to recognizing that our inevitable relatedness requires us to remain accessible to the other. Remaining accessible to the other may not directly and necessarily trigger "I must"—there are individuals who only want to *be* with others or who are fully happy only in others' presence. However, for Noddings, it is the ontological foundation that obligates us to feel "I must" and call it forth if it does not arise spontaneously.

Pragmatism and Existentialism

While caring relations involve obligation and autonomy, the fact that they are also experiential, situated, and concrete invites a discussion of the role of pragmatism in those relations. The very root of care and thus of her educational thinking,

Noddings (1995) acknowledged, may "properly be identified with pragmatic naturalism" (p. 145), which leaves two important points. First, the nature of human beings on earth evolves under changing dynamic conditions: Dewey shared Darwin's explanation of the origin of species, but not his conclusion, which is survival of the fittest. Second, human life is not essentially competitive but cooperative (Garrett, 2003). "Dewey started his ethical thought with the observation," Noddings (1995) tells us, that "human beings are social animals and desire to communicate" and "desire to be cared for" (p, 145) with languages and ideas.

Along with the recognition of the role of students' perspectives,[2] Noddings emphasizes the importance to her ethic of consideration of concrete circumstances. Our ethical ideas should not be frozen into one pattern for all time. They should change according to circumstances. She argues that the relational ethic remains "tightly tied to experience because all its deliberations focus on human beings involved in the situation under consideration and their relations to each other" (Noddings, 1988, p. 218). Noddings explained the significance of concrete experience to caring this way:

> I am interested not in ultimate structures of consciousness; I seek a broad, nearly universal description of "what we are like" when we engage in caring encounters. I am interested in what characterizes consciousness in such relations, but I do not claim to have found an essence or attempt to describe an ultimate structure; nor do I depend on a sense of consciousness as supremely constitutive of reality. Rather, the attributes or characteristics I discuss are temporal, elusive, subject to distraction, and partly constituted by the behavior of the partners in caring.
>
> *(Noddings, 2002b, p. 13)*

The essential interactiveness between humans and circumstances and the variety of human encounters causes those encounters themselves, as well as the carer and cared-for involved, to be "subject to change" (Noddings, 2002b, p. 14). "Reception, not projection," Noddings (2002b) argued, "marks the attention" (p. 15) that signals the carer's readiness to receive and respond to the needs of the other. That readiness can then be actualized only through the process of experience. These temporal and elusive characteristics of caring and of experience increase the complexity and but also the possibility of relationships. In recognizing these qualities, Noddings "returns us to the world of everyday experience, my life, and the lives of others I am pointed to" (Pinar, 1999, p. 57). She therefore does not see caring relationships as involving fixed structures, structures that, if we allow ourselves to be bound by them, distract us from existential problems. Essentially, then, Noddings "sacrifices neither the experience to the argument, nor the argument to the experience" (Pinar, 1999, p. 56)

This existential aspect of Noddings's philosophy encouraged Linda Stone (2006) and Bruce Novak (2012) to see Noddings's philosophy as phenomenological and Noddings as an existentialist. A former student of Noddings, Stone argues that Noddings's "pedagogy itself appears phenomenological" (2006, p. 27) and claimed that her philosophy is in part an "existential phenomenology" (p. 27). That is, Stone explains, "Working from a real world context, experiences, and relevant texts, she [Noddings] describes teaching that mirrors and/or is mirrored by her writing" (2006, p. 27). Stone (2006) contends that Noddings's analysis therefore arose from "a kind of existential phenomenology" (p. 27).

Like Stone, Bruce Novak affirms the existential attributes of Noddings's theory. Referring to Noddings's 1998 talk, "Caring About Is Not Enough,", Novak (2012) writes to Noddings:

> Clearly you [Noddings] knowingly adapt for everyday pedagogical use two of Heidegger's central terms: *Umsorge*, "caring about," interest, pure and simple, and *Füsorge*, "caring for," solicitude for another being *as* another being. In "caring for," as you put it in *Caring*, my ordinary interest is "displaced"; "my I becomes a *duality*," entering the realm of life Martin Buber calls the "I-Thou" relationship.
>
> *(p. 79; emphasis in original)*

If we understand *Umsorge* as "caring about the affairs of the world" (Novak, 2012, p. 79) and *Füsorge* as "caring for," *Füsorge* is indeed what Noddings's views assert. There is a difference between the two concepts; according to Noddings, the carer first considers neither the phenomenon nor problem but rather the person, the "cared-for": this is *Füsorge*. When caring is aimed at a problem, however, it is *Umsorge* and can easily become prescriptive, within which most education is occupied.

Both Stone's and Novak's interpretations of Noddings's thinking are persuasive in that they recognize Noddings's concerns with existential problems and with the specificity of people involved in caring relations. However, whether these aspects of her work suffice to identify Noddings as a phenomenologist or existentialist is arguable. I wonder whether a focus on experience, context, and Heidegger's *Umsorge* and *Füsorge* are sufficient to define her approach as phenomenological or existential; Noddings nowhere explicitly considers free will in a radical way. Nevertheless, I do see at least two phenomenological elements in her early work, Husserl's idea of *bracketing* and Heidegger's of *attunement*:

> [When we are acting as carers] we can switch from an assimilatory mode to a receptive-intuitive mode which, by a process we do not understand well, allows us to receive the object, to put ourselves quietly into its presence. We enter a feeling mode, but it is not necessarily an emotional mode. In such a mode, we receive what-is-there as nearly as possible without evaluation or assessment. We are in the world of relation, having stepped out of the instrumental world; we have either not yet established goals or we have

suspended striving for those already established. We are not attempting to transform the world, but we are allowing ourselves to be transformed.

(Noddings, 1984, p. 34)

In referring to a "receptive-intuitive mode," and describing how "we receive what-is-there as nearly as possible without evaluation or assessment," this passage first describes "bracketing," what Husserl (1964, p. xxi) called the "phenomenological *epoché*" (p. xxxiii), the prerequisite of phenomenological reduction that consists of "the suspension of judgment in regard to everything that, in the transition from the not-yet-evident to what-is-evident, is to be left out of consideration" (Kockelmans, 1994, p. 118). Bracketing is the putting aside of one's preconceptions in order to see what-is-there. Without conscious bracketing, one's preoccupations and memories of previous experiences trigger the evaluation or assessment process that is in opposition to Noddings's ethic. In a caring relationship, for instance, the latter process may consist of applying principles or following prescribed actions on the basis of our past encounters.

The second element of the passage above that seems to me existential is what Noddings called the "feeling mode," which resembles Heidegger's *attunement*, a "mood, being in a mood" (Heidegger, 1996, p. 126). It is our being thrown into the world or a state of mind in which we receive what-is-there, but not "yet-established" that allows our consequent transformation. Both Noddings and Heidegger recognize our possibility of being in certain openness to the experiences in which we find ourselves, in a world that we cannot control or transform but that speaks through us. The capacity for attunement comes neither wholly from inside nor wholly from outside (Wrathall, 2006, p. 34); attunement is therefore neither entirely objective nor entirely subjective but rather arises "out of being in-the-world" (p. 34). Between objective and subjective is certain kind of dialectical relationship. *Dasein* (our *being* or *existence*), Wrathall (2006) argues, "constantly *surrenders* itself to the 'world' and lets the 'world' 'matter' to it" (p. 35; emphasis added)—and I think Noddings's statement that "we are not attempting to transform the world, but we are allowing ourselves to be transformed" shows that she shares this view. I do not mean that I have to conform to the structures, but rather to be transformed through being-in-the-world.

Another existential interpretation of Noddings's care emerges from a juxtaposition of Gert Biesta's and Noddings's ideas. According to Noddings, the receptive character of caring genuinely welcomes the other's presence and transformation on both sides:

> Indeed, for the one-caring [carer] and the cared-for in a relationship of genuine caring, there is no felt need on either part to specify what sort of transformation has taken place. The intangible something that is added to the cared-for (and often, simultaneously, to the one-caring) will be an important consideration for us when we discuss caring in social institutions and, especially, in schools. It may be that much of what is most valuable

in the teaching–learning relationship cannot be specified and certainly not prespecified.

(Noddings, 1984, p. 20)

Noddings observed, as Pinar (1999) noted, "the unspecified nature of this something added" (p. 59); that is, that the "something" *cannot* be specified. This impossibility of prescribing the "something added" is also central in Biesta's (2013) *The Beautiful Risk of Education*:

> What I felt was missing from pragmatism was an awareness of what I would now call the deconstructive nature of "coming into presence," that is, the idea that the condition of possibility for anyone's "coming into presence" is at the same time its condition of impossibility.
>
> *(p. 143)*

Drawing on the Derridian concept of "impossibility" as something simply not foreseeable, and postulating in a chapter about Dewey's theory of communication that "most if not all education operates through communication" (Biesta, 2013, p. 25), Biesta goes on to suggest that "deconstructive pragmatism" is "a radically weak understanding of communication" (p. 26); as Derrida put it, "Communication is always already *in deconstruction*" (Biesta, 2013, p. 41; emphasis in original). By *weakness*, Biesta here means not incapability but the receptive ability to welcome "something added," something that cannot be foreseen but that can be valuable, through being in the world and encountering others. Given Noddings's and Biesta's similar views on the importance of openness and the unforeseeable in caring relationships, I think Biesta would see in Noddings's thinking "deconstructive pragmatism." This crucial, unspecified, and unforeseeable element of relations in caring is, unfortunately, missing from today's teaching–learning relationships (Pinar, 1999, p. 59), most certainly in a test-focused system.

Even though Noddings rejects characterizations such as Stone's and Novak's of her work as phenomenological or existential, saying "I never warmed to Heidegger" (quoted in Novak, 2012, p. 79), I think that in her emphasis on lived experience, in which existentialism and phenomenology converge, a phenomenological and existential element is indeed present in Noddings's work. Investigating the philosophical elements in her theory would certainly help to reveal the roots of Noddings's work. Her thinking on philosophical aspects and her ideas of relation are intertwined, as is best represented in her ideas on the feminine influence, discussed below.

Gender and the Feminine Influence

> [Noddings] unites [feminine and masculine into] an androgynous prose, which in the present historical moment is usually dissociated.
>
> —*William F. Pinar (1999, p. 59)*

> Nel's experiences as a teacher and scholar are seen through the eyes of a mother.
> —*Robert Lake (2012, p. 1)*

The umbrella theme of gender, which permeates almost all of the concepts that Noddings has developed, has provoked controversy and criticism. This section examines these responses. Noddings did not identify the gender aspect of her thinking in her first paper, "Caring" (Noddings, 1999 [1981]), although her thinking here hinted at the role that gender plays in caring. It was William Pinar who helped Noddings recognize the centrality of gender to her theory.

In her subsequent works, Noddings has explicitly discussed the influence of gender. When Noddings published "Caring" (1999 [1981]), Pinar responded, referencing Madeleine R. Grumet's (1981) "Contradiction, Conception and Curriculum," and writing that "the capacity to experience, understand, and articulate subjectivity tends to remain intact in the woman, while becoming repressed in the man" (Pinar, 1999 [1981], p. 57).[3] Pinar and Noddings both value feminine experience and capacities and criticize their sublimation in masculinity.[4] The Oedipal crisis, Pinar (1999) explains, is the process of the male becoming differentiated from his mother by characterizing himself as cognitive, rational, and logical and her as irrational, emotional, "intersubjective and undifferentiated" (p. 58). Although to different degrees and in different forms across age, race, class, and sexual orientation, women's characters and their inclinations toward their feelings and emotions have historically and culturally been considered by men as well as women to be inferior or subordinate to the characters and inclinations of men. The consequence is, as Pinar asserted, that "the politico-economic tendencies parallel the epistemological ones in the tendency to objectify and naturalize contingent and variable human experience into invariant laws and objective truth" (1999, p. 58). In contrast, by bringing the feminine into masculinized education, Noddings, as Pinar recognized, wanted to increase the value and respect accorded to feelings, experiences, and subjectivities.

Noddings (1984) initially dismissed as "nonsensical" (p. 128) the gender socialization Grumet and Pinar understood as an explanation for her theory. Noddings wonders

> why it is that women in virtually all societies are the care-takers of children. The biological view holds that women, having given birth and entered lactation, are naturally nurturant toward their infants.
>
> *(1984, p. 128)*

In this paragraph, Noddings's biological standpoint is evident without the socialization standpoint. Noddings thought the psychological gender socialization view that gender is socially constructed, developed by Nancy Chodorow (1978) and advocated by Pinar and Grumet, "denies natural instinct and nurturance and insists that mothering is a role—something learned" (Noddings, 1984, p. 128).

However, she acknowledges, "A woman's natural inclination to mother a newborn does not explain why she continues to mother a child into adolescence or why she mothers other people's half-grown children" (Noddings, 1984, p. 128). She concludes that "it may well be that a completely adequate theory will have to embrace both biological and psychological factors—and, perhaps, even socialization factors—if we are going to consider competence in mothering" (p. 128). Furthermore, agreeing with Pinar and Grumet with regard to socialization, Noddings (1984) argues that "man (in contrast to woman) has continually turned away from his inner self and feeling in pursuit of both science and ethics" (p. 87), the consequences of which have been "disastrous" (p. 87) with respect to ethics.[5]

Eventually, a decade after first proposing her ethic of care in her article "Feminist Fears in Ethics" (1990), Noddings abandoned the biological view of why women tend to be more caring than men and accepted the explanation based on socialization:

> I have always intended to rely on women's experience, not women's nature, to build my arguments for an ethic of care. But I wasn't as careful as I am now, and there are places where I've used the words "nature" and, more often, "naturally." I tried to explain this usage by referring to centuries of fairly stable experience that might indeed induce something like a "feminine nature." But now I think it may be best simply to avoid such language entirely.
>
> *(Noddings, 1990, p. 26)*

Here Noddings points out that "nature" and "naturally" were not referring in her work to women's generative ability but to women's experience: that is, the sociological and psychological rather than the biological aspects of gender.

What is more important for us than biology and the socialization debate in her ethic of care is probably why Noddings calls her ethic *feminine*; that is, "the approach of the mother" (Noddings, 1984, p.2), which she calls *natural caring*: that is, caring for others more naturally arises in women's experience than in that of men. Natural caring is the typical mother's inclination and attitude toward her child—although of course not all mothers care the same way and some fathers care more than their partners. Even those who are not biological parents—gays and lesbians, adoptive parents, and others—may be effective carers; and cultural and historical factors also affect ways of caring. When natural caring does not occur, the distinctions between moral rationalists' and ethical carers' approaches are clear; the "moral rationalist advises us to think conscientiously about the principles that should govern our behavior whereas care theorists advise us to draw upon our own ethical ideal—one built over a lifetime of natural caring" (Noddings, 2010d, p. 68). Noddings's ethical ideal is a picture of goodness that requires both that the carer's energies being directed toward the other and his or her project and that the carer reflect on the way he or she is simultaneously cared-for, which includes the "longing to be received, understood, and accepted" (Noddings, 1984, p. 49).

At the same time as it has this basis in feminism, however, Noddings's ethic of care also has other roots: she looked for a theoretical foundation beyond "add women and stir" (Noddings, 2001b, p. 29). Unlike progressive feminists, whose purpose is to change or subvert historical and cultural acceptance of the subordinate status of women, Noddings—along with other care ethicists such as Virginia Held (1995), Carole Gilligan (1982), and Claudia Card (1990)—has sought to articulate what we can learn from the female experience[6] rather than rejecting it. They are fully aware of the subordinate status of women in dominantly masculine private and public attitudes. The latter perspective is pervasive in school and cultural contexts, whose hallmarks are grades, competition, logic, and standardization. Although the consequences of masculine characteristics predominating may be disastrous, Noddings has written that women should not feel forced to discard "virtues and traits honored by men" (Noddings, 2002a, p. 109); rather, "the voice of [the] mother [should be] heard in both ethics and education" (Noddings, 1984, p. 182). It is important to understand that Noddings's gender-based claim here is not antagonistic—she does not argue that women are morally superior to men. Rather, she urges that we all "pay attention to a perspective on ethical life that is available (has been and will be) to us through women's experience and that may help all of us lead better lives" (Noddings, 2002a, p. 107).

Noddings suggests that our view of care "be analyzed anew from the perspective of women so that both women and men can be relieved of the burden of stereotypical expectations and of the violence and oppression that accompany them" (Noddings, 2002a, p. 109). Noddings further argues that we can gain "greater self-knowledge through studies that help [us] to accept [our] personal and group shadow sides" (p. 117). *To accept* in this claim means not to passively submit to them but rather to understand how they have shaped, conditioned, or arrested us. Thus, Noddings has aspired to a certain "dialectic between male and female [perspectives]" (p. 114).

Recently, Noddings has argued for "a convergence of care theory and traditional male ethics" (2010d, p. 9) over any choice between masculinity and femininity during the planning of curriculum and instruction. In her view, the least desirable human legacy is "the lingering male tendency to aggression and domination" (p. 8), a tendency that Noddings rejects. Further, she suggests that "instead of asking why women lag behind men in mathematics, we might ask why men lag behind women in early childhood education, nursing, and like activities" (p. 65). What makes Noddings's philosophy unique for me is that her primary interest is not to subvert the structures in which women have been oppressed—although they should be recognized and discussed—but rather to raise the awareness of men and women in valuing not only the tasks women traditionally gravitate to, but also what women are generally good at. This approach is nonviolent or non-antagonistic, with which current Korean education is dissociated.

An Ethic of Care and Ethics of Justice

> We want it [justice] tempered by care. And . . . care theorists speak often of "balanced caring," by which they seem to mean caring incorporated in a larger system of justice.
> —*Nel Noddings (2010d, p. 90)*

From the three roots of Noddings's ethic of care that I have discussed above, relation, philosophy (pragmatism and existentialism), and gender and the feminine influence, I want to discuss three themes—justice and care, coercive caring, and reciprocity and inclusion—that strongly challenge typical notions of caring. The dominant masculinized aspects of modern society and morality have relied primarily on justice, rationality, abstraction, and objectivity not only in theory but in practice. Some philosophers have argued that emotion and feeling have therefore typically been seen as leading to moral judgment and action rather than justice (Gilligan, 1982; Held, 2006; Hume, 1997; Noddings, 1984, 2010d). Noddings rejects Kantian ethics, particularly criticizing Kant's dismissal of women's inclination toward "the beautiful, [and,] in social relations, to be kind and loving" (Noddings, 2010d, p. 22). According to Kantian ethics, "Acts done from love or inclination have no moral worth. To have moral worth, . . . [Kant would say that] an act must be chosen in obedience to an ethical principle" (Noddings, 2010d, p. 36). Against Kant's dismissal of women's inclination toward love and to allowing feelings a role in morality, Noddings argued—as Hume would have—for the need to "give a central place to the role of emotions in moral life" (Noddings, 2010d, p. 31).

In emphasizing the importance of feelings in caring, Noddings's ethic of care directly conflicts with the Kantian idea of the traditional "lofty principles of institutions" (Noddings, 2005, p. 116), which demonstrate no interest in the perceptivity and receptivity of caring. Foucault (1983) restates what Kant says: "I must recognize myself as universal subject, that is, I must constitute myself in each of my actions as a universal subject by conforming to universal rules" (p. 280). Rather than following Kantian ethics (principles based on reason), Noddings agrees with Hume that the ideal caring relation is relational, reciprocal, and reactive, affected by emotions and experience. For Noddings, appreciation of the human tendency toward benevolence (see the discussion in the earlier section in this chapter, "Relation, Obligation, and Autonomy") is more evident in women than men. In other words, her care ethic's prioritization of emotion distinguishes it significantly from traditional justice-based ethics: the former is relational and situational, while the latter ignores those elements. For Noddings, because universal moral principles ignore the uniqueness of particular people in particular situations,[7] such principles have limited use in guiding moral actions. To explain this limitation, Noddings throughout her ethic of care uses contrasts: right vs. need, masculine vs. feminine, prescriptive vs. descriptive, principle vs. feeling, ethics of justice vs. an ethic of care, and coercive caring vs. an ethic of care.

At the same time, however, these contrasting concepts are not always irreconcilable opposites. Noddings does not entirely reject justice and reason; rather, she argues that these values, along with feelings, can be incorporated in her ideas about caring. In contrast, the Kantian ethic absolutely rejects the idea that women's inclinations have moral value, a clear difference between Noddings and Kant. For Noddings, reason should not come first. Referring to the research conducted by Gilligan (1982), Noddings argues that the female subjects involved in Gilligan's study "used reason, but they invoked it in assessing relationships and responses" (2010d, p. 23). According to Gilligan and Noddings, in ethics reason might need to be suspended—as in the "bracketing" discussed in the "Pragmatism and Existentialism" section of this chapter—in order for the carer to be able to be receptive to the needs of the other. For this reason, Noddings believes that reason should not dominate or subordinate the inclination to natural caring and that "care ethics may contribute substantially to a modification of justice" (2010d, p. 162).

What Noddings wants to do by rejecting the "lofty principles" is to avoid the objectification of the cared-for (1984, pp. 15–16)—that is, of other human beings and later ideas, other creatures and the planet. Thus, for example, her analysis of a mathematics teacher's approach to a student who was struggling in math was, as Pinar has noticed, "simple but powerful" (1999 [1981], p. 59): Noddings explains that for the teacher, students are infinitely more important than the subjects; the teacher shows "I am still the one interested in you. All of this is of variable importance and significance, but you still matter more" (Noddings, 1984, p. 20). Pinar (1999) further observed, as do I, that Noddings's language "is not the language of the Father, whose final commitments are to achievement and career; it is the language of the Mother, for whom, even in failure, her baby remains irreducibly important" (p. 59).

A universal principle of justice would, by its very nature, seem to depend on the assumption that human situations and predicaments exhibit a high level of uniformity; on that basis, they are proposed as useful abstractions of the specific, concrete situations in which we are involved. This necessity has, however, led Noddings to become interested in why the *particular* "condition which makes the situation different and thereby induces genuine moral puzzlement cannot be satisfied by the application of principles developed in situations of sameness" (1984, pp. 84–85). When we focus on the sameness of human situations, we quickly begin to objectify the individuals involved; simultaneously, that focus causes the individual's "I" to lose its uniqueness, its subjectivity.

Noddings also found objectification a topic of interest in the thinking of Tyler and Dewey: "Dewey spoke of learners whereas Tyler spoke of groups. Dewey directs our attention to individuals and their particular interests" (Noddings, 2008, p. 139). To treat people as "types" instead of individuals is objectification. When we are categorized under gender, grade, ethnicity, sexual orientation, age, and cultural background, "we become 'cases' instead of persons. . . . The fact is that many of us have been reduced to cases by the very machinery that has been instituted to care for us" (Gordon, Benner, & Noddings, 1996, p. 27). In terms of curriculum, a justice-based approach focuses on a curriculum that provides a specified knowledge and skill package that has been organized by outsiders applying certain values and criteria, whereas a caring approach puts aside "predetermined and externally imposed ends" (Doll, 1972, p. 309) in favor of students' needs in specific contexts.

The fundamental difference between Tyler's and Dewey's views in regard to what constitutes curriculum—and we could also consider Kant's and Hume's views here—is in the value they place on students' needs. For Tyler, students' expressed needs are irrelevant to educators' superior understanding of educational goals. Noddings, however, invites us to question what is probably our biggest and most detrimental assumption as educators: that we know what children need. She argues that when we try to meet these inferred needs, unfortunately "we often neglect the expressed needs of our students" (Noddings, 2005, p. 147); that is, our preoccupation with inferring the needs of our students obscures the importance of their expressed needs, although the latter possibly have considerable intellectual and biographical significance. Furthermore, as a result of being focused on inferred student needs, we not only sacrifice "opportunities to develop [students'] individual talents, intrinsic motivation, and the joys of learning" (Noddings, 2005, p. 147) but also miss opportunities to develop caring relationships with students. These losses more often than not lead us into coercive caring.

Coercive Caring

Many parents and teachers, as Noddings (2005) pointed out, tend to think "someday you'll thank me for this" (p. xvi) when they impose particular knowledge, skills, or behaviors on the children in their care. Although they are sometimes right, the opposite possibility, that their actions may be pernicious, is possible too. And the consequences for subsequent generations of such coercion by teachers and parents may be "one of the greatest tragedies of traditional education" (Noddings, 2005, p. xvi). Yet coercion in the name of caring continues to be particularly prevalent in societies where educational systems explicitly objectify students and discourage "questioning [of] the pervasive instrumentalism associated with social engineering" (Pinar, 2011, p. 83). These educational systems are rife with the familiar, sad consequences of coercion: observed cheating by students, teachers, and administrators, and corruption in teacher–student and parent–child relationships.

In fact, considerable educational and parental coercion has taken place in the name of caring; how often have we observed that while parents and teachers are struggling to care, students are declaring, "nobody cares!" What is the source of these discrepancies? In her books *Prisoners of Childhood: The Drama of the Gifted Child and the Search for the True Self* (Miller, 1997 [1979]) and *For Your Own Good* (Miller, 1984), Alice Miller, a German psychoanalyst, explores this question through her groundbreaking analysis of how the roots of violence spring from our misguided child-rearing practices:

> It is the tragedy of well-raised people that they are unaware as adults of what was done to them and what they do themselves if they were not allowed to be aware as children. Countless institutions in our society profit from this fact, and not least among them are totalitarian regimes. . . . Conditioning and manipulation of others are always weapons and instruments in the hands of those in power even if these weapons are disguised with the terms *education* and *therapeutic treatment*.
> *(Miller, 1984, p. 227)*

Noddings, agreeing with Miller's description of such "poisonous pedagogy" (Noddings, 1984, p. x), asserts that "the oppressed often fall into collusion with the oppressor and then, with the best intentions, pass that oppression on to others" (Noddings, 2001a, p. 36) from generation to generation. Miller described how for her, the results of this destructive pedagogy "for a long time . . . separated me [Miller] from my true feelings, from myself" (Miller, 1984, p. x). The same kind of pedagogy leads some adults "to the emotional blindness responsible for the absurd attitude they act upon as parents and educators. The denial of endured violence leads to violence directed toward others or oneself" (p. x). This "poisonous pedagogy" and other coercive childrearing practices often confuse love with abuse and violence (Miller, 1984). Furthermore, in engaging in this kind of violence, some parents or teachers substitute abstract conceptions of life for "lived life," thereby distracting their attention from the actual children in their care, whose existence cannot be reduced to an abstraction and who are irreplaceable.

What can educators and parents do in the face of this traditionally acceptable form of coercion? No ethicist, including Noddings, can explain how to act in every situation so as to ensure that coercion does not occur; it is never a simple question, even for psychoanalysts like Miller. However, Miller (1984) urges us to recall how we have been raised, treated, and educated; having accessed her own past through painting, she suggested we each find our own ways to recall our early experiences. Above all, Miller (1984) calls on us to do the following:

> Affirm and lend our support to the human objects of manipulation in their attempts to become aware and help them become conscious of their malle-

ability and articulate their feelings so that they will be able to use their own resources to defend themselves against the soul murder that threatens them.

(p. 277)

In the face of the "soul murder," which may reside in ourselves and/or in others, we can use our own resources to activate our capacity to understand our past and reconstruct it. However, coercion is not completely avoidable: sometimes we knowingly choose to use coercion, believing it is necessary. In this situation, Noddings explains, "Carers know that the relation is at risk" and carers therefore need to ensure that "the cared-for [is] allowed to express her hurt, and help must be offered; every act of coercion [needs to be] followed by negotiation, not authoritarian demands for compliance" (Noddings, 2001a, p. 37). At other times, however, we unwittingly act coercively. In this situation, Miller's idea of self-analysis is helpful: it is a way to reveal parts of the self that the one might not have recognized yet. The place of self-understanding in caring is discussed further in the conclusion of this chapter. Now I turn to reciprocity and inclusion, which are necessary in avoiding coercion.

Reciprocity and Inclusion

Writing about the caring relationship, Noddings agrees with Martin Buber that "one should not try to dilute the meaning of the relation: relation is reciprocity" (Noddings, 1984, p. 73). The two essential parties in Noddings's ethic of care, the carer and the cared-for, are united in their reciprocal relationship. To consider caring as an ethical act, both sides should reciprocate a sense of care for one another. In turn, acknowledging and building this reciprocal sense of care requires inclusion. What Buber called the "relational process [of] 'inclusion' [means] that the one-caring assumes a dual perspective and can see things from both her own pole and that of the cared-for" (quoted in Noddings, 1984, p. 63). Yet it can be very difficult for teachers to read the needs of students. Educational institutions and teachers therefore often err at this stage, relying on presuppositions or social norms in categorizing students or in assuming that they understand students' needs—both of which are forms of objectification and therefore of oppression.

To avoid this trap, Noddings urges us to ask "What part does the cared-for play in caring?" (1984, p. 69). Reciprocity emphasizes the importance not only of the carer acknowledging the cared-for's needs and desires, but also, and more fundamentally to a relationship, the cared-for helping to build and continue the caring relationship. The cared-for's initial participation is acknowledgement, a response to the carer that is the source of the carer's energy. It is neither contractual payback nor is it necessarily gratitude. Reciprocity in female experience, Noddings (2010d) argues, "often involves no expectation of compensatory action. A mother hopes for *response* from her infant, but there is nothing in her conduct that corresponds to contractual reciprocity" (Noddings, 2010d, p. 40; emphasis in original).

How then should the cared-for respond to the one-caring? What response from the cared-for makes the one-caring feels that his or her caring has been received by the cared-for? What does the one-caring expect to see in the cared-for? Noddings explains:

> She meets him [the cared-for] as subject—not as an object to be manipulated nor as a data source. Indeed, this recognition of the freedom-as-subject of the cared-for is a fundamental result of her genuine receiving of the cared-for. The responsive cared-for, in the fullness of the caring relation, feels the recognition of freedom and grows under its expansive support. The child genuinely cared for is free to respond as himself, to create, to follow his interests without unnecessary fear and anxiety.
>
> *(2010d, p. 72)*

Essentially, then, the ultimate goal of the one-caring is open-ended: the one-caring wants only "to help [the other] grow and actualize himself" (Noddings, 2002b, p. 20). For this reason, like a mother delighting in her child's inventiveness, the teacher is/shall be captivated by students who use in their own ways and for their own purposes the educational experiences that they have shared with the teacher. In these reciprocal relationships are strong elements of subjectivity, self-understanding, and agency on both parts. Students' personal delight or happy growth in their freedom-as-subject completes the picture of genuine reciprocity.

Conclusion

> Possibly no goal of education is more important—or more neglected—than self-understanding.
>
> —*Nel Noddings (2006, p. 10)*

> Of all the concepts associated with self, reflection is probably the most important and useful.
>
> —*Nel Noddings (2002b, p. 117)*

While gender is the overriding theme in Noddings's ethic of care, self-understanding is my main theme in understanding her thinking. Responding to Socrates's statement "know thyself, an unexamined life is not worth living," Noddings argues that "unexamined lives may well be valuable and worth living, but an education that does not invite such examination may not be worthy of the label education" (2006, p. 10). Ethical caring requires "reflection and self-understanding" (Noddings, 1995) and an "understanding of self and others" (Noddings, 1995, p. 139).

For the one-caring, self-understanding helps not only to recall "natural caring" and thus reveal the nature of feminine care, but also to unlearn coercive care and poisonous pedagogy. We all should strive to become aware first of how we have been cared for and then of how we care-for-others, work that requires us to examine "how external and internal forces affect [our] lives" (Noddings, 2006, p. 10) and our engagement with the forces based on "what we believe and how we believe it. What do I feel? Why? What am I doing? Why? And even, What am I saying? And, again, why?" (p. 10). Since the caring relation and its roles are not fixed (Noddings, 2011, p. 8), this kind of understanding is often not a single event but continual and recursive, what William Doll (1993) described as a "looping back," an ongoing process of self-reflection that allows one to create "one's own conscious self—the highest expression of human awareness" (p. 289). Self-understanding in an ethic of care requires us educators to sensitize ourselves to the very essence of our mode of being, what Pinar (1994) calls our capacity for "first-person subjectivity" (p. 105).

It is fortunate that thinkers like Pinar and Grumet have provided us with a way out of our conditioned selves, a way into first-person subjectivity. By recalling our past, we can understand, deconstruct, and then reconstruct our selves, and by doing so we might be able to avoid reenacting "poisonous pedagogy," coercive caring, and unthinking conformity. I have to admit that I am ambitious here, perhaps too optimistic, while acknowledging there were difficult moments over the process of self-understanding, which is discussed in the section on anxiety and paradox in Chapter 2. What *currere* offers me is not guarantee but a possibility.

For Noddings, the one-caring's open-ended goal, if it has direction at all, is for the cared-for to achieve self-actualization, as I mentioned earlier. Self-actualization of the cared-for also requires that the carer engage in self-reflection by activating his or her subjectivity. Obvious examples of the failure to engage in this process can be found in Alice Miller's (1984) analysis of cruelty in childrearing, what Noddings calls the "pathology of care" (2002b, pp. 39–49). Alice Miller observes, Noddings (2002b) explains, that those who do not come to realize that they were treated cruelly when they were young continue to believe that:

> their childhood sufferings really were "for their own good." Miller contends that these people never developed real selves, and it did not (perhaps could not) occur to them that authority could be questioned. Pain suffered without acknowledgement becomes like a commodity; it is stored up and passed on without reflection.
>
> *(p. 40)*

When the cared-for lacks awareness of the goal of care, that person may surrender his or her subjectivity to coercive outer forces and then eventually, as a carer, reenact this kind of pathological caring. Similarly, but in a perhaps more tender manner, this lack of awareness can result in mutual sacrifices; that is, both the one-caring and the cared-for fail to understand that the goal of caring is open-ended in nature but is aimed at promoting the growth and actualization of the cared-for. The cared-for, for example, may sacrifice his or her need in order to show that he is cared for, while the carer may sacrifice his or her own subjectivity for the sake of the cared-for. In this situation, the caring relation is particularly complicated or even paradoxical, which emphasizes how necessary reflection is in caring. To be reflective, one has to return to his or her everyday experience, and the experience of those others whom one is "pointed to" (Pinar, 1999, p. 57).

Ontologically, we are relational selves that are ever-changing. This quality of our existence—which includes Husserl's idea of *bracketing* and Heidegger's of *attunement*, and the ability to welcome unforeseeable possibilities—makes our caring relations remarkably difficult and complicated. The nature of our being thus increases the difficulty of our understanding our relationships; yet if we are attuned to the world, without resorting to universal principles, the same qualities in our being also strengthen the possibility of developing caring relationships.

Nevertheless, more often than not educational institutions instill discipline, propaganda, and competitiveness that culminate in an emphasis on cognitive aspects of learning at the expense of emotional, maternal components. The vision of caring that Noddings has shared is based on her strong maternal nurturing of children as well as the influences that have colored her life and scholarship. Noddings's educational philosophy, professional collegiality, and private life are all welded together in an ethic of care that has provoked important debate, appraisal, and criticism. Throughout her work, Noddings's language, as Pinar (1999) approvingly emphasizes and as I would like to reiterate, acknowledges that the baby remains irreducibly important to the mother. In the originality and sincerity of her thinking, Nel Noddings is a caring, courageous, and inspirational scholar.

Notes

1. See Seo Won Lee and Yong Eun Jang's "A Study of the Effect of Adolescent's Academic Stress on Suicidal Ideation" (2011) conducted in Korea, and Rebecca p. Ang and Vivien S. Huan's "Relationship Between Academic Stress and Suicidal Ideation" (2006) conducted in Singapore. Both studies argue that there is a strong relationship between academic stress and adolescent suicide rates. The academic pressure derives mainly from an overemphasis on testing, a phenomenon that also causes corruption and waste. The problem is not exclusive to students, as Noddings (2007) laments, but includes "sympathetic teachers and desperate administrators" (p. 71).
2. To explain the primacy of incorporating students' experiences into education, Noddings approvingly quotes Dewey:

    There is, I think, no point in the philosophy of progressive education which is sounder than its emphasis upon the importance of the participation of the learner in the formation of the purposes which direct his activities in the learning process, just as there is no defect in traditional education greater than its failure to secure the active cooperation of the pupil in construction of the purposes involved in his studying. (quoted in Noddings, 2010c, p. 193)

This passage points to the primacy of students' participation in the whole process of their learning, a component that has been missing from traditional education and even from progressive education, such as open education, child-centered education, and numerous school reforms, because they did not genuinely incorporate students' experiences into education. It is presumptuous for teachers to assume that what they bring into the classroom is meaningful to their students. Recognizing this problem, both Dewey and Noddings feel that their foremost educational goal is "to guide students in well-informed exploration of areas meaningful to them" (Dewey, 1916, p. 67). This pragmatic understanding of the centrality of students' subjectivity in their education is also fundamental to Noddings's idea of caring.

3. In his response to Noddings, "Caring: Gender Consideration," Pinar (1999) discusses "the receptivity of caring" (pp. 56–59), a propensity or disposition to receive the other as he or she is rather than fully understand or project into the other. Using Freudian psychosexual terms, Pinar (1999) explains:

> "Receiving the other" is, classically and specifically heterosexually, the women's posture. It suggests a certain passivity, a certain openness to the Other. Classically and specifically heterosexually, the male is the asserting, even aggressive one. . . . "Caring" is classically a woman's preoccupation, especially when it is described as receptivity. (p. 57)

Using Nancy Chodorow's psychoanalytic phrase, he continues:

> It may be that man—by virtue of his gender formation—has "stunted relational potential". . . . In a word, we men may have reduced capacities to care. (p. 57)

4. Here is a difference between Pinar and Noddings: Pinar's emphasis is on subjectivity, and Noddings's emphasis is on relationality. This is, I believe, because they are from different disciplines: Pinar, psychoanalysis, phenomenology, and existentialism; and Noddings, pragmatism and feminism. This issue is certainly big enough for another project, so I will be looking forward to working on it.

5. The radically different ethical views between men and women are discussed in more depth in the following section, "Ethic of Care and Ethics of Justice."

6. Specifically, their theories have challenged the traditional patriarchal, masculine moral approach, but Noddings (2010d) still thinks that "scholars rarely look at female experience" (p. 1).

7. Caring takes culturally variable and situation-specific forms in historical moments that invite complicated conversation across contexts and peoples who deal with different issues; for example, the neoliberal agenda has been prominent in many places around the world, while many parts are still dealing with colonial agendas; perhaps some places deal with both.

4
SELF-CARE AND SELF-UNDERSTANDING

Introduction

The first chapter, a historical analysis of hakbeolism, contextualizes this study. The second chapter, an autobiographical study of my subjectivity, is an example of subjective reconstruction through self-understanding. The third chapter contains a theoretical analysis of an ethic of care, which, I argue, requires self-understanding. Over the study journey, I have realized that there are two big issues, self-care and care-for-others, and that there seems to be a certain relationship between them. In the next three chapters I engage with these three topics: self-care, care-for-others, and the association between them.

In this chapter I discuss how self-understanding can be a form of self-care. To do so, I first need to explain what I mean by self-care, and I do so with the help of three thinkers: Socrates, Si-Hyung Choi (who wrote under and will be referred to here using the pseudonym Haewol, 1827–1898), and Foucault. After discussing Socrates and Haewol's thoughts on self-care, I turn my attention toward the question of the way in which self-understanding can be a form of self-care. My response to this question is to suggest that I create my own standards for my life rather than resort to the constraints from social structures.

Self-Care

> You concern yourself with your wealth, your reputation, and with honors, but you don't worry about your virtue and your soul. . . . It [care for the self] is a mission that was conferred on [you] by the deity.
> —*Socrates (quoted in Foucault, 1982b, p. 93)*

> One serves a human as he or she serves God since a human is God. Every human being, even a seemingly worthless one, is where hanul [God] resides.
>
> —Haewol (quoted in Huh, 2010, p. 89)

Juxtaposing Michel Foucault's analysis of Socrates's notion of *epimeleia heautou* (care of self), and Haewol's, the second leader of *donghak*,[1] idea of Hyang-A-Seol-Oui reveals what I mean by self-care. In addition to the similar accusations that led to the execution of both Socrates in 399 BC and Haewol in 1898, there are shared qualities in their thoughts, their insistence on the significance and primacy of care for the self.

It is Foucault through whom I read Socrates's notion of care of the self. In "The Hermeneutic of the Subject" (Foucault, 1982b) and "On the Genealogy of Ethics: An Overview of Work in Progress," Foucault (1983) urges us to bear in mind that "know thyself" has regularly been associated with "the theme of care of the self" (p. 93). *Epimeleia heautou* in Ancient Greek, Foucault tells us, was powerful. It meant "working on or being concerned with oneself. . . . It describes a sort of work, an activity; it implies attention, knowledge, technique" (Foucault, 1983, p. 269). Foucault argues that "[taking] care of oneself is doubtless[ly] obscured by the radiance of the *gnōthi seauton*, the Ancient Greek aphorism 'know thyself'" (Foucault, 1982b, p. 93). In his later works, Foucault shows us through genealogy how the theme of care for the self had been obscured under the "evidence" of Descartes, the "reason and universality" of Kant, and the emphasis on "self-renunciation and self-sacrifice" throughout the history of Christianity (Foucault, 1983, p. 279).[2] Foucault explains what Socrates in *Apology* says about care of the self:

> Socrates is the man who takes care that his fellow citizens "take care of themselves." Socrates says three important things in the *Apology*: it [care of the self] is a mission that was conferred on him by the deity, and he will not give it up before his last breath; it is a disinterested task for which he doesn't ask any payment, he performs it out of pure benevolence; and it is a useful service to the city-state, more useful even than an athlete's victory at Olympia, for by teaching citizens to attend to themselves (rather than to their possessions), one also teaches them to attend to the city-state itself (rather than its material affairs). Instead of sentencing him, his judges would do better to reward Socrates for having taught others to care for themselves.
>
> (Foucault, 1982b, p. 94)

The idea of Hyang-A-Seol-Oui (向我設位) found in Haewol's preaching on April 5, 1897, a year before he was killed by hanging, directly reversed the idea of Hyang-Byuk-Seol-Oui (向壁設位)—both are ways of conducting a memorial service, a kind of religious ceremony to remember God or one's ancestors.

The difference that A (我, I) and Byuk (壁, wall) make is radical. For Hyang-Byuk-Seol-Oui, which is the traditional service, the alter is put on the wall; for Hyang-A-Seol-Oui, the alter is put on the side of the one performing the ceremony. The practice of Hyang-A-Seol-Oui is revolutionary in that it believes that God is within every individual. Haewol preaches:

> In hanul (God) is the mind; in the mind is hanul. Thus mind is hanul; hanul is mind. Outside of mind there is no hanul; outside of hanul there is no mind. They are not two. They are not different entities. Each individual is hanul. Thus, one has to serve not only the self but also all other individuals as one serves God. This requires three premises. First is that the formation of hanul is universal, that it is in every individual. Second is that to be as hanul requires that I, here and how, am ethically and practically responsive to hanul. When I am egoistic or unethical, I am not any more one where hanul resides. Third is that the most important foundation of donghak is that I contain hanul and my existence and my life are cosmologically and ecologically holistic. When these three premises are met, hanul is in me and I can see myself as "a small hanul."
>
> *(quoted in Huh, 2010, p. 93)*

Let me discuss the two long passages quoted previously. First, the imperative of care for the self is essential in both Socrates and Haewol, although the ways they rationalize it are different. For Socrates, the responsibility to care for oneself is given by God, and it is not possible to deny or reject it; for Haewol, the imperative is stronger, since not caring for the self is not serving God. The second point is that care for the self is extended to care-for-others. Socrates says that care for the self is "more useful even than an athlete's victory at Olympia" since the one who properly cares for the self will care for the other and the city.[3] For Haewol, this imperative is not secondary but a primary obligation, because individuals all have God in them. Thus, if one serves God, he or she serves himself, herself, and all others, regardless of gender, age, class, and any other categories. This egalitarian and democratic view is represented by Hyang-A-Seol-Oui. This view not only rejects any discrimination and stratification in society—during the lifetime of Haewol Korean society was stratified—but also includes the endowed rights of women and children, which were not included in the notion of human rights at that time in Korea.[4] Third, Socrates and Haewol share the ethical responsiveness of oneself to the self. They warn us about falling into materialism, egoism, and self-absorption. To take care of the self and to live in Hyang-A-Seol-Oui, one has to be "here and now" (Huh, 2010, p. 100).

"Here and now" emphasizes the imperative to consider the circumstance in which one exists, which requires one's ethical decisions. "Here and now" obligates us to attend to the specific moments we face. What we can learn from Socrates and Haewol is not guidance for our daily tasks but their insights on the imperative of care for the self and others. Foucault, in "On the Genealogy of Ethics: An Overview of Work in Progress," makes clear that he did not want to find an attractive and plausible *alternative* through his genealogy of ethics. Actually he dislikes Ancient Greek culture, its virility, dissymmetry, and exclusion of others. He says, "All that is quite disgusting" (1983, p. 258). What he wants, Rabinow (1997) understands, is "to make visible a bygone way of approaching the self and others which might suggest possibilities for the present" (p. xxvii). Foucault's (1983) point is not that "everything is bad but everything is dangerous" (p. 256), and thus there is always something we can do with situations. He calls not for "apathy" but for "a hyper and pessimistic activism" (p. 256) through which we participate in difficult situations with a certain possibility for alterity. In his studies, "to demonstrate the arbitrariness of the extant order and the exclusions it contains" (Pinar, 1985, p. 213). Foucault defines his role as:

> to show people that they are much freer than they feel, that people accept as truth, as evidence, some themes which have been built up at a certain moment during history, and that this so-called evidence can be criticized and destroyed.
>
> *(quoted in Dreyfus, 2004)*

Foucault seems to have no doubt about our ability to think and act otherwise through our creative relationship to our unique, concrete, and many times difficult everyday tasks.

In a similar way, Huh (2010) warns us not to be bound by the Hyang-A-Seol-Oui of Haewol, not to structuralize it as a definite Truth. He understands that Hyang-A-Seol-Oui is not epistemological but ontological. Huh argues that "it is a belief, [a] practical viewpoint, a way of living at the same time" (2010, p. 100). There are no definite and fixed answers for our questions about how to conduct everyday struggles. Regarding Haewol's Hyang-A-Seol-Oui, "What we are expected to do" is, Huh (2010) argues, "to attend to the 'here and now,' not the 'there and that' of Haewol" (p. 101), that is, to be fully aware that I am the subject of Hyang-A-Seol-Oui and thus continuously and responsively work on how to live in Hyang-A-Seol-Oui.

It seems to be worth considering Foucault's "mode of subjectivation" (Rabinow, 1997, p. xxxi), which might help us understand living in Hyang-A-Seol-Oui. The mode of subjectivation is the way that one freely relates to him- or herself and, further, to things and others. Subjectivation for Foucault is a mode of being that he calls the *aesthetics of existence*, which is the ethical practice of the self in the relationship with him- or herself. We are all selves conditioned by histories, cultures, and social, economic, or political structures. However, it does not necessarily mean that we are always bound by them. In this mode of being, the principles that constrain one's behavior may be rudimentary—perhaps for the sense of belonging—but "greater attention is paid to the methods, techniques, and exercises directed at forming the self within a nexus of relationships" (Rabinow, 1997, p. xxvii). The other modes of being for which Foucault seeks, Rabinow (1997) understands, "were already in existence" (p. xxvii). In other words, Foucault believes, Rabinow (1997) tells us, that our moral conduct, ethical practices, can be otherwise by "denaturalizing the subject of desire, not to invent philosophical system per se, but to contribute to the mode of being" (p. xxvii).

Similarly and interestingly, Hyang-A-Seol-Oui requires us, Huh (2010) understands, "to endlessly problematize our perception, conduct, and understanding of our daily lives" (p. 106). In this matter, it is not different from Foucault's ethics. Through problematizing what has seemed to be normal, we can think, conduct, and eventually live otherwise, not entirely resorting to the external forces that constrain us. Foucault's technology of the self is all about how to do it. Hyang-A-Seol-Oui constitutes, Huh further argues, the "art of existence" (p. 106) in that existence is "not different from the self–self relationship of the subject, the hermeneutic of the subject, and the self-forming techniques of Foucault" (p. 106).

It is one's decision to "create" relationships with oneself, and one has the possibility of doing so in any oppressive circumstances since there are no completely absolute or eternal "power relations" (Foucault, 1984, 293)—where power relations exist, for Foucault, is where resistance can develop. Foucault explains:

> In antiquity, this work on the self with its attendant austerity is not imposed on the individual by means of civil law or religious obligation, but is a choice about existence made by the individual. People decide for themselves whether or not to care for themselves. We have hardly any remnant of the idea in our society that the principal work of art which one must take care of, the main area to which one must apply aesthetic values, is oneself, one's life, one's existence.
>
> *(Foucault, 1983, p. 271)*

Self-referential authority seems to be central in the quote above. Foucault argues that how one's life is and how one's relationships "[are] still and always defined by the rule of the individual over himself" (Foucault, 1986, p. 68). One has the authority to have a certain kind of relationship with oneself or to be a certain kind of person. One makes the decision not because society, or anybody else, obligates one, but because one wants to. Thus for Foucault, the cultivation of the self is not the consequence of socialization or an ideology conflict; rather it emerges out of one's relationship with oneself in creative ways. This kind of creative relationship of one to oneself should not be referred to as creative activity. The relationship itself should be creative. The self, for Foucault, always should be in the process of creation in the relationship with itself in that he argues that "there is no true self that [can] be deciphered and emancipated," but that "the self [is] something that had been—and must be—created" (Oksala, 2007, p. 98).

Then, one of the questions that remains with us is how to create the relationship that Foucault talks about.

I would like to ask Foucault what he thinks about the understanding of the self that I articulated in Chapter 2. I think that self-understanding can be a creative form of self-care that has a certain therapeutic and aesthetic quality. To elaborate on this idea, I turn my discussion to the way in which self-understanding can be a form of self-care.

Self-Understanding Through Autobiographical Study As a Form of Self-Care

> Autobiography is an architecture of [the] self.
> —*William F. Pinar (1985, p. 220)*

> The creation of the *hupomnemata* is the creation of the self. It is not a detached documentary. The *hupomnemata* make the writer just as surely as the writer makes the *hupomnemata*.
> —*Matthias Swonger (2006, p. 1)*

> They [*hupomnemata*] must form part of ourselves: in short, the soul must make them not merely its own but itself. The writing of the *hupomnemata* is an important relay in this subjectivation of discourse.
> —*Michel Foucault (1997, p. 210)*

"To create ourselves," as Foucault argues, means not to be bound by histories, cultures, and social, economic, or political structures, although sometimes we are haunted by them. We understand through our reading of Foucault how sexuality has been shaped over the history of the West and how care of the self has lost its ethical quality or relation to the truth. We cannot find any directions for our actions here and now from what Foucault has told us, nor from Socrates or Haewol. In "Technologies of the Self," Foucault (1982a) shows us "the correlation between disclosure of the self, dramatic or verbalized, and the renunciation of self in the history of Christianity" (p. 249). What strikes me is that he finds that self-disclosure or verbalization from the eighteenth century to the present has been reinserted in different contexts by the so-called human sciences so that self-disclosure can be used without self-renunciation "but to constitute, positively, a new self" (p. 249). Foucault insists that "to use these techniques without renouncing oneself constitutes a decisive break" (p. 249), a break in the unnecessary connection between our ethics and oppressive structures. How then can we start to work on building the *creative* relationship with ourselves to which Foucault aspires? Foucault introduces Ancient Greek techniques such as reading, writing, meditation, and self-reflection.

Of these techniques, Foucault seems to have paid much attention to writing in creating a self–self relationship. Although the emergence of writing, as Foucault

(1983) understands, was "as disrupting as the introduction of the computer into private life today" (p. 272) for people in antiquity, the context of this criticism of writing is its "administrative use in Plato's time" (p. 272). From *hupomnemata*, a notebook or journal of sorts for the Ancient Greeks, Foucault finds certain desirable, or valuable, qualities. He says:

> They [*hupomnemata*] constituted a material memory of things read, heard, or thought, thus offering these as an accumulated treasure for rereading and later meditation. They also formed a raw material for the writing of more systematic treatises in which were given arguments and means by which to struggle against some defect (such as anger, envy, gossip, flattery) or to overcome some difficult circumstance (a mourning, an exile, downfall, disgrace).
>
> *(p. 273)*

"The objective of the *hupomnemata*," Foucault explains, is not the writing itself; it is "not to pursue the unspeakable, nor to reveal the hidden, nor to say the unsaid," but "to capture the already said, to collect what one has managed to hear or read, and for a purpose that is nothing less than the shaping of the self" (Foucault, 1997, pp. 210–211). In other words, that the objective is "to make of the recollection of the fragmentary *logos* transmitted by teaching, listening, or reading a means to establish as adequate and as perfect a relationship of oneself to oneself as possible" (Foucault, 1983, p. 274). It seems obvious to me that Foucault's analysis of *hupomnemata* expresses a certain quality of analysis, reflection, and thus understanding of the writings, which is an important technique for the care of the self. Arguing against the assumptions about understanding the self in psychology and psychoanalysis and the use of writings for self-renunciation in Christianity,[5] Foucault shows his rejection of the possibility of "deciphering" (1983, p. 274) or "[telling] you what your true self is" (p. 271). I find Foucault's position to be somewhat radical; although I think that one's subjectivity is not fixed but is constantly developing and expanding as much as it is fragmented, which makes it impossible to grasp it exactly or totally, his analysis of writing expresses and requires certain forms of reflection, analysis, understanding, study, or contemplation. I think what Foucault rejects about writing can be incorporated into what he insists on in writing practice. That is, the objective of the *hupomnemata* should not be limited to revealing the hidden or saying the unsaid or already said but should be extended to the beyond. I believe that without seeking the true self or absolute understanding of the self, we still can try to understand our selves "however nonunitary, dispersed, and fragmented" (Pinar, 2006b, p. 3). I suggest that self-understanding through the method of *currere* can be what Foucault might call an example of working with *hupomnemata*. To me the "decisive break" can be led by rigorous study through autobiographical inquiry.

What I mean by self-understanding is first to *unlearn*—"one of the important tasks for self-cultivation" (Foucault, 1982b, p. 97)—the false or inauthentic relationships to my self, and then to create a new, neither definable nor predictable, relationship with myself, which is only the beginning of education. I have started this project in my doctoral program when in my late thirties. *It is my belief that self-understanding, through autobiography, can provide one with opportunities to create the new relationship with oneself that Foucault aspires us to seek. It is a journey of "self formation, deformation, learning, and unlearning through writing" that "discerns new landscapes, new configurations, especially those excluded by proclamations of Government, State, and School"* (Megill, quoted in Pinar, 1985, p. 217, emphasis added). Pinar (1985) calls that kind of self-understanding "an architecture of self" (p. 212), which is a desirable consequence of autobiography. For the architect of self, Pinar tells us, "should judge his current edifice obscuring its foundation in ways that keep him ignorant of himself" (p. 212).

How can we create the space for us to judge our current obfuscating edifice? Intellectual activities are recommended for understanding how history and culture have influenced the constitution of ourselves, and not always negatively. Yet understanding how the history and culture has been or can be reproduced through us requires another means. Such work, as Pinar (1985) tells us, involves "bracketing and distancing" (p. 203) that renders for us "a psychologically possible a politico-cultural critique" (p. 203). "Bracketing," in a phenomenological sense, is a mode of distancing in that it brackets one's taken-for-grantedness and already built-in perspectives. *Currere* provides me with that possibility in that it allows for me to *analyze* and *synthesize* the educational experiences through which I enter into "a third space" (Wang, 2004, p. 16) where I create, deconstruct, or reconstruct my subjectivity, making the relationship with myself anew. One's false or inauthentic relationship with oneself can be reconstructed through *currere*, as I have shown in Chapter 2.

"Self-knowledge" (Pinar, 2011, p. 8) conceived through self-understanding is not "self-searching and preoccupation, . . . drawing one into a false inner contemplation" (p. 159) but occurs "in active involvement in the world" (p. 159). Through the world and its history and culture I have been conditioned to be, and also I am one of the many who contribute to the constitution of the world. Thus, the two are co-constructive; understanding the self and the world is coextensive, reciprocal, and indeed inseparable. Such a realization inevitably forces us from private study to return to the world. That is, an architecture of self requires one to study historical facts and lived experiences, through both of which I reconstruct my subjectivity, "the lived sense of self" (Pinar, 2009, p. 3). The general conclusion of the discourses on the ancient educational injunction "know thyself," Pinar (2011, p. 8) explains, is that "we are able to distance ourselves from our experience and the world wherein it occurs, what we remember, what we underwent, and that we can exercise some choice" (p. 8) in what to value or devalue. That is one of the possibilities that *currere* offers us.

In this sense, *self-understanding* is *allegorical*, and is "individual and social, directed to the present (including the fantasies of the future we experience in the present) as it is informed by the past" (Pinar, 2011, p. 7). Allegory juxtaposes "facts and lived experience in creative tensionality . . . that can trigger transformation" (p. 7), and Pinar shares Rauch's assertion that the impact of allegory on cognition "causes a constant transformation of attitudes and thoughts about reality" (quoted in Pinar, 2011, p. 7). In this study, the juxtaposition of the analysis of hakbeolism (Chapter 1) and my *currere* (Chapter 2) can be allegorical.[6] The analysis of the historicity of aspects of Korean education and my lived experiences constitutes the understanding of my subjectivity.

The consequences of this kind of self-understanding cannot be definitely graspable nor can the process be terminable since self-understanding is not limited within the boundary of an epistemological interrogation—although this study requires a certain quality of the interrogation—but extends to an ontological attitude. It requires *"ascesis,"* "permanent battle" for Foucault; that is why, I think, Earle (1972) calls it "ontological autobiography" (p. 10). Self-understanding is not a one-time event or celebration but rather a way of living or a form of consciousness.

Having grasped the seemingly unbearable weight of Korean culture and history, I understand in part how my educational experiences have suffered and my subjectivity has been arrested. Over the process of my study to unlearn my relationship with myself, I have become more generous to myself, making a new relationship with myself, a desirable consequence of autobiography. I cannot get rid of my anxiety, both fear and existential freedom. Not only is getting rid of it impossible, it is also undesirable. I decided to "create" a new relationship with myself, a rather generous one. I do not have to blame myself for feeling anxiety. I do not need to be ashamed of having it. I am a little more revealed to myself than I was. *I am less concerned about other's objectification of myself but more concerned about my relationship with myself. In this way, self-understanding through autobiography has been a form of self-care. In other words, creating one's relationship with oneself anew means making one's own standards for one's life rather than conforming to standards externally given.*

Having One's Own Standard

Why can't we make our own standards?
—Jin-Seok Choi (2013)

In an outer-directed culture, children are socialized from early on to care very much about others' objectifications. . . . Those who can free themselves from the power of others' objectifications without trading their outer-directedness for a form of autism can achieve a degree of independence that is political as much as it is social and psychological.
—William F. Pinar (1979, pp. 105–106)

What can happen in one's life when, through having an authentic self–self relationship, one makes of one's life a work of art? Jin-Seok Choi's question in the epigraph strongly speaks to us: *Why can't we make our own standards?* One of his examples for his argument is Dr. Jung-Ryong Kim, who is called the Korean liver doctor. Doctor Kim invented the first vaccine for hepatitis B in 1977; however, the vaccine could not be used until it was certified in 1983. The reason that the Ministry of Health and Social Affairs (MHSA) of Korea could not certify the vaccine was that there was no "standard" by which to certify it in Korea at that time. After other hepatitis B vaccines had been certified in the U.S. and France, the MHSA of Korea could certify doctor Kim's vaccine, adopting the other countries' standards for Korea.

Choi (2013) suspects that the incapability of the MHSA of Korea to certify the vaccine was because we, Koreans, are used to being "the consumers of standards" rather than "the producers or creators of standards." He argues that to be the master of oneself is to be the standard creator for oneself. Of course, I would add that one's standards are subject to change. Choi's observation intrigues me, although his accusation seems to be hastily made and the reason the MHSA could not certify Dr. Kim's vaccine at that time may be much more complicated, in that the lack of ability to make one's own standards makes me think about the psychological consequences of the standardization and accountability discourse epidemic in Korean education. Standards from outside are legitimized by the strong force of universality and objectivity, under both of which individuals are abstracted into *numbers* (Taubman, 2009). One's dependency in one's study on others' objectifications is, as Pinar (1979) is keenly aware, "political as much as it is social and psychological" (p. 106).

Self-understanding through autobiography can be a way of resisting, or at least challenging, the haunting external standards. Those who rely exclusively on outer force, universalized and objectified standards, are less capable of making their own standards. They continually try not only to conform to external standards but often times to impose the standards on others. What educators have to do instead is not make curricula for students but also not prohibit students from doing so. A specific example is the test-focused system that I critiqued in Chapter 1. Those who believe that they have to control the curriculum with given standards for students remain in the "political and intellectual trap" (Pinar, 2006a, p. 120) that only increases students' dependency on their teachers in their study and "teachers' culpability" (p. 118) "under the twin banners of standards and accountability" (Taubman, 2009, p. 2). *Self-understanding through which one understands how he or she has been constituted and that there are alternatives is only the starting point toward avoiding or overcoming the traps and culpability. Self-understanding does not give us solutions to or guidelines for our daily problems but cultivates our ability to make our own standards.*

Making one's own standards, a way of resistance, is a possible way of self-care. One who can make his or her own standards is one who is capable of disallowing the reproduction of the imposed standards through the oneself. This is also a way to fight for the intellectual and political freedom of students and teachers. In this way, self-understanding *is* a political action. To live as the master of one's own life is not to be a consumer of imposed standards but to be a creator of one's own standards.

Conclusion

Can education allow and encourage students to come up with their own standards in their studies? All of us, students and teachers, are hardly immune to the inexorable and arbitrary demands by neoliberal and corporatized forces. Since the standards that forcefully structure our educational experiences require our culpability for their activation and reinforcement, we can resist by strengthening our immune system through self-understanding. We are freer, as Foucault tells us, and stronger than we think. This by no means implies that we can simply keep our naïve "hopes." The forces do not seem to be going away in the near future. However, by not allowing their reproduction through ourselves, we still have the ability, and chance, to resist. Our professional comment in this devastating historical moment, as Alan Block (2009) tells us, is for teachers "to be brave" (p. 115) in our ethical decision making and "to help others achieve bravery" (p. 116). "We must," Pinar (2012) urges us, "abandon infantilized positions from which we pretend helplessness, demanding to know 'what works,' the authoritarianism of instrumental rationality" (p. 231). What we need is "courage" that is constituted of several parts: the "intellectual courage" to study embodied in the concrete lives of students as people and citizens and the "political courage" to resist the authoritarianism of instrumental rationality, both of which require "psychological courage" (Pinar, 2012, p. 231). It is our choice either to be drifters who allow the world to author their lives or to be the authors of our lives.

However, there is a paradox in the self-care I have discussed here. Self-respect can be made only from relations with others, but from the early days of our educational lives we are taught, evaluated, and eventually turned into numbers (Taubman, 2009). Developing one's intellectual, psychological, and political independence is inevitably associated with one's relationship to others, especially significant others (I discuss this point further in Chapter 6). To theorize how care-for-others contributes to self-understanding and then self-care, I discuss "voice" in curriculum studies, not only because it expresses a certain quality of subjectivity, but also because it provides me with a concrete example for analyzing the association between self-care and care-for-others.

Notes

1. *Donghak* (or *chun-do-kyo*, Religion of Heavenly Way) is a kind of religion combining Confucianism, Buddhism, Taoism, and even Shamanism that opposes Roman Catholi-

cism, which was called *seohak* (Western Learning) at that time. It is closely related to the Korean *Minjung* revolution, called the "*Donghak* Peasant Revolution" (1984). Donghak (Eastern Learning) arose in the middle of the19th century in Korea. The donghak leaders, such as Jae-Woo Choi, Si Hyung Choi, and Byung Hee Son, are not only religious leaders but also considered philosophers and thinkers who tried to help the people overcome societal problems: the depravity of the feudal system, invasions of Western countries, and the absence of thinkers that might lead the people (Cho, 2013).

2. Foucault (1983) understands that "the relationship to the self needed to be ascetic to get into relation to the truth" (p. 279). Further, he argues that before Descartes "one could not be impure, immoral, and know the truth" (p. 279). After Descartes, he says, "[One] can be immoral and know the truth" (p. 279). Then, Foucault laments that that change made possible the "institutionalization of modern science" (p. 279). After Descartes it is Kant, according to Foucault, who introduced ethics as an applied procedural form of rationality—this criticism of Kantian ethics overlays agrees with that of Noddings. Furthermore, Foucault criticizes Christianity, saying that "salvation in Christianity is attained through the renunciation of self" (p. 285). That is, one is born a sinner, one has to accept that the truth and confess the sin, and then one will be saved by God. Foucault acknowledges the paradoxical quality of care of the self in seeking for salvation as a way of self-care in Christianity. Foucault explains, "Christianity is usually given credit for replacing the generally tolerant Greco-Roman lifestyle with an austere lifestyle marked by a series of renunciations, interdictions, or prohibitions" (p. 270). Foucault goes further, without entirely accusing Christianity of the loss of the self: "Clinging to the self was opposed to God's will" (p. 271). The desires from within in the culture were conceived as having a negative influence on people's lives and beliefs.

3. It seems obvious that Ancient Greek society prioritized care of the self over care for the other. Defining the relationship between self-care and care for the others is not simple. It is discussed in Chapter 5 in detail.

4. Learning from the thought of Haewal, Jung Hwan Bang, the father of children's literature in Korea, contributed to organizing theater festivals and public readings and to instituting Children's Day in Korea, first celebrated on May 1, 1992.

5. Foucault finds a linkage between the problem of self-purification and self-renunciation and the use of writings in Christianity: "The problem of ethics as an aesthetics of existence is covered over by the problem of purification. . . . The self was no longer something to be made but something to be renounced and deciphered" (Foucault, 1983, p. 274).

6. In his theorization of allegory, Pinar (2012) understands that the concept "forefronts both History and questions of its representation as central to understanding self and society through study" (p. 52). Allegory embraces, Pinar explains, "the past's significance for the present moment" (p. 50) for "reconstruction" (49). Understanding self, and reconstructing one's subjectivity invites understanding History and one's past experiences. Chapter 1 on hakbeolism and Chapter 2 on my *currere* work may be allegorically juxtaposed.

5
CARE-FOR-OTHERS

Introduction

> At every stage we need to be cared for in the sense that we need to be understood, received, respected, [and] recognized. . . . Not all of us learn to care for other human beings. . . . Some impoverished and dangerous people care for nothing; their lives are not directed by care or ultimate concern. Still others develop a distorted notion of care and do dreadful things in its name. These people, too are dangerous.
> —*Nel Noddings (1992, p. xi)*

> At this time in capitalism, at this place-nation-state, within educational institutions, the prospects for "authentic being" and "authentic self-knowledge" are few. So it is that calls for a "return to things themselves," to the discovery of "authentic voice," have political as well as epistemological and pedagogical content.
> —*William F. Pinar (1985, p. 203)*

In the previous chapter I articulated how self-understanding can be a form of self-care, a way of having creative standards and an authentic relationship with oneself. This kind of self-understanding can be achieved, although in a limited and temporal way, through reconstructing one's subjectivity *allegorically*. By allegorically, I mean studying one's lived experiences and the history and culture one is from, both of which are constituent parts of each other. Through self-understanding one "returns to things themselves," as Pinar (1985) says in the epigraph, "to discover one's authentic voice." Self-understanding for me is a way to activate my authentic voice. The "authentic voice" stands against the self-renunciation that Foucault has criticized. One's "authentic voice" in one's education symbolically expresses one's subjectivity, and one's capacity to be sensitive, or receptive, to one's inner voice. Thus finding one's authentic voice—although "not a definitive event but rather a continuous and relational process" (Miller, 1990, p. xi)—can be a way of activating, revitalizing, or reconstructing one's subjectivity.

Then, how can one discover one's "authentic voice?" Private endeavor is necessary and thus self-understanding, for many people, as Pinar (1976) points out, "is work with others that is a medium through which they work with themselves" (p. 53). A Chinese four-character idiom that I introduced in the section concerning the reciprocity of *currere* in Chapter 2 is suggestive here: 啐啄同時 (mutual pecking out and pecking in, referring to the process of a chick and hen pecking at each other as the chick hatches; the hen never leads the process—rather, she observes, listens, and responds to the chick as necessary). *I am by no means arguing that self-understanding cannot be pursued in solitude but rather suggesting that we need to rethink how others might contribute to the journey of self-understanding; this is the focus of this chapter.*

The thinkers Foucault, Noddings, and Pinar, whom I am drawn to in this section, all insist on the significance of others' influence on one's self-understanding or self-actualization. Among them, Foucault's position in the relationship between self-care and care-for-others can be conceived of as problematic. In "The Ethics of the Concern for Self as a Practice of Freedom," he says that while recognizing one's "complex relationships with others" (Foucault, 1984, p. 287), "care-for-others should not be put before the care of oneself. The care of the self is ethically prior in that the relationship with oneself is ontologically prior" (p. 287). Foucault positions the self–self relationship first as "ethically prior," suggesting that if one, let's say, has an false, inauthentic, or abusive relationship with oneself, "the relationship is most likely bound to express itself, despite one's effort to hide it, in one's relationship with others" (Pinar, personal communication, Feb. 25, 2014). Sharing Foucault's concern, I want to raise another of Foucault's points in this regard. In "The Hermeneutic of the Subject," Foucault (1982b) considers rather explicitly the self–other relationship:

> It was a generally accepted principle that one could not attend to oneself without the help of another. Seneca said that no one was ever strong enough on his own to get out of the state of *stultitia* [stupidity, foolishness] he was in: "He needs someone to extend him a hand and pull him free." In the same way, Galen said that man loves himself too much to be able to cure himself of his passions by himself; he had often seen men "stumble" who had not been willing to rely on another's authority. This principle is true for beginners but also for what follows, and even to the end of one's life. Seneca's attitude, in his correspondence with Lucilius, is characteristic: no matter that he is aged, having given up all his activities, he gives counsel to Lucilius but asks him for advice in return and is thankful for the help he finds in this exchange of letters. What is remarkable in this soul practice is

the variety of social relations that can serve as its support. . . . In this way there is constituted what one might call a "social service," which is performed through multifarious social relations.

(pp. 97–99)

Foucault acknowledges the significance, intensity, and complexity of the self–other relationship and its reciprocal quality in care for the self, although he does not analyze it in considerable depth. However, the self–other relationship is hinted at in Foucault's pedagogical concerns. The practice of the self, he tells us:

must enable one to get rid of all the bad habits, all the false opinions that one can get from the crown or from bad teachers, but also from parents and associates. To "unlearn" (*de-discere*) is one of the important tasks of self-cultivation.

(Foucault, 1982b, p. 97)

What Foucault is concerned about seems to be twofold. One has to "unlearn" not only an inauthentic self–self relationship but also false forms of self–other relationships or "poisonous pedagogy" (Miller, 1984), both of which have been discussed in Chapter 3 and will be further discussed in succeeding sections of this chapter. It is Nel Noddings and her ethic of care that initiated my (re)thinking on the perspectives and approaches care-for-others should take.

Having in mind the significance of care-for-others and Noddings's philosophy about it, I want to discuss how care-for-others can contribute to self-care. To do so, I choose to analyze a movie, *The King's Speech* (KS), using the theme of voice and speech, which metaphorically express one's subjectivity. My focus is neither to analyze the totality of KS and show the admiration of the royalty for King George VI nor to discuss the worldwide acknowledgement of the movie[1] and the historical accuracy of KS.[2] My special attention is on its pedagogical significance, that is, finding one's own voice; the self-understanding that leads to agency and to speech that gestures toward *orality* (Pinar, 2011, p. 176; 2012, pp. 13–14); *and* others' contribution to the process of finding one's voice and self-understanding. In doing so, I try to articulate how self-care requires care-for-others and how the form of care-for-others can be seen in the two men's relationship, the king and the therapist.

The King's Speech: A Jungian Take[3]

Bertie (Colin Firth), later King George VI, approaches the microphone as in a death march, to give a public address at the 1925 Empire Exhibition in Wembley. Bertie's eyes widen in terror as he begins the address, so begins the movie. The end of the speech is poignantly devastating for Bertie. Bertie cannot give his speech; he has lost his voice in public. The movie quickly raises Bertie's problems, which are evident to us in the scene when Bertie first visits his therapist, Lionel (Geoffrey Rush):

Lionel: What was your earliest memory?
Bertie: What on earth do you mean?
Lionel: First recollection.
Bertie: (stammer growing) I'm not here to discuss personal matters.
Lionel: Why are you here then?
Bertie: (exploding, stammer free) Because I bloody well stammer.
Lionel: You have a bit of a temper.
Bertie: One of my many faults. . . . I've always been this way.
Lionel: What do you think was the cause?
Bertie: I don't know. I don't care. I stammer. No one can fix it.

Bertie's problem is not only the loss of his ability to make a speech but also his false relationship with himself. He can hardly touch this problem as long as he understands it as only physical or technical, which is the mind/body dualism and the separation of private and public life. The separation in Bertie and Elizabeth's, Bertie's wife, minds is evident when Elizabeth says, "My husband has a mechanical difficulty with his speech," and when Bertie says, "Strictly business. No personal nonsense." This separation is understandable given their social status as royal family members and the common understanding of stammering at that time. Bertie's false self–self relationship becomes explicit when Lionel blocks Bertie's false self–self relationship. Lionel asks Bertie to put on a headphone, which plays a loud music and then asks him to read *Hamlet*. By putting on the headphone, Bertie cannot hear his voice while reading *Hamlet*. Bertie's false self–self relationship is blocked by the loud music. He reads flawlessly. "You were sublime," says Lionel, but Bertie says, "Hopeless. Hopeless." When he explodes, Bertie's anger is aimed not at Lionel but at himself; he says "One of my many faults," and "I don't know. I don't care." Bertie has lost hope: "No one can fix it" and (self-deprecatingly) "I have been always this way. I cannot remember not doing it." Furthermore, his attitude toward his stammer is problematic because he blocks himself and Lionel from accessing "personal matters," something related to his inner self, the dualism and separation.

Bertie is overtaken and hidden by his persona: that is, his ego is weakened and his persona is that of a stammer. The essence of his stutter, as Palmer (2013) diagnoses in Jungian terms, is that "he lacks a way to confront the shadow of his abusive childhood or to establish a desperately needed viable persona" (p. 68). Robert H. Hopcke (1995) describes patients who lack an adequate persona:

> First, there needs to be the development of awareness that something is missing, a consciousness-raising process which can at times be slow in that it requires an awareness of an absence rather than the identification of an active, present dynamic. How can one miss something which one has

never had? As always with persona issues, feedback from other people, their responses or lack thereof, including the therapist's own reflections to the patient of what he or she experiences with the patient in the room, is vital in developing the kind of awareness of this lack of persona which lays the foundation for the next step, namely, the development and use of a workable, authentic persona.

(p. 58)

This passage characterizes Lionel's struggle "to address what is missing and to create [to help create would be better because an authentic persona has to be created] an authentic persona for Bertie, one founded on friendship, trust, shadow work, active imagination, and equality" (Palmer, 2013, p. 69).

The issue of the cure is how to make Bertie's self–self relationship healthy: that is, how to help Bertie's ego face his shadow boldly. Bertie's authentic persona and his awareness of his shadow have to be developed. What is vital is to develop the awareness, which requires feedback or responses from other people. For the responses to be welcomed, the relationship between patient (Bertie) and therapist (Lionel) must be positive, based on friendship, trust, and equality. The healing process is not controllable by either of the two but it progresses through the development of their relationship.

Regarding building a relationship based on trust and equality, the tension between Lionel *vs.* Bertie and Elizabeth is strong. When Elizabeth first visits Lionel's office, Lionel tells her, "Well, have your hubby pop by . . . to give his personal history and I'll make a frank appraisal." Elizabeth stubbornly rejects Lionel's request: "I do not have a 'hubby.' We don't 'pop.' We never talk about our private lives. You must come to us." "Sorry, Mrs. J. My game, my turf, my rules," replies Lionel. He continues, "For my method to work there must be trust and total equality." And during Bertie's first visit, Lionel asks to be called by his given name and suggests that he call the prince "Bertie." Bertie counters: "Only my family uses that." Lionel says, "Perfect! In here it is better if we're equals." That brings Bertie's insistence, "If we were equals, I wouldn't be here. I'd be at home with my wife and no-one would give a damn." Later, Bertie reacts to Lionel's calling him "Bertie": "Stop calling me that! . . . Then we shan't speak!" The establishment of trust is slow in coming and "must surmount the defensive strategies of Bertie and Elizabeth" (Palmer, 2013, p. 77).

Bertie and Elizabeth's defensiveness is persistent and obstinate. After they listen to a recording of Bertie's sublime reading of the beginning of *Hamlet* in their room and find that Lionel's approach worked, although momentarily, Bertie and Elizabeth revisit Lionel to ask for help, but with restrictions that they want to apply to Lionel's treatment, as the following exchange among the three shows:

Bertie: Strictly business. No personal nonsense.
Elizabeth: I thought I'd made that very clear in our interview.

Lionel: Physical exercises and tricks are important, but what you're asking will only deal with the surface of the problem.
Elizabeth: Isn't that sufficient? As far as I see it, my husband has mechanical difficulties with his speech. May we just deal with that?
Bertie: I'm willing to work hard, Dr. Logue.
Lionel: Lionel.
Bertie: Are you willing to do your part?

Although Lionel makes it clear that they have to *go beyond the surface of the problem* and go deeper, as he emphasizes later, Lionel agrees to dealing with mechanics. Thus starts the building of their relationship.

During Bertie's visit after King George V's death the defense of *no personal nonsense* starts to dissolve. This scene is a turning point in the two men's relationship, Lionel's treatment, and most importantly, Bertie's revelation of poignant traumas that opens up access something deeper, something "closer to active imagination" (Palmer, 2013, p. 78). In this scene Bertie gives Lionel a hint that he is trying to open himself. Entering the consultation room, Bertie opens their conversation: "I've been practicing. An hour a day. In spite of everything." When Lionel asks him, "Do you feel like working today?" And "I'll put on some hot milk," Bertie says "Logue, I'd kill for something stronger." Bertie still uses Lionel's last name, but without "Doctor." Eventually Bertie accepts a closer relationship with Lionel:

Lionel: Do you want a top-up?
Bertie: Please.
You know, Lionel, you're the first ordinary Englishman . . .
Lionel: Australian.
Bertie: . . . I've ever really spoken to. Sometimes, when I ride through the streets and see the common man staring at me, I'm struck by how little I know of his life, and how little he knows of mine.
Lionel: What are friends for?
Bertie: I wouldn't know.

The two men's sharing their memories of their fathers evokes Bertie's revelation of the traumas that also moves Lionel's treatment to a deeper level, beyond mechanics. After sharing with Lionel King George's dying words, "Bertie has more guts than the rest of his brothers put together," Bertie cannot continue; he cannot talk about his brother David. Lionel suggests, "Try to sing it. . . . My brother David, he said to me, doo-dah doo-dah. . . . Continuous sound will give you flow." Lionel's technique is no longer mechanical but "an integral part of a psychological process" (Palmer, 2013, p. 78). Bertie initially resists singing but when he sings, as Palmer explains, he achieves "something closer to active imagination,[4] where dialogue between the unconscious and conscious occurs in a waking state" (p. 78). Under Lionel's questionings, using the singing technique,

86 Care-For-Others

Bertie reveals a train of traumas in his relationships to his significant others, father, mother, brothers, and nannies.

Lionel: Did David tease you?
Bertie: Oh, yes. They all did buh-buh-buh-Bertie. Father encouraged it. "Get it out, boy!" It would make me stop. Said . . . "I was afraid of my father, and my children are damn well going to be afraid of me."
Lionel: Are you naturally right handed?
Bertie: Left. I was punished. Now I use the right.
Lionel: Yes, that's very common with stammerers. Any other corrections?
Bertie: Knock knees. Metal splints were made . . . worn night and day.
Lionel: That must have been painful.
Bertie: Bloody agony. Straight legs now.
Lionel: Who were you closest to in your family?
Bertie: Nannies. Not my first nanny, though . . . she loved David . . . hated me. When I was presented to my parents for the daily viewing, she pinched me so I'd cry and be handed back to her immediately. And then she would . . .

Bertie cannot continue to talk because his memory of the first nanny halts him. Lionel whispers, "sing it." Bertie sings a poignant description of the nanny's behavior that includes a fragment from Sewanee River, "Then she wouldn't feed me, far far away." The singing technique prevents/circumvents stammering. Bertie continues, "Took three years for my parents to notice. As you can imagine. That causes some stomach problems still." With a sympathetic face, Lionel carefully and calmly asks the last question: "What about your brother Johnny?" (Bertie's epileptic brother Johnny, who was always hidden and died at age thirteen.) Bertie remembers him: "Johnny, he was a sweet boy. . . . " Bertie is in a poignant mood, almost crying: "He was a little different. I am told it is not catching."

What we learn from the key scene is not only that the dynamics of active imagination give rise to the transcendent function,[5] but also that "Bertie is isolated from both family kindnesses and the commoners, 'far far away indeed'" (Palmer, 2013, p. 80). "The specifics of Bertie's personal traumas are intense," Palmer (2013) emphasizes, "but the sense of [his] isolated and utterly friendless existence is heartrending" (p. 80); that is, Bertie's lack of proper relationships with significant others. Now the status of their friendship in the movie is upgraded from a requirement for curing stammering to the fundamental problem of Bertie's life. As their relationship develops, Lionel does his job through shadow work.

There are two scenes in which shadow work is employed; they are separate events but seem very similar in that they show two sides of Bertie's shadow: anger and courage. The first shadow work happens when Bertie returns from King Edward's party after the harsh exchange with David, Edward VIII. Facing David's mockery and accusations of treason, Bertie's stammering is strongly reactivated.

In Lionel's consulting room, a disappointed and tempered Bertie says, "All that work down the drain. My own brother . . . I couldn't say a single word to him in reply." The profanity scene, "both comic and seemingly out-of-character for Bertie acts as a kind of therapeutic shadow eruption" (Palmer, 2013, p. 81). After Bertie's fluent string of obscenities, Lionel says, "Well, that's a side of you we don't get to see all that often," to which Bertie replies, "No. No, we're not supposed to really, not publicly." Palmer (2013) interprets this scene as "an ideal prelude to Lionel's role as a target for Bertie's shadow projection" (p. 81). The scene is followed by the Regents Park scene.

Bertie: I know my place. I will do anything in my power to keep my brother on the throne.
Lionel: You can outshine David.
Bertie: Don't take liberties! That's bordering on treason.
Lionel: I'm just saying you *could* be king. You could do it!
Bertie: That *is* treason! [They face each other, as though in combat.]
Lionel: I'm trying to get you to realize you need not be governed by fear. What are you afraid of?
Bertie: Your poisonous words.
Lionel: Why did you come to me? You're not some middleclass banker who wants elocution lessons so you can chit-chat . . .
Bertie: Do not instruct me on my duties. I am the son of a king and the brother of a king. You're the disappointing son of a brewer. Jumped up Jackaroo from the outback. You are nobody. Your sessions are over.

Palmer's (2013) analysis of this scene is that "Lionel over plays his hand here as he later admits, but Bertie's vehement, wounding, cruel characterization and rejection of Lionel confirms the power and threatening truth of Lionel's words" (p. 81). Bertie's reaction to Lionel definitely seems to be anger but it indicates something else, the lack of healthy anger, courage.

Bertie's shadow work culminates at the coronation rehearsal scene. Bertie is haunted by his insecurities and projects his own inadequacies and insecurities about assuming the throne onto Lionel by attacking Lionel's lack of credentials as a speech therapist. Bertie says, "Fraud! With war looming, you've saddled this nation with a voiceless king. Destroyed the happiness of my family. All for the sake of ensnaring a star patient you knew you couldn't possibly assist!" His desperation spilling out, Bertie pulls himself out of the chair, striding past Lionel: "It'll be like mad King George the third, there'll be Mad King George the Stammerer, who let his people down so badly in their hour of need!" Lionel sits down on the chair of Edward the Confessor.

Bertie: What're you doing? Get up! You can't sit there!
Lionel: Why not? It's a chair.

Bertie: No, it's not. That is Saint Edward's Chair.
Lionel: People have carved their initials into it!
Bertie: That chair is the seat on which every king and queen . . .
Lionel: It's held in place by a large rock!
Bertie: That is the Stone of Scone. You are trivializing everything.
Lionel: I don't care. I don't care how many royal . . .
Bertie: Listen to me. . . !
Lionel: Listen to you? By what right?
Bertie: Divine right, if you must! I'm your king!
Lionel: Noooo you're not! Told me so yourself. Said you didn't want it. So why should I waste my time listening to you?
Bertie: Because I have a right to be heard!
Lionel: Heard as what?
Bertie: A man! I HAVE A VOICE!!!

In a few seconds, Lionel quietly responds, "Yes you do. You have such perseverance, Bertie. You're the bravest man I know. And you'll make a bloody good king." Bertie's anger turns into courage. Bertie himself is surprised by his coming out of his shadow. About shadow work, Palmer (2013) explains:

> If the shadow speaks for the dark thoughts in the psyche—for what is repressed, unspoken, and denied, or for potentialities, for the undeveloped traits that must be acknowledged and embraced— Lionel surely enacts that role for Bertie.
>
> *(p. 81)*

Through the shadow work, Bertie realizes and declares, "I have a voice"—as a king to the others and more importantly to himself. This moment when Bertie's shadow emerges to the level of consciousness so that Bertie admits and incorporates his false persona to become a more authentic self is a healing moment of self-realization, and self-actualization. During the preparation for the first wartime speech, Bertie self-deprecatingly says, "I'm the solemnest king who ever lived. Lionel, I can't do this! The nation believes when I speak, I speak for them. Yet I cannot speak!" Lionel encourages Bertie: "In your head, I have a right to be bloody well heard." Bertie reminds himself "Bloody well heard, bloody well heard, bloody well heard myself." Before the final speech, Lionel advises Bertie: "Forget everything else and just say it to me, say it to me as a friend." After complimenting Bertie on the speech, Lionel points out, "Bertie, you still stammer on the w." "I had to throw in a few so they knew it was me," replies Bertie. According to Palmer (2013), "It confirms his acceptance of a hard-earned kingly identity" (p. 83), but for me Bertie's acceptance, rather than a denial or rejection, of himself seems to indicate a transformation of Bertie's *false* persona into an *authentic* one; "an internal change in Bertie has taken place" (Seidler, 2010, p. xi). Bertie accepts and holds on to the side of himself he used to reject and deny, but now he willingly lives with it as a father holds onto his son.

The essence of the King's speech problem is his relationship with himself, which seems to be related to his relationships with various significant others in his life. I am not arguing that his speech problem is solely caused by his family and nannies (simply because I do not have the whole picture of his early life), but that Bertie's false self–self relationship seems to have been developed by them and internalized in Bertie, as he shows in the living room scene after the death of his father. Internalization is an important educational problem. How much of our oppression and punishment is justified? I think that Bertie's words, "I was punished. Now I use the right hand," and "Bloody agony. Straight legs now" ring a few bells with many of us. I turn to a discussion about the nature of the problem of oppression and its internalization.

Disconfirmation, Love, and Anomaly

> Their parents were not merely more "strict"; they were sadists, engendering dependence, arresting the development of autonomy, and therefore, turning their children into things, being-for-others. Such "people" are dehumanized and dehumanizing; they have lost themselves to others; they are mad.
> —*William F. Pinar (1975c, p. 367)*

> Foucault, in a variation on Heidegger's account of research, sees that our current practices, supposedly grounded in sciences such as social psychology, produce anomalies, such as delinquents, and then take every anomaly, every attempt to evade them, as an occasion for further intervention to bring the anomalies under scientific norms. All this is done, of course, for the anomaly's own good.
> —*Hubert L. Dreyfus (2004)*

In "Sanity, Madness, and the School," Pinar (1975c), drawing from British antipsychiatrists such as R.D. Laing, David Cooper, and A. Esterson and from existentialism and phenomenology, deeply and scathingly criticized how *maddening* American schooling in the 1970s was. His criticism is of the banking concept of education, which had little respect for students' own resources; its predominant emphasis was on control and management, which turns both teachers and students into things rather than into organically transforming creatures. The maddening quality of schooling in the 1970s was not exclusive to the oppression of students by teachers but—more importantly and heartbreakingly—extended to students' internalizing the oppressor and eventually becoming numb to the oppression. Thus, oppression in education functions to transform "deficient people" (Pinar, 1975c, p. 368)—in banking education, students are buckets to be filled—into "efficient things" that absorb what is given to them and perform as they are supposed to based on "rules of others," rather than "one's own rules" (Cooper, quoted in Pinar, 1975c, p. 366). Ultimately students do not know what has been taken away from them. What they have had taken away is their inner lives, feelings, fears, imaginations, and aspirations, that which expresses their uniqueness as human beings.

The substitution of madness for sanity necessarily requires the "disconfirmation of students' inner selves" (Pinar, 1975c, p. 378) and ultimately the numbing of their autonomy and freedom. By autonomy, Pinar means "[making] one's own rules" (Cooper, quoted in Pinar, 1975c, p. 366), and "making external laws conform to the internal laws of the soul, . . . and [creating] a new world according to the laws of one's own heart" (Cooper, quoted in Pinar, 1975c, p. 366). Disconfirmation forces children to conform to external laws, then internalize them, and eventually become someone else rather than themselves. To learn to be someone else, "children must learn to be dissatisfied with themselves. That is 'maddening' and 'schizophrenic'" (Pinar, 1975c, p. 376) and embalms the subjectivities of individuals. Madness is substituted for sanity. Madness becomes normal; sanity becomes an anomaly.

"Dissatisfaction with oneself," Pinar (1975c) tells us, "is almost always the introjected nonacceptance by a significant other" (p. 363). As long as teachers and students are trapped within the banking concept, a system that produces and reinforces the introjection of the disconfirmation of self, the oppression functions almost automatically in students, without external forces. Such introjection, Pinar (1975c) continues, "is necessarily violent, . . . a self turned against itself, a divided self, or, in extreme cases, a self lost to others" (p. 364). It is commonly termed "self-hatred" (Pinar, 1975c, p. 364), as we see in the case of Bertie.

Often that kind of disconfirmation has been justified, as Foucault insists in the epigraph, for anomaly's own good. While parents and teachers are desperate to help students' study, as can be observed through *education fever* (Seth, 2002) in Korea, how often do we hear students saying, "Nobody cares!" and teachers and parents saying, "I am doing this for your own good. I am doing this because I care about you and love you." In Korean culture, corporal punishment has even been conceived of as "a rod of love"—which is a Korean way to express "tough love" but at the same time to justify parents' and teachers' oppression in correcting children's deficiencies from the perspective of the oppressor—the use of which the majority of Koreans today agree with.[6] When love is claimed for (or stands for] banking education, it is faulty. What do I mean by love? R.D. Laing (1960) is worth quoting here:

> Love lets the other be, but with affection and concern. Violence attempts to constrain the other's freedom, to force him to act in the way we desire, but with ultimate lack of concern, with indifference to the other's own existence or destiny.
>
> *(p. 50)*

To love is to acknowledge, confirm, and respect others as they are, without forcing them to be somebody that the other wants them to be. For me, love is the inverse of disconfirmation. Love is a synonym for confirmation, one of Noddings's (1992) four components of moral education. Noddings explains:

> Martin Buber (1965) described confirmation as an act of affirming and encouraging the best in others. When we confirm someone, we spot a better self and encourage its development. We can do this only if we know the other well enough to see what he or she is trying to become. Formulas and slogans have no place here. We do not set up a single idea or set of expectations for everyone to meet, but we identify something admirable, or at least acceptable, struggling to emerge in each person we encounter.
>
> *(p. 25)*

Regarding love and confirmation, what Laing and Buber, thus Pinar and Noddings, share is giving up our expectations, often our preferences, for our children, or for any others. Let them be who they want to be. Let them truly enjoy their search for who they are, what they want to do, how they want to live their lives.[7] Through days and years of experiences of the disconfirmation, "one hemorrhages (Sartre, 1943), loses one's life-blood, is filled with embalming fluid, which is the alien that is the estranged self, the self fabricated by unaware compliance and collusion with significant others" (Pinar, 1975c, p. 374). Alas, maybe I am one of the victims of the tragic phenomenon. I suspect so was the boy in the poem (see Chapter 1). In the area of speech, disconfirmation has been a historically significant area of consideration.

Semantic Environment and Speech

> It is likely that if you have never been regarded as a stutterer, you can come nowhere near appreciating the uncanny, crushing power of the social disapproval of whatever is regarded as stuttering. It is probably one of the most frightening, perplexing, and demoralizing influences to be found in our culture.
>
> —*Wendel Johnson (1944, p. 76)*

> Speech defects are among the evils of civilization; they are almost unknown among native races.
>
> —*Lionel Logue, quoted in Logue and Conradi (2010, p. 100)*

What can be summarized from the epigraphs from Lionel Logue and Wendell Johnson[8] is that stuttering *is* a product of our culture. Johnson made this argument empirically concrete. His 1944 article, "The Indians Have No Word For It," started with a possibly exaggerated statement by an English stutterer, William Nuttall: "Whoever finds a cure for stuttering will have found a cure for all the ills of society" (quoted in Johnson, 1944, p. 65). Johnson comments, "Mr. Nuttall was pointing a finger in the direction of 'semantic environment'—the environment of attitudes and evaluations, opinions, and beliefs—as a source of his difficulties" (p. 65). He understood that "the aspects of the environment most important in relation to stuttering are semantic, or evaluational, in a broad sense" (p. 65). That insight led Johnson to further studies among Native Americans.

A few years before Johnson wrote the paper, his student, Miss Harriett Hayers, had become a teacher on an Indian reservation in Idaho. She intended to study stuttering among Shoshone and Bannock tribes, but surprisingly she returned without any information because she was unable to find any stuttering Native Americans (Johnson, 1944, p. 65). The superintendent and teachers of the schools, who had been in close relationship with the Native Americans for 25 years, reported that they had never seen any stuttering Native Americans (p. 65).[9] Johnson continued his study by sending his student John Snidecor, to continue the investigation in two areas: "the language of the Indians, and their policies and standards concerning the care and training of their children" (Johnson, 1944, p. 66). Snidecor interviewed several hundred Native Americans. From his investigation, Snidecor reported:

> First, these Indians had *no word for stuttering* [emphasis in the original] in their language. He had to demonstrate stuttering for the chiefs and the members before they could understand what he was talking about. . . . Second, their standards of child care and training appeared to be extraordinarily lax in comparison with our own.
>
> *(Johnson, 1944, pp. 66–67)*

With the absence of a word for stuttering, Johnson (1944) argued that the Native American child-rearing culture explained the lack of stutterers. This insight is followed by his five-year study of "the onset of stuttering" (p. 67), starting in 1935. An interesting argument made in the study is that "the so-called stuttering children were found to have been apparently normal, even with respect to speech, at the time when someone, usually the parents, first regarded them as stutterers" (Johnson, 1944, p. 68). Then Johnson came to the rather brave conclusion, although he acknowledged the limitation of his study, that "stuttering is a *diagnosogenic disorder* in the sense that diagnosing their child's speech [as] stuttering or as defective, or abnormal, [is] a very important part of the child's semantic environment" (Johnson, 1944, p. 68; emphasis in original); that is, "Stuttering as a clinical problem, as a definite disorder, was found to occur, not before being diagnosed, but *after being diagnosed*" (Johnson, 1944, pp. 66–67; emphasis in original).

Although it seems to me that Johnson was hasty in assuming causality between the semantic environment and stuttering—because the relation is not necessarily causal and opponents have argued against Johnson's theory (Shell, 2005; Zimmerman, Liljeblad, Frank, & Cleeland, 1983), his theory has been much discussed in the field. For instance, Barry Guitar's (2014) discussion of the environmental factors of stuttering in his frequently cited, and much-used book *Stuttering: An Integrated Approach to Its Nature and Treatment*, first published in 1991, is largely based on Wendell Johnson's studies and conflicting findings.[10] Although researchers (e.g., Shell, 2005; Yairi, 1999) do not entirely agree with Johnson, it is not difficult to see that they share his concern about and recognition of the semantic environment, whether or not they support causality, demonstrating how influential Johnson's studies have been in the field.

The educational implication of Johnson's studies and his theory is his insight about one's relationship with others. First, the long-recognized importance of the semantic environment in stuttering entails consideration of the relationship between stuttering children and others. Johnson's success in curing stuttering children through changing their semantic environment is not disputed, although it cannot be applied to all cases: "Every case must be handled on its own merits. There are no rules of thumb" (Johnson, 1944, p. 75). With the evidence of a cure through changing stuttering children's semantic environment,[11] Johnson argued that:

> It was essential, although it should be stressed that it was not possible in all cases, to get the parents and teachers to evaluate the child's speech and to react to it—*regardless of how he spoke*—in ways that would convince the child that his speech was approved. As the child appeared to sense that his speech was being thoroughly approved, his reluctance to speak, his exaggerated hesitancy and caution and effort in speaking all decreased. The eventual result tended to be speech that was free, spontaneous, a source of evident enjoyment to the child and speech that was *normally* fluent—not perfectly fluent, for perfect fluency is as 'abnormal,' or unusual, as very severe stuttering.
>
> (Johnson, 1944, p. 70; emphasis in original)

In Johnson's approach is a strong sense of the "receptivity of caring" (Noddings, 1984, 2010c; see also Chapter 3), which is a disposition to receive the other as he or she is rather than to project social expectations of speech, or anything else, onto the other. Almost all of us are somehow stammerers in an extreme sense. Most of us pause, hesitate, stop, reiterate, and mispronounce when we talk. In Korean schools, students are expected to be almost *perfectly fluent* through constant disconfirmation. Or else, students are constantly informed, through standardized tests, how fluent or nonfluent they are in the given areas of school subjects. To fix the students' nonfluency, the system imposes more and more treatments, such as tests, regulations, policies, reforms, and kinds of curricula. The assumption is that with appropriate methods we can reduce nonfluency, but the approach seems to me to have been strengthening students' stammering instead. Is not education under the two banners of standardization and accountability a form of semantic environment that continually diagnoses students as stutterers? I have many memories of when I was frightened, not knowing the answer to the questions I was asked, standing in the classroom being ashamed, and eventually blaming myself. The influence of the semantic environment is not always so explicit; many times it is implicit, as Pinar (1975b) tells us: "The degree of nonacceptance need not be that extreme to cripple and even paralyze the self" (p. 364). As sanity is substituted for madness, could the direction of stammering can be reversed? Let me explore that possibility below.

Compliance of Others in Disavowing a Student's Inner Voice

Stammering to oneself is one's inability to make one's own voice, possibly without noticing the inability, and to activate the subjectivity that "orality" (Pinar, 2011, p. 13) expresses, as I have shown in Chapter 2. What is weakened is their autonomy and self-respect, which are validated and developed by the confirmation of different significant others. The violence of disconfirmation of the other is often times internalized. The internalized disconfirmation does not always cause an extreme pain like stammering. This devastating state of internalized oppression is also strengthened when children vie for the love of teachers and parents.

Instead of listening to students' voices, parents and teachers show nonacceptance and disconfirmation and offer presents, rewards, or promises of material gain because they are desperately looking for ways to motivate students to learn. From the first day of teacher education, I was told that motivation is the key to instruction, the fundamental assumption, which is based on instrumental rationalism, banking education, and educational psychology. "Why" is always replaced by "how." Always how! Children are treated like the animals in the labs of Pavlov, Thorndike, and Skinner. With appropriate stimulation, which is understood by progressive educators as students being taught in the way they want to be taught, students will "produce" the expected outcome or behavior.

Parents and teachers unwittingly become accomplices of the system as long as they consider that the purpose of schooling is to fill students with given knowledge and skills. How commonly we hear parents and teachers telling students they will be rewarded if they reach this grade, that achievement, and those levels of performance. "If you get all As, you will get a Mac computer. If you reach the top, you will get into the best university and eventually have a high-paying job." Parents feel their efforts for their children's education are rewarded by their children's university acceptance letters. Schools, teachers, and principals are also rewarded financially, and all of these "rewards" are calculated as numbers, either grades or money. What is substituted for the "reward" is the freedom and autonomy of students and teachers, who become unaware of what has been taken away from them. It is their soul, or heart, as the high-school boy in the poem at the beginning of this book lamented: "I cannot endure this pain any more. My brain nibbles my heart." Children's inner voices are psychologically, culturally, and institutionally ignored, and the children themselves are deceived. That is not your fault, boy! The symptoms are invisible; the disavowed inner voice is hard to detect and thus even harder to treat. Is this an educational question, a medical question, or both? I think both.

Schooling has been detecting delinquency, anomalies, and deficiencies and then fixing them by inventing and applying treatments for the good of those with the anomalies. Those who do not want to study are believed to have something wrong with them. Thus they have to be treated one way or another. Once the treatments for the anomalies' own good is internalized, again, it becomes a strong inner force supporting Social Darwinism, which I want to call "educational Darwinism"—part of the problem is also that meritocracy supports the roots of which hakbeolism shares. It is interesting at this point to learn that in Ancient Greece, education and medicine were not clearly separated areas. Foucault (1982a) explains:

> It [self-cultivation] is much closer to the medical model than to the pedagogical model. . . . One should recall the principle—familiar to the Epicureans, the Cynics, the Stoics—that Philosophy's role is to heal the disease of the soul. Plutarch was able one day to declare that philosophy and medicine constituted *mia khora*, a single area, a single domain. Epictetus did not want his school to be regarded merely as a place of education but also as a "medical clinic," an *iatreion*; he intended it to be a "dispensary for the soul"; he wanted his students to arrive thinking of themselves as patients: "One man has a dislocated shoulder, another an abscess, another a headache."
>
> (p. 97)

What strikes me is the curative function of self-cultivation; Epictetus wanted his school to be a medical clinic and saw his students as patients. In Ancient Greece, the practice of the self is therapeutic because it enables one to get rid of negative influences and false opinions from others, such as teachers or parents. Thus to "unlearn" the influence of the semantic environment is one of the important tasks of self-cultivation. The unlearning of those in my case happened in my Ph.D. program in Canada, after I had reached almost 40 years of age, completed 18 years of education, nine years of teaching, and had two children. Unfortunately, not everybody has the privilege of studying for a Ph.D. with the greatly caring teachers that I had. I suggest that the therapeutic quality of the practice of the care of the self needs to be incorporated into our education. Doing so can be approached by getting rid of the oppressive semantic environment that diagnoses students as anomalies, as Johnson did with his child patients.

Implications of *The King's Speech* on the Self–Other Relationship

> *The King's Speech* is about much more than stammering, but about friendship, mentoring and support. We lose these deep, meaningful friendships at our peril.
>
> —*David Seidler (2010, p. xv)*

My discussion focuses here on the implications for education in Lionel's approach to curing Bertie's stammer in the journey to find Bertie's authentic voice, self-realization, authentic persona, and eventually a positive self–self relationship. The recovery of Bertie's voice cannot be attributed only to Lionel; it comes through the relationship built by the contributions of both.[12] One of my study questions is *how self-understanding requires care from others and what kind of care is desirable rather than detrimental.* In thinking of the answers to both parts of the question, I want to discuss some characteristics of Lionel's approach from the perspective of care.

Lionel's exact approach remains unknown, since he did not write about it.[13] However, what I observed in the movie, and how his patients and relatives felt about him indicate what kind of person he was and his approach. Therefore it is possible to discuss Lionel's approach as caring, and Lionel as the caring one. A major secondary source of information is Lionel's biography, *The King's Speech: How One Man Saved the British Monarchy* (Logue & Conradi, 2010).

First, in the treatment, one's carer should remain humble under (or should not dominate) the primacy of the self-understanding of the patient. Lionel was sure that patients have their own voices, and they are only the ones who can recover their voices and achieve self-understanding. Seidler (2010) tells us that Lionel would never say "I can eliminate your stutter," but rather, "You'll get rid of your stutter; I'll show you things that'll help, but you'll do the real work and I know you'll succeed" (p. xi). Lionel lets Bertie know Bertie has a voice, a right to be heard, and the ability to find his voice. In this regard, Logue might agree with Habermas and Freud in thinking that "emancipatory self-understanding cannot come through the analyst's imparting information to the patient, or merely by applying psychoanalytic theory in a technical or strategic manner" (Pinar, 1978, p. 88). What is necessary, Pinar argues, is "a coming to consciousness by the patient, a process that functions to dissolve resistances" (p. 88). What Habermas, Freud, Jung, and Pinar teach us is that the only one who can cure Bertie, with help of others, is Bertie himself. The role of Lionel in curing Bertie's stammer is influential, but it is not great enough to say that *Lionel cured Bertie*. In today's hospitals, it is commonly said that doctors cure patients, but more accurately, it is the patient's mind and body that actually do the work with the help of doctors' treatments; that is, what is less recognized regarding the curing process is the imperative and significance of a patient's desire to be cured and his or her body's endurance over the process. Lionel makes recommendations; Bertie makes decisions and acts. In education, students are responsible for their studies, more than their teachers and parents, but in the discourse of accountability, the responsibility is on the teachers. For self-understanding to start, Bertie needs to be conscious of his ability and voice.

Lionel seems to be certain that assisting his patients in overcoming their debilitating symptoms can be successful only to the extent that he succeeds "in assisting the patient to become conscious of his distinctive self-formative process" (Pinar, 1978, p. 88). That is process of understanding that guides one to self-reflection. In Pinar and Grumet's *currere*, it happens through free association; in Lionel's approach in the movie, it is through shadow work based on friendship. What *currere* and shadow work intend to do is to bring to the surface memories, experiences, and shadows now frozen in the unconsciousness; in Jungian terms, it is the *individuation process*. The surfacing of memories, Pinar warns us, "must be attended to cautiously, and control—of some fundamental sort that is not repressive—maintained" (p. 91).

To develop the relational, communal, and receptive quality of the relationship, Lionel discloses himself to Bertie as a human being, not as a therapist, rather than forcing Bertie to open up. Through his disclosures, he achieves Bertie's acceptance as a friend.[14] When Bertie visits Lionel's consultation room after his father's death, Lionel opens the conversation with his memories about his own father, a brewer: "I wasn't there for my father's death. Still makes me sad." His disclosure leads to Bertie's disclosure. Also, when Bertie and Elizabeth visit Lionel's home, Lionel, with full confidence, tells Bertie to be "his own man." Mystle, Lionel's wife, enters her house and is flabbergasted to see Elizabeth because Lionel did not tell Mystle about the king and queen's visit. As soon as Lionel hears Mystle, he presses himself up against the wall. Bertie asks Lionel, "Are you all right, Lionel? You are being a coward!" "You're damn right!" says Lionel. Opening the door, Bertie tells Lionel, "Get out there, man!" Now their situations are reversed. Bertie opens the door for Lionel, and for Bertie to open the door and face his hesitancy, fear, and insecurity is also a self-affirmative action. Lionel shows the power of self-disclosure that might evoke the other's disclosure or more. The first disclosure seems to be intentional in that Lionel's disclosure is congruent with Bertie's; the latter one seems accidental but might give Bertie a feeling that although Lionel always seems confident, he is also a weak, insecure, normal man.

Individualization is another significant part of Lionel's approach; it means that Lionel's approach does not conform to principles. His methods are "in sharp contrast to rather more brutal methods, including electric shock therapy" (Logue & Conradi, 2010, p. 31), as we see in the movie after Bertie's painful speech in Wembley. Lionel wrote in the *Daily Express* on March 22, 1932, "Every patient requires slightly different handling and a study of each individual's psychology is necessary. Conditions that give one man sufficient confidence to overcome a defect will actually set up a similar defect in another" (p. 100). Lionel sees Bertie as a singular being, not a "type or case" (Noddings, 1984, p. 66). When one treats us as a type instead of an individual, strategies are simply exercised on us, objectify us (Noddings, 1984, p. 66). When we ignore the singularities of others, we make them "cases instead of persons" (Noddings, 1984, p. 66).

I have no doubt that Lionel is a "carer" from Noddings's perspective. When Lionel's daughter-in-law Anne, who was married to his middle son, Valentine, was asked about the secret of Lionel's success, she said, without giving a definitive answer, "Anyone can do tongue twisters and breathing exercises, but he was a first class psychotherapist. He was a super good daddy where George V had been a ghastly one" (Logue & Conradi, 2010, p. 228). This opinion carries more weight because of her career as a consultant in child psychiatry at the Middlesex Undergraduate Teaching Hospital. When Lionel died (April 12, 1953), a reader who was Lionel's patient, commented on the obituary in *The Times*: "I can testify to the fact that his patience was magnificent and his sympathy almost superhuman" (Logue & Conradi, 2010, p. 227). The scriptwriter, Seidler's "rather eccentric uncle," David, was also a patient of Lionel's. When Seidler asked him about Lionel's approach, he responded, "Absolute rubbish. All he wanted to do was talk about Australia and his childhood and his parents and get me to talk about my parents and my childhood" (Seidler, 2010, p. xi). However, David was cured. It is not overstatement to say Lionel shows the attitude of one caring about the other, displaying "receptivity" (Noddings, 1984, p. 30) and "sympathy, feeling with the other" (Noddings, 2010a, pp. 55–57). It seems that Lionel knew how to make his patients feel comfortable talking to him. Lionel's strategy was to let patients know that he was there to listen, and to share stories, rather than to correct them from the position of a man who is himself without flaws. Interestingly there seems to be a commonality between Lionel Logue and Nel Noddings in that they both weld their private life and professional life. In other words, Lionel's persona as a speech therapist does not mask the self. When I think about this point, Lionel as a carer from the perspective of Noddings's ethics and the power of his self-disclosure, I cautiously suggest that Lionel's treatment is ontological, a way of being. Is not teaching a way of being, when a teacher welds her public and private life and genuinely engages with the students and the subject that she teaches?

Lastly, the goal of his treatment is for one to recover one's relationship with oneself. Lionel could "give [Bertie] faith in his voice," which becomes evident in the war speech scene when Bertie says, "I had to throw in a few so they knew it was me." Bertie accepts himself as himself rather than blaming or denying himself. What becomes authentic is not only Bertie's voice but also his self–self relationship. Bertie is not afraid of being himself anymore; he builds his own rules in his speech, is not bound by those of others. The self-denial transforms into the self–self relationship.

Conclusion

Korean education today can be conceived of as a process, or continuation, of disconfirmation. Through the institutionalization of students, today's Korean educational institutions perpetuate the politically oppressive and psychologically detrimental characteristics of teaching and learning. Korean education, in which many teachers and parents are complicit, is responsible for the negative influence on students' development, political and intellectual as well as psychological. Students' and teachers' voices are disavowed and sometimes they stammer, not to others but to themselves. What kinds of approaches should others—teachers, parents, peers—take? The analysis of *The King's Speech* invites us to rethink our semantic environment not only in institutions but also in our relationships. Care-for-others, if approached in caring ways, not in disconfirmation, can certainly contribute to self-care.

Notes

1. *The King's Speech* has gained much attention and has received several nominations and awards. In addition, reviews and articles in disciplines such as history, literature, film, psychology, and therapy have analyzed the movie, but little work has been done on the film from an educational perspective, and even less from a curriculum studies angle. Nevertheless, I see the story of King George VI (Albert Frederick Arthur George; December 14, 1895–February 6, 1952), as one that has powerful implications for current education practices and educators not only in South Korea but elsewhere.
2. In his Jungian analysis of KS, James Palmer (2013) addresses the omissions: "Examples of historically significant details omitted include King George VI (Bertie) giving a royal welcome to Prime Minister Chamberlain on his return from Munich; the fascist leanings of Bertie's brother Edward VIII (Guy Pearce); and the glossing over of the steadfast support that Winston Churchill (Timothy Spall) offered the irresponsible Edward VIII" (p. 69). Palmer also acknowledges two attacks on the historical accuracy of KS, namely Christopher Hitchens's "Churchill Didn't Say That" (*Slate*, January 24, 2011, http://www.slate.com/id/2282194), and Peter Hitchens's "The Real King's Story versus 'The King's Speech'" (*Daily Mail Online*, Peter Hitchens's Blog, January 2011, http://hitchensblog.mailonsunday.co.uk/2011/01/colin-firth-in-the-kings-speech-versus-the-real-story.html).
3. This section title is from James Palmer's title, "The King's Speech: A Jungian Take," which helped me with the psychoanalytic analysis of the movie.
4. For a detailed explanation, Palmer quotes Jungian analyst Robert Johnson's summary of the dynamics of active imagination:

    In dreams, the events happen completely at the unconscious level, In Active Imagination, the events take place on the *imaginative* level, which is neither conscious nor unconscious but a meeting place, a common ground where both meet on equal terms and together create a life experience that combines the elements of both. The two levels of consciousness flow into one another in the field of imagination like two rivers that merge to form one powerful stream. They complement each other; they begin to work together; as a result, your totality begins to form itself into a unity. The dialogue of conscious mind with unconscious gives rise to the transcendent function, the self, that stands as a synthesis of the two. (Johnson, quoted in Palmer, 2013, p. 79)

5. In Lionel's consultation room, Bertie is relaxed on a couch, and drinking whisky. With help of Lionel's techniques, Bertie tells his traumas to Lionel, and then Bertie's unconscious starts to be integrated with conscious. This is a necessary process for individuation.
6. A survey by Gallup Korea in 2013 shows that 80% of Koreans think that physical punishment is acceptable, or should be allowed, for the purpose of education. The survey asked people, "What is the biggest problem in Korean education." The responses were private supplemental education (36%), university-exam-focused education (16%), the lack of continuity of educational policies and university student selection policies (11%), and school violence and bullying (8%). None of them deals with the loss of self in education.
7. I suggest this approach as a way of care-for-others given dire consequence of hakbeolism and its internalization. However, I also want to make clear that this is not a universal way of caring. Caring takes culturally variable and situation-specific forms that invite complicated conversation across countries and peoples and historical circumstances. What is necessary is an individual's receptivity, attuned relationship with self and others, and a deep understanding of the distinctiveness of the individuals and specificity of the situations. My thanks to Professor Karen Meyer for bringing me attention to this important point.
8. Wendell Johnson, an American psychologist and actor, is one of the earliest and most influential speech pathologists. The Wendell Johnson Speech and Hearing Center of the University of Iowa Hospitals and Clinics is named after him. He is also famous for his unethical study, the Monster Study, in 1939, which led to compensation of the participants from the Iowa University in 2007.
9. Two Native American stutterers have come to the Iowa Speech Clinic over a 25-year period: one was an individual of mixed ancestry from South Dakota who had lived almost his entire life among white men; the other one was of full Native American ancestry, but it was eventually found that his silence was intentional because of his relationship with his God—that is, the boy had interpreted the stuttering to mean that God intended him to be silent. Later he was cured and entered a monastery (Johnson, 1944, p. 66). Dr. C. Esco Obermann, a doctor at the clinic, was assigned to the boy's case. He convinced the boy by reinterpreting the boy's faith that God would be pleased if the boy would continue to talk and spread God's words. A couple of days later the boy came back with excitement: he was able to talk with only slight stammering. Johnson's point is that the boy was the only case of stutter over the series of studies they have conducted. Johnson makes the rather brave statement that "It may be said, so far as the writer [Johnson] is aware, that there are no stutterers among North American Indians living under conditions comparatively free from the white man's influence" (*Johnson, 1944*, p. 66).
10. Barry Guitar (2014) argues that the causality that Johnson assumed is misleading because "it is highly possible that the differences between parents of stutterers and parents of nonstutterers may be the result of stuttering" (p. 89). Marc Shell (2005) who, bringing in his family history, supports a genetic predisposition to stuttering, calls Johnson's theory an "iatrogenic theory" (p. 12). It is unfortunate for me that he did not provide his familial culture of child-rearing. It is not clear whether Shell's experience in stuttering was affected by a genetic preposition or the semantic environment or both.
11. Johnson's approaches to curing stuttering did not aim at the child stutterer but were directed toward "relevant evaluations—the attitudes, assumptions, beliefs, etc.—and the resulting policies and reactions, of the child's parents and teachers and the other persons who affect his own evaluations and reactions" (Johnson, 1944, p. 71). The purpose was to change the conditions under which the child stuttered. He tried to lower high standards of behaviors, such as table manners, cleanliness, toilet habits, and

obedience or the prohibition of certain words, innocent to the child but profane or vulgar to the parents and encouraged a more affectionate and friendly relationship between the parents and their child (Johnson, 1944, p. 71).
12. Lionel would not sit on Saint Edward's Chair without his sure knowledge that his relationship with Bertie was "as family," shown in the following exchange: Bertie says to Archbishop, "I should like the Doctor to be seated in the King's box." The Archbishop responds, "But members of your family will be seated there, Sir." "That is why it's suitable," replies Bertie. Bertie's acceptance of Lionel as family allows Lionel's blasphemy, to sit in the divine chair.
13. My guess about this lack of information is that it is related to the confidentiality that Lionel has to keep, as Logue and Conradi (2010) tell us:

> Although he [Lionel Logue] wrote a few articles for the press about the treatment of stammering and other speech impediments, he never set out his methods in a formal way and had no student or apprentice with whom to share the secrets of his work. Nor—probably because of the discretion with which he always treated his relationship with the king—did he write up his most famous case. (p. viii)

14. Bertie's role in the relationship is by no means minor, which can be understood in Noddings's term "apprehension of caring" (1984, p. 59) or "reciprocity, . . . [the] contribution of the human cared-for" (p. 69). It is Bertie's acceptance that completes the reciprocity. "The cared-for," as Noddings insists, "must 'receive' the caring" (p. 69).

6
SELF-CARE AND CARE-FOR-OTHERS

Introduction

> It was a generally accepted principle that one could not attend to oneself without the help of another. Seneca said that no one was ever strong enough on his own to get out of the state of *stultitia* [stupidity, foolishness] he was in.
> —*Michel Foucault (1982b, p. 98)*

> I need to acknowledge how surely an ethics of caring needs to attend to care for oneself as well as others. Can we care-for-others if we are not caring for ourselves?
> —*Carl Leggo (2011, p. 77)*

> The engagement with the other and the engagement of the self go hand in hand.
> —*Hongyu Wang (2009, p. xiv)*

The focus of this chapter is on *how self-care and care-for-others are associated with one another*. In other words, this chapter is about the association between the self–self relationship and self–other relationships, since to have an authentic self–self relationship is a form of self-care, as I have shown in Chapters 2 and 4, and care-for-others is about self–other relationships, as discussed in Chapters 3 and 5. I do not intend to seek a causal or sequential priority between them—there seem to be various formations of the association between them depending on the people involved, their relationships, and their (cultural, historical, and political) circumstances—but rather to discuss the complexity and challenges of the relationship between self-care and care-for-others.

The relationship between self-care and care-for-others is neither a matter of sequence nor of choice—although one can be suspended for the other for certain moments depending on the circumstances. There is an inextricable and complementary quality to the relationship between the two. It is inextricable in that they are not discrete; it is complementary in that each implies and requires the other. That is, care-for-others necessarily requires self-care, and care-for-others is frequently a way of self-care; self-care also may require care-for-others, and at the same time self-care can be a way to care-for-others. However, this relationship is by no means without possible confusion, risks, challenges, and of course failures, to which I will turn after discussing the seemingly inseparable connection between them.

The connection between self-care and care-for-others *is* inseparable, which is more evident in intimate relationships such as between a parent and a child, first because self and other are ontologically interconnected and constantly changing, hand in hand. That is, "I-for-myself" does not exist in an extreme sense, but rather, for Bakhtin, "The self is coauthored with others" (quoted in Wang, 2004, p. 43). "Such a relationship between self and other," Wang (2004) understands, "enables both to become active consciousness" (p. 43). She further argues that "relationship and individuality are both claimed and transformed through open-ended interaction" (p. 43). Second, the connection is inseparable because the purpose of care-for-others is part of one's self-care; the purpose of self-care is part of care-for-others. Let me explain it using a mother and her son. I postulate that mother wants her son to be happy; the son wants his mother to be happy. In other words, the happiness of the son makes his mother happy and vice versa. Thus, the mother's care for the son is not only care-for-others but also self-care, because she is pleased and happy to see her son in his happiness—in fact, the act of care-for-others already in part fulfills one's desire to be a carer. Volunteers often say that working for the people in need and for the society makes them feel good and makes their lives worth living. In this way, care-for-others is of a part of self-care and vice versa. "As I care-for-others and am cared for by them [and by my act of care-for-others I would add]," Noddings (1984) contends, "I become able to care for myself" (p. 49).

For one to remain ethical, neither self-care nor care-for-others should or can be sacrificed, nor one sacrificed for the other. In this regard, Foucault's prioritization of self-care over care-for-others needs to be questioned. Although he does not disregard the significance of the other in one's care of the self through what might be called a "soul service which is performed through multifarious social relations" (Foucault, 1982b, p. 99),[1] he makes a strong vertical order between them—maybe because of his critique of self-renunciation in the Christian confession tradition. Is not Wang (2004, p. 43) right in claiming that Foucault fails to directly address how to work through differences within and between self and other without doing violence to either? The problem of Foucault in this regard is the consequential quality, or character, of care-for-others resulting from self-care. I agree with Wang (2004) arguing that Foucault's emphasis on self-care may need to be diluted to a certain degree by "simultaneous relationships with others" (p. 37).

Care-for-others cannot fulfill self-care without "self-affirmation" (Wang, 2004, p. 37). Self-affirmation for a woman, Wang contends, is attending to her inner voice and speaking women's languages. However, the primacy of self-affirmation in the relationship of self-care and care-for-others is not exclusive to women. "Without attending to her inner voice," Wang (2004) argues, we all, not only women, are "susceptible to others' gaze" (p. 37), and we speak "others' languages" (p. 37). Without self-affirmation, care-for-others can be subsumed either to servitude or self-renunciation. In this regard "care-for-others," Wang argues, "depends on the care of the self" (p. 37).

The relationship between self-care and care-for-others is not as simple, or straightforward, as it might sound here. There is no way to structure our actions upon/between them. My ethical intention cannot be guaranteed in any way and to any degree, but only "attempted and approached" (Britzman, 1998, p. 43). There is no simple answer to the important question of how and to what extent I can creatively (re)construct my relationship with myself and others as a work of art without resorting to oppressive structures in my already-built relationships with myself and others. What has to be clear for my discussion here is that the shared aim of care-for-others and self-care is to be ethical through an authentic relationship of one with oneself and with others so that neither of them is sacrificed, but through both of which one makes one's own voice, and indeed educational life, authentic. In this matter, Wang (2004) suggests that one needs "a certain sense of turning away from others in order to cultivate [one's] own space" (p. 37); in other words, one needs "a room of one's own" (Woolf, quoted in Wang, 2004, p. 37). I agree with Wang's insight that having distance is crucial. Yet, there are layers of distance in the association between self-care and care-for-others. I wonder whether distance can be created through rethinking, if not breaking, the unnecessary connection between ethics and oppressive structures and between love and preference.

For me, the relations between social and political structures and our ability and possibility to be ethical and between love and preference are somewhat odd. I discuss the former from an intellectual and political point of view with the help of Michael Foucault and William F. Pinar, the latter from a psychoanalytic and ethics viewpoint of Deborah p. Britzman and Nel Noddings. Then I suggest a contemplative or meditative mode to keep my balance between self-care and care-for-others with the help of Catherine Ingram. The viewpoints are, however, not exclusive since the self is a totality of intellect, emotion, and spirituality, all of which are always embodied.

Distance Between Ethics and Repressive Structures

> For centuries we have been convinced that between our ethics, our personal ethics, our everyday life, and the great political and social and economic structures, there were analytical relations, and that we couldn't change anything, for instance, in our sex life or our family life, without ruining our economy, our democracy, and so on. I think we have to get rid of this idea of an analytical or necessary link between ethics and other social or economic or political structures.
> —*Michel Foucault (1983, p. 261)*

> Through distance and engagement one discerns the paradoxes and antinomies of determinacy. Distance and engagement are two intertwined if tensioned modalities of study, always altering their forms and intensities according to the project at hand, its historical situatedness, its subjective meaning, or its social significance.
> —*William F. Pinar (2011, p. 18)*

> There is no philosophy, it's true, but a philosophy or rather philosophy in activity. The movement by which, not without effort and uncertainty, dreams and illusions, one detaches oneself from what is accepted as true and seeks other rules—that is philosophy.
> —*Michel Foucault (1980, p. 327)*

The topic in this section is how we engage with oppressive structures—the verb could be "overcome," but I chose "engage" instead because it expresses rather a dynamic relationship within the structural relationship. I do not mean that we have to invert the structure, get rid of it entirely, or get out of the relationship, but I want to engage with these structures, tweaking the question into thinking about what prohibits us from doing it. There are two common modes of response to oppressive structures: mere resistance, and nihilism or cynicism, both of which we have to resist. First, resisting or denying one's current relationship with oneself, others, and society only for the sake of resistance results in effacing "subjectivity, and the embodied historical individual" (Pinar, 2011, p. 31). Without reconstruction of subjectivity, "the critical pedagogue is paralyzed by reproduction, left to cry 'resistance' without the subjective means to enact it" (Pinar, 2011, p. 35). And the result is "impossible praxis" (Lather, quoted in Pinar, 2011, p. 31). Individuals and structures are not entirely separate entities but "reciprocally related, indeed mutually constitutive" (Pinar, 2011, p. 31). We are not subjects determined by structures, but rather we have the ability to constitute structures and their acts upon us through engagement. Without addressing subjectivity, social reconstruction is moving into an old village with new signs. New signs might seem like a radical change, but the constraining structures are the same.

The cynicism or nihilism of our time forces us to believe that the only possible world is the one in which we are suffering. One might say "I know how the system works, and it is not desirable. But what else can I do beside struggling to survive in the system?" The seemingly unavoidable influence of the neoliberal, commercialized, and politically oppressive structure of education, in Pinar's (2011) criticism, suffocates teachers and "*Just do it* becomes the anthem of our time: acting now, suspending judgment, and ignoring ethics; only outcomes matter, and outcomes are numbers, only" (p. 11). Yes, I cannot agree more with Pinar's claim about the undervalued status of subjectivity, agency, and the intellectual and political freedom of students and teachers in their study. It is not exclusive to the U.S. but stronger, I believe, in Korea (see Chapter 1). But however oppressive the system is, Pinar does not forget to mention, "students squirm and teachers struggle to create opportunities to teach" (2011, p. 9). We do not need to be cynical or nihilistic even though we cannot change the system today. I do not see that the system will change in the near future, but we can change, or engage with, its ability to reproduce itself through us.

Foucault's urging, in the epigraph, that we break the unnecessary link between ethics and social, economic, or political structures fascinates me. His insistence, as Pinar (2011) understands, is "simultaneously a politics against social submission and a private politics against an essentialized self, creating a passage to a politics of cultural creation, that is, to think, to perceive, and to live 'otherwise'" (p. 109). To make this more complicated, let us add Wang's understanding of Foucault's analysis of the care of the self:

> There is a peculiar paradox. On the one hand, he emphasizes that self-mortification is not the cultivation of the self; the self must not be shadowed by sacrificial ethics. On the other hand, his call for tearing away from oneself in order to become a new person necessarily requires a certain sense of self-negation.
>
> *(2004, p. 48)*

Now the one Foucault advocates against is the one who was characterized by social submission, self-sacrifice, and self-negation. Between who one was and who one can be otherwise, Wang (2004) finds "a third space," "an ambiguous zone in which the individual can decide his style of life only in an uncertain way" (p. 48). Both Wang and Pinar recommend that we cultivate a certain space or distance from what seems to be normal or one's taken-for-grantedness, where we might feel unstable, uncomfortable, uncertain, but where we can taste, indeed enjoy, the "dizziness of freedom."

Entering into a third space requires us to "cultivate noncoincidence between self and the world through the cultivation of distance, even estrangement and exile" (Pinar, 2011, p. 17). Pinar's "noncoincidence" resides in subjective, social, and political realms that can be cultivated by "understanding" through autobiography and allegory, which are informed by rigorous academic study. Academic study, for Pinar, can cultivate a certain distance—often distance also makes possible a new understanding of one's reality—between one and one's experience, which is "not always reliable" (p. 17), and indeed questions one's "self-evident experience" (p. 17).

"Cultivating such noncoincidence supports the cultivation of virtue, [which is] key to a self-conscious and chosen commitment to others" (Pinar, 2011, p. xiii), a "moral excellence and firmness," one of the definitions, or characteristics, of the word "character" that Pinar uses in his book *The Character of Curriculum Studies*. Pinar's use of "noncoincidence" fascinates me because it requires from us both intellectual rigor and the quality of morality, virtue, or ethics. There is seemingly no necessary linkage between oppressive structures and ethics. The linkage is, I think, one of the greatest challenges we are facing today. The consequence of the linkage between the two is disastrous, not only in schooling but also on this planet.

On the other hand, Foucault's insistence on getting rid of the link between ethics and oppressive structures invites us to think about the broken linkage between knowledge and ethics. Knowledge devoid of ethics functions as a weapon to destroy the humanity. On this matter Foucault's accusation goes back to Descartes (see Note 2 in Chapter 4). After Descartes, Foucault (1983) laments, "I can be immoral and know the truth" (p. 279). We should cultivate a certain distance between self and reality, and in that space rehabilitate the linkage between knowledge and ethics. Our era, more urgently than ever, needs the cultivation of the linkage between knowledge and ethics, since with the help of technology, "knowledge" is everywhere and anybody can produce and spread any information.

Regarding the unnecessary linkage between ethics and the constraining structures, a passage from an interview with Foucault, first published anonymously in 1980, lingers with me:

> Those who, for once in their lives, have found a new tone, a new way of looking, a new way of doing, those people, I believe, will never feel the need to lament that the world is error, that history is filled with people of no consequence, and that it is time for others to keep quiet so that at last the sound of their disapproval may be heard.
>
> *(Foucault, 1980, pp. 327–328)*

The passage contains no doubt, only assurance about the human possibilities of the agency of subjectivity. There are always certain possibilities to create one's own ethics, one's own way of life. The remnants of the oppressive structures might not leave us forever; but we can change our relationship with them via what is called understanding[2] through study. Through understanding we can learn that we do not have to limit our relationships within the structures and resorting to their rules.

Understanding Love

> Virtually no word in our language has been abused as much as *love*.
> —*Nel Noddings and Paul J. Shore (1984, p. 154)*

> The care of the self cannot itself tend toward so exaggerated a form of self-love as to neglect others or, worse still, to abuse one's power over them.
> —*Michel Foucault (1984, p. 288)*

> [Bettelheim] is concerned with how one learns to move from the early fear of losing the other's love—one of the central methods Fenichel notes—to "the fear of losing self-respect." The paradox is that self-respect can be made only from relations with others.
> —*Deborah p. Britzman (1998, p. 43)*

Beside the structural constraints, there is a psychological challenge in the relationship between self-care and care-for-others that I discuss here through love. I first briefly discuss what I mean by "love," and how it is abused. Then, I will suggest "ethicality" as an approach toward love.

There are countless definitions of love: affection, attraction based on sexual desire, warm attachment, an act of kindness, benevolence, liking, and so on (see the Merriam-Webster Online Dictionary for more). So many different uses of the term "love" result in a "cacophony of confusing and contradictory meanings that often stymies serious discussion of love"[3] (Noddings & Shore, 1984, p. 154). What I mean by love is, as R. D. Laing defines it, letting the other be as he or she is, and wants to be, but with affection and concern. What is violent in this love is to constrain the other's freedom and being and "to force him to act in the way we [the educators or parents,] desire" (Laing, quoted in Pinar, 1975c, p. 368). The strong sense of directedness and consequential force that "desire" expresses has to be given up if it remains on the side of love—love in self-care (self-love without selfishness) and care-for-others—for personal growth living in harmony with a greater whole, and with goodness. Ted T. Aoki's (1992, p. 195) "pedagogical watchfulness" expresses a certain quality of this love.

Love is often unwittingly associated or confused with aggression, or even violence. Two common concepts that I conceive as abused love are "for your own good," which I have already discussed with the help of Alice Miller in Chapter 3, and "tough love," which is frequently misunderstood and misguided. My focus is that the two often become, through conditioning and manipulation of others, "weapons and instruments in the hands of those in power even if these weapons are disguised with the terms *education* and *therapeutic treatment*" (Miller, 1984, p. 227). The disguise of "for your own good" in education has become harder to notice since its physical form has mostly disappeared, though it nonetheless remains in our psyche.

Self-Care and Care-For-Others **109**

"Tough love" is also often misleading. Bill Milliken—the winner of the Jefferson award in 2009 for his lifelong service to teenagers in need of help, many of whom were drug-addicted—coined the term (Milliken & Meredith, 1968). The general approach of tough love is to have courage and take the risk of saying, "I don't care how this makes you feel toward me. You may hate my guts, but I love you, and I am doing this because I love you" (Milliken, 2007, p. 45). Milliken says it to drug-addicted children who agree that their condition needs to be corrected. The most important thing in applying tough love, as Milliken emphasizes in his books and speeches, is *relationship*. On the main page of the Communities in Schools website, which he founded in the1970s, is the following sentence, "It's relationships, not programs, that change children" (http://www.communitiesinschools.org, n.d.). A great program, for Milliken, creates environments for the development of healthy relationships, relationships based on full care and love—I should not forget to mention that the main goal of the organization is to help children remain in school and earn a high school diploma. Although the emphasis on community surely has educational value, the approach of Communities in Schools does not pay much attention to "educational issues." It is understandable given the high drop-out rate in U.S. high schools and the problems those without a high school diploma face in the future. The point that I want to emphasize is that a relationship based on care and love gave birth to "tough love."

However, some have testified about how "tough love" has been applied in different contexts. Maia Szalavitz is the author of *Help at Any Cost: How the Troubled-Teen Industry Cons Parents and Hurts Kids*. As a former troubled, and drug-addicted teenager, she finds that many parents whose children are out-of-control, bewildering adolescents fall into "traps" when they seek help. After interviewing hundreds of children, parents, psychiatrists, psychologists, sociologists, and juvenile justice experts, she concluded that "the [troubled teen] industry is dominated by the idea that harsh rules and even brutal confrontation are necessary to help troubled teenagers" (Szalavitz, 2006). She recalls her experience:

> I have never understood the logic of tough love. I took drugs compulsively because I hated myself, because I felt as if no one—not even my family—would love me if they really knew me. Drugs allowed me to blot out that depressive self-focus and socialize as though I thought I was okay.
>
> *(Szalavitz, 2006)*

Proclaiming that the residential treatment programs available to her to cure drug-addicted adolescents never helped her, Szalavitz points out the problems of "tough love." One of them I want to emphasize is the underlying philosophy that pain produces growth. Since "tough love" has to rely on unwarranted authority or disciplinary rules, the consequences of inflicting it on children are psychological. It turns out, Szalavitz (2006) argues, that "the experience of being emotionally terrorized can produce compliance that looks like real change."

A prominent traditional part of Korean educational culture is the absolute authority of teachers over students. Corporal punishment has long been justified as a "whip of love," which can be translated into "a faulty tough love." In the majority of traditional drawings of any kind of school in Korean history are teachers, who were considered as significant as parents, holding whips. I have hundreds of experiences of being punished by whips and other torture methods because of bad marks or behavior. The necessity of the use of these "whips of love" is strongly controversial in Korea.

Following the inauguration in 2010 by Sang-Gon Kim of a rule prohibiting corporal punishment in Kyung Ki Province, the superintendents of education of the cities of Seoul, and Kwangju joined the movement and other provinces and cities are in the process of adopting the rule. However, prohibiting corporal punishment in schools is highly controversial. Some cry that without such punishment schools are failing. Some others argue that there is no other way to control troubled students at school. A survey conducted by Korean Gallop in May of 2013 shows that 79% approve of allowing educational punishment.

The fear of losing control and of student resistance stems from the beliefs that support the use of the whip of love. In that framework, students are conceived of as needing to be controlled, empty buckets to be filled, and whose souls, indeed, should be "murdered" (Miller, 1984, p. 278). Authorities know that students will resist aggression against them. Students are punished "for [their] own good." I confess that the countless punishments I was given did not do me any good but increased the dependency of my study on teachers and strengthened my "outer-directedness." In my middle school years, I was afraid of the "whip of love" but in my high school years, I did not care. I was punished and laughed. I was a so-called punk. It was not the punishment but self-motivation that led me to become a teacher. I studied all the subjects for the Korean SAT within seven months, while students normally study for three years. I received a fairly good grade and was able to enter Chinju National University of Education.

The philosophy of "for your own good" and "faulty tough love" not only increases students' compliance with and dependency on adults—we have been prolonging their childhood and delaying their maturation—but also disguises the real problem. This perspective makes it really difficult for us to question what we do for children and how we do it. No discussion, negotiation, or conversation is encouraged. The worst thing is that when this view is coupled with curriculum dictated by the government,[4] it is hardly possible for the approach to incorporate students' and teachers' subjectivities into their study, which is the death of education.[5] The camouflaged love confuses both teachers and students, which leads me to emphasize "self-understanding" in care-for-others, as I discussed at the end of Chapter 3.

The strategies using the frame of faulty love are threefold: "direct threat, mobilization of the fear of losing love, or the promise of special reward"[6](Britzman, 1998, p. 40). The three strategies are not exclusive; one can be explicit and another implicit. The strategies, Britzman contends, "are not meant to invoke insight into the ethical dilemmas of thought or the harshness of life. Nor do these methods or strategies of address consider how they might sustain identificatory thinking as opposed to understanding" (p. 40). The approaches instead invoke "a rather rigid sense of guilt and fear, which then incite[s] the ego's defenses" (p. 40). The consequence of the approaches can be detrimental; they disguise one's attention to his or her id, or unconscious, strengthen the fantasy in education that there is a direct link between teaching and learning, increase students' dependency on teachers, delay students' maturation, and prohibit one from experiencing his or her "existential angst."[7] Am I making unwarranted assumptions? I think my *currere* work and the analysis of *The King's Speech* support my argument here. There are no systemic ways to halt these developments. Alice Miller understood that state as "soul murder" (1984, p. 213). She suggests that:

> All that we can do, as I see it, is to affirm and lend our support to the human objects of manipulation in their attempts to become aware and help them become conscious of their malleability and articulate their feelings so that they will be able to use their own resources to defend themselves against the soul murder that threatens them.
>
> *(Miller, 1984, p. 278)*

What we, as teachers and parents, have to know and help others know is not only a consciousness of our malleability but also our culpability in the soul murdering. In the epigraph for this section, Britzman articulates the problem. Britzman's thorny question can be restated: *How can one move from being concerned about others' standards to being concerned about one's own standard?* I am not arguing that one does not need categorical imperatives, but we have to remain vigilant for the state that one is excessively in compliance with categorical imperatives. For the transition from learning for love to love of learning to occur, Britzman (1998) suggests that teachers "reckon with their own psychic events" (p. 41). Drawing from Bruno Bettelheim's concept of the "good enough mother" (1987, p. 13), Britzman (1998) explains:

> The "good enough teacher" is one who transfers, in exchange for her or his love, not a learning but a demand that students learn to make their own demands in learning. The "good enough teacher" leans upon Winnicott's suggestion that the work of the "good enough" mother is composed of two different actions toward the infant, and upon the mother's own self: "active adaptation to the infant's needs, an active adaptation that gradually lessens, according to the infant's growing ability to account for failure of adaptation

and to tolerate the result of frustrations" (Winnicott, 1982, pp. 13–14). The mother must help the infant in the illusion and in the disillusion of demand. The "good enough" teacher must engage the student's capacity for illusion and disillusion, the capacity to express and understand, and the capacity to tolerate times of being misunderstood and not understanding. The "good enough" teacher must also help herself in tolerating the result of her or his own frustration.

(pp. 41–42)

Students, Britzman (1998) suggests, deal with "twofold ethics" (p. 42), "an ethic that can tolerate scrutinizing itself [with which] we can tentatively posit that the work of education might attempt to transform neurotic anxiety into existential angst" (p. 42). Britzman explains:

something from within must pressure the learner. Fenichel describes this pressure as the beginning of a "twofold ethics," one set in tension when one feels oneself watched by an outside authority, and the other effective when one is alone. What would education be like if it could engage in such a twofold ethic: watching itself as it watches others and watching itself when alone? Can a twofold ethic disturb the identificatory thinking that provokes "the violence of innocence"?

(p. 42)

Ideally, as students' abilities to deal with "twofold ethics" increase, teachers' care has to lessen. Lessening affective actions on children is perhaps a difficult task for parents and teachers. My school experience and today's Korean education seem to be exactly the opposite of the "good enough teacher." Rather than reducing intrusion as children grow, it is increased and strengthened to the level that students are traumatized. Teachers might think that they give students freedom; actually, the freedom already belongs to the students, and it should not be taken away. This is almost precisely the approach that an ethic of care takes; it encourages students to come up with their own logic, or standards, rather than comply with laws, categorical imperatives, or oppressive structures. When teachers and students deal with ambivalence, loss, fear, and anxiety, learning emerges. Through "psychic events, " (Britzman, 1998, p. 118) fascinated by Freud's injunction, "where id was, there ego shall be" (quoted in Britzman, 1998, p. 44), Britzman questions:

if education is that other work of culture, can it become a place where one's life continues its own work of art, a place where one encounters the vicissitudes of love, a place to refind the means whereby love of ideas can be made from the stuff of one's dreams, from the otherness offered from within, and from the otherness encountered in the world?

(1998, p. 44)

This is a rhetorical question for us, educators, to ponder, and on which to linger. Is not Britzman raising almost the same question as does Foucault, to make one's life a work of art? However, from the perspective of practice the psychic events that Britzman urges do not occur easily. We should not underestimate the difficulty of the pedagogy Britzman proposes.

Psychic events, I think, can be initiated by one's study. My *currere* work discussed in Chapter 2 is simultaneously intellectual and psychic. I doubt if the psychic event occurs without understanding through one's study, study of one's past. Understanding psychoanalytic theories does not directly lead one to understand the characteristics of social psychology, Britzman explains, not only because of the difficulty of understanding the theory and practicing it, but also because of particularities in one's situation and the impossibility of guaranteeing psychic events. Perhaps that is why Britzman (1998, p. 43) calls this work "ethicality." "To act ethically," Britzman argues, is "already to place the act in question" (p. 43); learning must begin with a question that places the ego in question. This journey is difficult and teachers and students may experience frustration, delay, failure, denial, fear, or existential anxiety. Love in the struggle should not be founded on authority but on "ethicality" (p. 43). Teachers and students should not give up tolerance and frustration. I advocate the love with "ethicality" which "cannot be guaranteed, only attempted and approached" (p. 43).

How do we deal with the uncertain, challenging, and demanding task of keeping our balance between self-care and care-for-others? That can start from understanding "love" differently, letting the other be with a passionate affection and concern for the common good, for wholeness. This thinking invites me to go beyond intellectual and psychological pondering.

Discernment and Distance

> Discernment provides a natural equipoise between caring for oneself and caring for others, and it knows when an imbalance occurs.
> —*Catherine Ingram (2004, p. 144)*

I have to confess how much I, as a father, friend, or teacher, have hurt others I cared about and loved. It is surprising how precisely Carl Leggo (2011) expressed the same feeling when he visited my classroom[8]: "I was never malevolent or malicious, not even mischievous, but I have hurt others, and I have hurt a few even monstrously" (p.66). Why have we hurt those we care about? I sincerely believed that the tough love I have exercised on my students was/ would be good for them in their future. How often do I regret what I could have done otherwise! Remembering the moments that I have hurt those I loved also hurts me tremendously! Thank god, many of my former students are incredibly generous to me since they find me through Facebook and still call me "my teacher."

Why do we in our daily lives—without being malevolent or malicious, and not being confused by coercion or abusive love—have difficulties with care-for-others and care for the self? I have found myself struggling with caring for myself and even more with caring for my children. Contemplating these challenges, I happen to recognize that I have had a strong preference in my actions, rather than having "ethicality." I have had a rather strong desire to see what I want to see in others and in me. Failure to live up to my preference, or accept consequence of my deeds, even the humblest ones that are only for the betterment of the other and myself, brought me disappointment, distress, and frustration. How do I understand this? Is this a failure of care for the self? Is this why I need to be cared for by others? Besides understanding the communally dependent relationship between self-care and care-for-others, what will help me deal with it?

I suggest that one way of acting can be found in/through *discernment*, which means to "surrender to the truth of the situation" (Ingram, 2004, p. 136); in other words, it means to accept the truth that there is no guarantee of anything in my life. About discernment, Catherine Ingram (2004) explains:

> While it is only human and reasonable to have preferences, discerning awareness knows that we win some and lose some and that our inherent peace need not be disturbed in any case. We can have a light relationship to our preferences, the lighter the better, and this promotes clarity in assessing any situation. It also fosters trust. Trust comes from knowing that however things go, we will be fine; we will be at peace in any storm of life.
>
> *(p. 136)*

Discernment recognizes the truth that we cannot control reality. The most politically powerful or the richest person probably knows that much of what brought them where they are today is the arbitrariness and coincidences in their lives and histories. Clear discernment comes, Ingram (2004) tells us, "when we have no need for reality to conform to our fantasies for us to be happy" (p. 136). However surely we accept the truth, it is hard for us to give up our preferences. I agree. But we can at least momentarily have a "light relationship to our preferences" so that we can clearly see situations we are involved in and make decisions for the greater good. Through discerning awareness, we remind ourselves that sometimes our preferences are met and other times not, but "our inherent peace need not be disturbed in any case" (p. 136). What discernment can bring us is a certain kind of calmness and peace with trust knowing that "however things go, we will be fine; we will be at peace in any storm of life" (p. 136). Surrendering to the truth of reality, in other words, is being open to "whatever is unfolding rather than chasing after things or pushing away what is presenting itself" (p. 138). Surrendering to reality is not simply being passive or skeptical or unable to commit to the life. One does what one wants and has to do while being open to the consequences of one's action since "reality is [can be] fantastic enough without help" (p. 136). I am writing this, and you are reading this, and we think and understand through the thinkers and texts through whose thoughts we engage. The genes passed down through thousands of generations in our eyes, fingers, and brains are working almost perfectly. Look out the window: trees, animals, and people—they are all miracles. Is it not fantastic? Ingram even tells us that "the actual feeling of surrendering is sweet in itself, like floating downstream" (p. 138), and that we do not need to look for peace because it *is* already with us, in our passionate presence. We simply let the numerous good or OK moments leave us without recognizing them while overreacting to our pain, loss, frustration, and dissatisfaction. That "peace [in discernment] . . . mitigates the pain of loss" (and the dissatisfaction toward preferences, I would add; Ingram, 2004, p. 135). What does discernment in peace in our everyday lives do? It brings us calmness producing a certain distance between myself and reality that "decreases the violence and fear in the world" (p. 32). This calmness we can find in silence:

> This adaptation to silence also dissolves barriers between us. Although words are mainly intended to form bridges of communication, they often have the opposite effect. Many people use words simply to fill the quiet.
> *(Ingram, 2004, p. 18)*

This kind of silence, Ingram (2004) explains, is our "inherent intelligence that is available when we are quiet, when our minds are not running the show" (p. 21). How many of us practice or enjoy calmness, or silence? One may walk in a forest or garden, another takes a shower, another meditate, another lie under a tree feeling the wind and sunshine. Suddenly a brilliant thought or insight comes to us "like a comet through the sky of awareness" (p. 21). Furthermore in silence the powerful work of discernment can be done. Ingram explains:

> While discernment knows that it is important to take care of the organism known as *me*, it also cares deeply for other creatures and the environment in which we all live. This caring tends to serve the greatest good, so if personal sacrifice provides something greater for the whole, discerning awareness will choose it. In fact, in clear discernment it doesn't feel like sacrifice. Just as a mother, in a shortage of food, would want to feed her child before herself, discerning awareness naturally prefers serving the greater good.
> *(p. 143)*

This discernment gives us time to rest as necessary and courage to withdraw, not as a failure but to recharge, as needed, and go back to our own tasks, or our acts of care-for-the-self and care-for-others.

116 Self-Care and Care-For-Others

However, how do we find and keep peace in our everyday struggles and in this world of chaos, with environmental devastation, starvation, terrorism, violence, and wars? There is no, as Ingram (2004) tells us, "lasting peace to be found in the world" (p. 32) but our "recognition of the silence contains it" (p. 32). In silence we find the fundamental and ineradicable peace that has been always with us. The aloneness we can enjoy in silence is not the "hardship of isolation but a refuge from the demands of constant mental and physical activity" (p. 26). Our obsession to be connected through "smart" phones definitely challenges the possibility for us to enjoy calmness, silence, and aloneness. There seems to be confusion about loneliness and aloneness. We need a space, physical, emotional, and spiritual, for aloneness so that we can find fundamental peace, not from anywhere else but from within us. It is discernment that "enables us to choose between suffering and peace" (p. 134).

In discernment we might witness or grapple with who we are becoming, what we want to do, and how situations are going in the relationship with the other, and then question whether we are subordinating the other under the name of education or parenting. In the quality of discernment of passionate presence, Ingram (2004) contends, "[we are] able to distinguish the types of thoughts and emotions" (p. 134) that arise from us and then "to determine how much interest we will pay them" (p. 134). In discernment we may be able to keep a balance between care-for-the-self and care-for-others.

Conclusion

In this chapter I have discussed the inseparable and complementary association between self-care and care-for-others. Undoubtedly, the difficulty we face in/between self-care and care-for-others requires us not only to engage with the specific situation and people in it but also to cultivate a certain distance or non-coincidence between self and the world, our ethics and oppressive structures, and our preferences and reality. Through our study, our understanding, or our discernment we might be able to find a peaceful space for education for ourselves and for others, as well as for society. Through discernment, without forgetting the inextricability and inseparability of self and other and private and social, one can connect and separate one's relationship with oneself and with others.

Notes

1. Foucault (1982b) says that exercising one's power over another for the purpose of domination occurs precisely because one fails to take care of oneself, since one becomes the slave of one's desires. One's false, or abusive, relationship with oneself often violates one's relationship with the other despite one's efforts to hide it. Sometimes one exercises power destructively on those one loves.
2. Understand what? "The relations among academic knowledge, the state of society, processes of self-formation, and the character of the historical moment in which

where our ancestors lived, we live, and our decedents will live" (Pinar, 2012, p. 190). It is understanding that enables us "to think and act with intelligence, sensitivity, and courage in both the public sphere—as citizens aspiring to establish a democratic society—and in the private sphere, as individuals committed to other individuals" (Pinar, 2012, p. 190).

3. Drawing from the ancient Greek notion of love—*eros*, *agape*, and *philia*—Noddings and Shore (1984) coined the term *educational caritas*. They explain love in education thusly:

> It is a desire to come into direct, undiluted contact with the human partner of the educational enterprise, to go beyond superficialities and become involved with the other person. Notice that we emphasize "desire"; this desire may not be fulfilled as external circumstances intervene, yet the desire is the evidence of love, not the elusive material result. Educational caritas may also involve a deep interest and even passionate commitment to the subject matter being taught. . . . [another facet of educational caritas] is a sense of rightness and of appropriateness, what might even be called a sense of mission or a "calling" that teachers have often felt through the ages. (Noddings & Shore, 1984, pp. 157–158)

Their concept of love goes toward teachers' desire for undiluted relationships with students and teachers' knowledge and affection for the subject and the profession. Their emphasis on *desire*—although they make it clear that the desire for love is not the "elusive material result"—concerns me a bit, since the word expresses a strong sense of directedness. But this concern can be weakened by R. D. Laing's type of love, as discussed in Chapter 5.

4. The stupidity of the governmental educational policy is culminating with strange laws. First in August 2014, the law prohibiting *preceding learning*—referring to students' out-of-school-learning, which precedes the progress of learning at schools—took effect. Preceding learning is a primarily Korean phenomenon in which students are introduced to material they are *going to be* learning in schools by tutors or shadow educators. The purpose of this law is to control the excessively high cost of shadow education. However, I do not think that the law contributes to reducing the cost; there has been no sign of the cost going down. The point I am making here is that the law is another form of educational dictatorship that rules what students study. The current president, Geun Hye Park, is dictating education, as did her father, Jung-Hee Park. Another law President Park inaugurated is the *free semester* law, which states that for the first semester of the first year of the middle school, students will take no standardized tests but have more extracurricular activities that may help them find their dreams. As one can imagine, shadow education uses the law for the sake of their business. Private educational institutions' marketing strategies increase the fear of parents that their children might lose their competency in taking tests.

5. "'There is no 'pure' school subject to be transmitted uncontaminated by those who study and participate in it. That does not mean there are no essential facts in each discipline—what we can call 'canonicity'" (Anderson & Valente, 2002, p. 13)—but it does mean that these are to be engaged, even translated, if they are to be understood" (Pinar, 2011, p. 6). Teachers have to carefully forge connections between the subject they love to teach and the students.

This is a matter of human dignity and civil rights. If I remain a school teacher, I will seriously consider suing, with colleagues and students, the Ministry of Education for taking away our intellectual and political freedom. But this is another story.

6. "One of the central fantasies of omnipotence in education [is] that there can be a direct link between teaching and learning and that both of these dynamics are a rational outcome of the teacher's conscious efforts" (Britzman, 1998, p. 41). This mythic assumption justifies teachers' strategies: "direct threat, mobilization of the fear of losing love, and the promise of special rewards" (Britzman, 1998, p. 40).

7. For a critique about the assumption that there is a direct link between teaching learning, see Gert Biesta's (2014) *The Beautiful Risk of Education*. For the problem of students' dependency on teachers in students' learning, see William Pinar's(2006a) *The Problem With Curriculum and Pedagogy*.
8. When I was taking Dr. Anne Phelan's course, Storying Teachers' Lives, Dr. Carl Leggo visited our class on March 6, 2012. It was the first time for me to listen to him reading/talking/singing his paper.

CONCLUSION

Awakened by learning about my arrested subjectivity through the history and culture of Korean education (and indeed internalizing), and inspired by self-understanding through *currere* and an ethic of care, I have written to elucidate the association between self-care and care-for-others.

The first chapter dealt with *What is the character and what are the dire consequences of the Korean test-focused education?* and the second chapter with *How can self-understanding through currere contribute to my relationship with myself?* The two chapters contextualize this research: the former is historical research; the latter is an autobiographical study of my subjectivity. These two questions allegorically juxtapose the "facts and lived experience in creative tensionality . . . that can trigger transformation" (Pinar, 2011, p. 7).

Seeing the horrendous, terrifying incidents of children who decide not to continue their lives and recognizing that the major cause of that kind of disaster is the academic pressure on the victims, I studied the character of Korean education, centering around hakbeolism—a uniquely Korean concept of symbolic capital based on hierarchical status or on the reputation of the school a person graduates from. The examination system has been considered by many as offering the possibility of advancing not only their education but also their social status. In its current state, Korean society seems to be "the most exam-obsessed culture in the world" (Seth, 2002, p. 5), an "examination hell" (p. 4). The examination system has provided "a sense of fairness and served to enhance the authority of teachers and principals" (Seth, 2002, p. 31). The system reflects, as Seth (2002) keenly observes, "one of the great contradictions of South Korean culture," which is "the concern for assigning rank and status in a society where egalitarian ideals were [and are] strong" (p. 145).[1] In the name of egalitarianism, equity, or fairness, examinations have become indisputably central, not only in Korean education but, I argue, in the society, which historically is a stratified clan society.

This seemingly egalitarian approach has contributed to, or strengthened, the failure to recognize the significance of students' subjectivities in their study, a component of utmost importance in one's education. The system, I argue, has contributed to enhancing social Darwinism through aggressive competition. In this system there is no doubt about the answer to the canonical curricular question: what knowledge is of most worth? In this system, teachers and students face the risk of being caught within an "intellectual and political trap" (Pinar, 2006a, p. 120). The dire consequences of it do not remain on the intellectual and political level but sink to the deeply psychic level of individuals, as Chapter 2 testifies. In this highly outer-directed culture, individual egos can be almost totally objectified, what Pinar calls "arrested" (1994, p. 40). Arrested individuals are unable to act freely, without completely resorting to the constraining structures; to make their own ethical judgments in their study and in what they are doing (not only to overcome governmentality or constraining structures but also to do the assigned work ethically);[2] and to reconstruct their relationships with themselves and others.

How can self-understanding through currere contribute to my relationship with myself? Chapters 2 and 4 respond directly to this question: the former is my testimony of self-understanding through *currere*; the latter is a theorization of how *a subjective reconstruction through self-understanding contributes to making one's relationship with oneself authentic, which, I argue, can be a form of self-care*. In Chapter 2 I study the breakdown I experienced during my graduate program, during which I discuss paradoxical elements of existence, the dialectic of anxiety, and the dialectical relationship between the world and myself. The study, for me, served to build my "autobiographical consciousness" (Pinar, 1976, p. 42), enabling me to understand, deconstruct, and reconstruct my subjectivity. Through this *currere* work—juxtaposed with my study of hakbeolism—I have come to understand, at least partially, how I, as a student and a teacher, have been conditioned, *not defined*, by the history and culture of Korean education, what my breakdown meant to me, and what I can/want to do with it. I have begun to understand the complexities and paradox of my being-in-the-world, an awareness that may signify what Pinar calls the "ontological shift from outer to inner" (Pinar, 1974, p. 15).

The ontological shift may alter one's relationship with one's self, making authentic the self–self relationship (as we see in my case and in the case of Bertie in Chapter 5). In an authentic self–self relationship, one may be able to dance with one's arrested self, a dance in which "one holds one's damaged ego like a father tenderly holding his son [or a mother holding her child]" (Pinar, personal communication, Nov. 25, 2012).[3] An important function of *currere* is for one to aspire to become aware of one's physical, emotional, and intellectual states through resensitizing one's subjectivity and revealing its biographical and educational meanings and then inviting one to imagine who one wants to be. However, the results of this work are implicit rather than explicit, complicated rather than simple, recursive rather than linear, descriptive rather than prescriptive.

This kind of understanding is often not a single event—since the caring relation and its roles are not fixed (Noddings, 2011, p. 8)—but continual and recursive, what William Doll (1993, p. 289) described as a "looping back," not only to what one was taught or learned but also to what one did or experienced. It is an ongoing process of self-reflection that allows one to create "one's own conscious self—the highest expression of human awareness" (Doll, 1993, p. 289). Self-understanding in an ethic of care requires us educators to sensitize ourselves to the very essence of our mode of being, what Pinar (1994) calls our capacity for "first-person subjectivity" (p. 105).

I suggest that self-understanding through *currere* can be one path to what Foucault calls care-for-the-self through *hupomnemata*, a technique that constitutes "a decisive break" (Foucault, 1982a, p. 249) without renouncing oneself, a break in the unnecessary connection between our ethics and oppressive structures. For me the "decisive break" was started with rigorous study through autobiographical inquiry.

What I mean by self-understanding is first to *unlearn* the false or inauthentic relationship that one has with oneself—which is inextricably related to one's relationships with others—and then to create a new relationship with oneself, a process that is only the beginning of education. This kind of self-understanding Pinar (1985) calls "an architecture of self" (p. 212). To be the architect of the self, Pinar tells us, one "should judge his current edifice [that is] obscuring its [authentic self–self relationship] foundation in ways that keep him ignorant of himself" (p. 212). The edifice is both within oneself and in the world: structural and psychological. Allegory, which juxtaposes facts and lived experience, the analysis of hakbeolism, and my lived experience, for example, can make visible the obscuring edifice. In my case that understanding increases the possibility of being less concerned about others' objectification of me and more concerned about my relationship with myself and then eventually building the self–self relationship anew. In this way, self-understanding through autobiographical inquiry can be a form of self-care.

Creating one's relationship with oneself anew, conceiving one's life as a work of art as Foucault suggests, means making one's own standards for one's life, and of course one's education, rather than conforming entirely to standards externally given. In other words, one can set one's own standards in life, in education (this does not require entirely rejecting or getting rid of external ones). I imagine an education that allows and encourages students to come up with their own standards in their studies. The standards from the inexorable and arbitrary constraints imposed by neoliberal and corporatized forces that forcefully structure our educational experiences require our culpability for their activation and reinforcement; therefore, we can resist through self-understanding by not allowing them to be reproduced through us.

The forces do not seem to be going away in the near future. However, when we do not allow their reproduction through ourselves, we have the ability, and the opportunity, to resist. Such resistance, many of us may know, is not easy. It requires that we (teachers, parents, and educators) "be brave" (Block, 2009, p. 115) in making our professional decisions ethically and that we "help others [each other] achieve bravery" (p. 116). We need to cultivate our "courage" (Pinar, 2012, p. 231), intellectual courage, political courage, and psychological courage, abandoning our "infantilized positions from which we pretend helplessness, demanding to know 'what works,' the authoritarianism of instrumental rationality" (Pinar, 2012, p. 231). We are, as Foucault tells us, freer and stronger than we think. We often, however, find how weak we are in recognizing our inability to change the structures that oppressively work upon us: We should know that our infantilized status feeds the weakness. Focusing on immediate change in the structures is not the only way to fight against them. Self-understanding is also a way of resisting the structures. One who experiences the "ontological shift from outer to inner" may be able to live as the architect of one's own life, not to be a consumer of imposed standards but to be a creator of one's own standards.

However, there is a paradox in self-care, which is that while self-respect can be developed only from relations with others, from the early days of our educational lives we are objectified by external standards: we are taught, evaluated, and eventually turned into "numbers" (Taubman, 2009). Developing one's intellectual, psychological, and political independence is inevitably associated with one's relationship to others, especially significant others. Private endeavor is necessary for self-understanding, but for many, as Pinar (1976) points out, it is "work with others that is a medium through which they work with themselves" (p. 53). Self-understanding can be pursued in solitude but many times others' contribution to the journey of self-understanding is significant. For that, discussion of Nel Noddings and her ethic of care is helpful.

What is the significance of Noddings's "ethic of care" and how does it require self-understanding? Over three decades, Noddings has developed an ethic of care that outlines a specific feminine position on moral theory and on educational practice. Caring, Noddings argues, is relational, not a principle or form of ethical deliberation nor a virtue in the sense of a list of personal qualities or lofty principles. It is in direct contrast to traditional ethics—such as "principled Kantian ethics" (Stone, 2006, p. 31) based on justice and principles—which are often "short-sighted and arrogant [approaches to] . . . what it means to be moral" (Noddings, 1988, p. 218). Kant says, "I must recognize myself as [a] universal subject; that is, I must constitute myself in each of my actions as a universal subject by conforming to universal rules" (quoted in Foucault, 1983, p. 280).

Rejecting Kantian ethics (principles based on reason), Noddings argues that the ideal caring relation is relational, reciprocal, and reactive, affected by emotions. Because universal moral principles ignore the uniqueness of particular people in particular situations, such principles have limited use in guiding moral actions. A universal principle of justice, by its very nature, depends on the assumption that human situations and predicaments exhibit a high level of uniformity; on that basis, universal principles are proposed as useful abstractions of the specific, concrete situations in which we are involved. Noddings, however, is concerned about why the *particular* condition makes the situation different and thereby induces "genuine moral puzzlement [that] cannot be satisfied by the application of principles developed in situations of sameness" (1984, pp. 84–85). When we focus on the sameness of human situations, we quickly begin to objectify the individuals involved; simultaneously, that focus causes the individuals' "I" to lose its uniqueness, its subjectivity.

While gender is the overriding theme in Noddings's ethic of care, self-understanding is my main theme in understanding her thinking. Responding to Socrates's statement "Know thyself; an unexamined life is not worth living," Noddings argues that "unexamined lives may well be valuable and worth living, but an education that does not invite such examination may not be worthy of the label education" (2006, p. 10). Ethical caring requires "reflection and self-understanding" and "understanding of self and others" (Noddings, 1995, p. 139).

For the one caring, self-understanding—recalling one's relationships with one's significant others and reflecting on how one engages with others—helps not only in recalling "natural caring" and thus revealing the nature of feminine care, but also in unlearning coercive care and poisonous pedagogy "for the children's own good." We all should strive to become aware first of how we have been cared for and then of how we care for others. That work requires us to examine "how external and internal forces affect [our] lives" (Noddings, 2006, p. 10) and our engagement with these forces based on "what we believe and how we believe it. What do I feel? Why? What am I doing? Why? And even, What am I saying? And, again, why?" (p. 10).

How then can an ethic of care contribute to self-understanding? Self-understanding achieved through reconstructing one's subjectivity *allegorically* is, for me, a way to activate my authentic voice.[4] In the film *The King's Speech*, Bertie's struggle to find his own voice (see Chapter 5) helps me understand how care-for-others contributes to self-understanding. I pay special attention to Lionel's approach to helping Bertie find his own voice, and indeed the self-understanding that leads Bertie to agency and to speech that gestures toward *orality* (Pinar, 2011, p. 176, 2012, pp. 13–14). In three different times and spaces (the 1930s in the U.K. through Bertie's case, the 1970s in the U.S. through Pinar's analysis of American schooling as "maddening," and today in Korea through my poem), we can see how "maddening" the situations were and are. Rather than transforming students organically, disconfirmation, control, management turn both teachers and students into things, and internalizing the oppressor in the oppressed, who eventually become numb to the oppression. Thus, oppression in education functions to transform "deficient people" (Pinar, 1975c, p. 368)—in banking education, students are buckets to be filled—into "efficient things" that absorb what is given to them and perform as they are supposed to based on the "rules of others," rather than their "own rules" (Cooper, quoted in Pinar, 1975c, p. 366). Ultimately, students may not know what has not been acknowledged through their education. What they have been missing are their voices, inner lives, feelings, fears, imaginations, and aspirations, that which expresses their uniqueness as human beings, the irreplaceability of one's being.

Lionel's work with Bertie can be summarized as an endeavor with love to turn the internalized disconfirmation into courage, bravery, and self-affirmation by helping Bertie achieve self-understanding, recover his relationship with himself. Understanding the dire consequences of the semantic environment and one's compliance in the maddening situation is a decisive break for education. The recovery of Bertie's voice cannot be attributed only to Lionel; it comes through the relationship built by the contributions of both. It is Bertie who struggled and finally achieved his authentic voice, self-realization, authentic persona, and eventually a positive self–self relationship, while Lionel assisted Bertie in becoming "conscious of his distinctive self-formative process" (Pinar, 1978, p. 88). Why can we not exercise "love," letting students live with confirmation rather than disconfirmation? Is it not because of the fear we are projecting onto them? What are we fearful of? Losing control or authority? Is much of it not our fear of the reality over which we have no control? Chapter 6 responds to these queries.

How is self-understanding as a form of self-care associated with care-for-others? The relationship between self-care and care-for-others is neither a matter of sequence nor of choice—although one can be suspended for the other for certain moments depending on the circumstances. There is an inextricable and complementary quality to the relationship between the two; inextricable in that they are not discrete and complementary in that each implies and requires the other. That is, care-for-others necessarily requires self-care, and care-for-others is frequently a way of self-care; self-care also may require care-for-others and at the same time self-care can be a way to care-for-others. However, this relationship is by no means without possible confusion, risks, challenges, and of course failures.

Self-care and care-for-others are *inseparable*, as is more evident in intimate relationships, first because self and other are ontologically interconnected and constantly changing, hand in hand. They are inseparable because the purpose of care-for-others is part of one's self-care; the purpose of self-care is part of care-for-others. For one to remain ethical, neither self-care nor care-for-others should or can be sacrificed, nor can one be substituted for the other. There is no way to structure our actions upon/between them: intentions in our actions cannot be guaranteed to be ethical. To act ethically is, as Britzman (1998) tells us, "already to place [our] act in question" (p. 43); our acts are only "attempted and approached" (p. 43). In our attempt to act ethically, we may experience frustration, delay, failure, denial, fear, or existential anxiety. There is no simple answer to the important question of how and to what extent I can creatively (re)construct my relationship with myself and others as a work of art without recourse to oppressive structures in my already built relationships with myself and others.

In speaking to this matter, Wang (2004) suggests that one needs "a certain sense of turning away from others in order to cultivate [one's] own space" (p. 37), "a room of one's own" (Woolf, quoted in Wang, 2004, p. 37). Entering into a third space requires us to "cultivate noncoincidence between self and the world through the cultivation of distance, even estrangement and exile" (Pinar, 2011, p. 17). Pinar's "noncoincidence" resides in subjective, social, and political realms that can be cultivated by "understanding" through autobiography and allegory, which are informed by rigorous academic study. Academic study, for Pinar, can cultivate a certain distance—and often distance also makes possible a new understanding of one's reality. Yet there are layers of distance in the association between self-care and care-for-others. I wonder whether distance can be created through rethinking, if not breaking, the unnecessary connection between ethics and oppressive structures and the linkage between love and preference. The former is one of the greatest challenges we are facing today; the consequence of the unnecessary connection between ethics and structures is disastrous, not only in schooling but also for this planet. The latter is perhaps the main source of coercion in childrearing and education.

Political debates are of course important, but we should not forget that we each work within ourselves to break the unnecessary linkage between ethics and the oppressive structures and create linkage between knowledge and ethics. We can change our relationship with these structures via what is called "understanding through study." Through understanding, we can learn that we do not have to limit our relationships within the structures and resort to their rules. We can activate our courage to make ethical judgments in our profession, abandoning mere resistance, and nihilism or cynicism. Doing so is part of our professional commitments, even though it might not be part of our job descriptions.

It is our "love" (Laing, quoted in Pinar, 1975c, p. 368), and "ethicality" (Britzman, 1998, p. 43) with "pedagogical watchfulness" (Aoki, 1992, p. 195) that compensate for disconfirmation, coercive caring, and the whip of love. Punishment and disconfirmation only increase students' conformity to authority and their dependency on others in their study. In many cases, and in the worst cases, it is not difficult to see that educators and parents treat their children in the ways they have been treated. It is our professional, familial, and indeed ethical commitment to break the reproductive force through us.

The difficulty we face in/between self-care and care-for-others requires us not only to engage with the specific situation and the people in it but also to cultivate a certain distance or noncoincidence between self and the world, between our ethics and oppressive structures, between teaching and learning, and between our preferences and reality. Through our study, our understanding, or our discernment (surrendering to reality), we might be able to find a peaceful space, at least temporarily, for education, for us and for others, as well as for society.

Through discernment without forgetting the inextricability and inseparability of self and other and private and social, one can connect and separate one's relationships with oneself and with others.

This book emerged out of my lived experience, my intellectual interests, and my engagement (and struggle) with myself and others. As I have been writing this book, I have often been struck by the challenges and complexity of self-care and care-for-others: can I live/am I living in the way that I advocate in this work? Am I treating myself and others with the perspectives that I articulate here? Sometimes I succeed; other times I fail. My humility overcomes my arrogance. It would be presumptuous if I said, "I am a better person now because of this research." My ethicality can only be attempted and approached, not guaranteed, as Britzman (1998) tells us. I try to question my acts.

I invite Korean educators and parents to join me in rethinking the nature of Korea's test-focused education and to undertake their own journey of self-understanding, understanding the devastating and suffocating neoliberal force in conjunction with historical and cultural remnants. The study of my subjective reconstruction and my analysis of hakbeolism is one possible way of doing so. I invite teachers and parents to find their own ways; nobody can do this for anyone else: being away from my country and people provided a certain distance, which triggered the struggle to understand both myself and the history and culture of Korean education. Without our individual study, understanding, and reconstruction, any structural change not only has the potential to subsume subjectivity, but may also strengthen our culpability and/or nihilism or cynicism. Although we know that hakbeolism and the constraining forces will not go away in the near future, we do not need to restrict ourselves to complaints, discontent, disappointment, and frustration—of course, we have to express how we feel and argue for changes—as if there were no space between total compliance and absolute freedom, both of which are unrealistic. Our ethics, combined with courage, can weaken our preoccupation with power and structural changes.

I conclude with the hope that the readers of this book will venture into their own journey of understanding self-care and care-for-others.

Notes

1. Egalitarianism in education has been expressed by the idea of the "uniformity of education" under the concept of equal opportunity. Specific policies have been developed to promote such equal opportunity, for example, teacher rotation (a teacher cannot stay longer than five or six years in one school) and a rotary system to assign students to public and private schools. While, ironically, the ranking of schools is obvious, the ranking in most cases is decided by how many students high schools send to the most highly ranked universities. It is ironic because the policies exist to make education fair, but at the same time they recognize the ranking.
2. One example of someone who failed to make ethical judgments is Adolf Eichmann, whom Hannah Spector (2013) describes as "such a notorious amoral careerist-opportunist" (p. 57) in her study of Hannah Arendt. The worst Korean example is the

captain of the Sewol ferry, which sank on April 16, 2014, with a loss of about three hundred victims. While the causes of the tragedy are still under investigation (including crew members, laws, and safety regulations, the corruption of officials and Chonghaejin Marine, and the family of the owner of the Sewol), the nation is suffering from the widespread social and political reactions and conflicts. Many Koreans and the opposition party are asking President Park to pass a special law governing the entire investigation (and ensuring ferry safety) and punishing those who are guilty. I agree with the argument that legal action should be taken; the incident should not be used for political conflict between the parties. I am shocked by the inability of the captain, Jun-Seok Lee, to make a professional and ethical decision by himself as the captain of the ferry. The captain testified that the reason that he did not make an evacuation announcement was that he was waiting for the decision from the company, Chonghaejin Marine.
3. Professor Anne Phelan comments, "Who will hold the damaged ego of the mother?" (2015). She explains that "given the stereotype of woman as care giver, it is this very stereotype with all its externalized expectations that makes it incredibly difficult for women/mothers to face the harmful effects of their relationships, often with their own children" (2015). This is a difficult point to discuss for me as a man whose wife is also taking on the stereotypical gendered roles. Hongyu Wang argues that "self-affirmation" (2004, p. 37) is necessary for care-for-others to reach the depths of a woman's own heart to transform itself, and my wife agrees with Wang. Self-affirmation also requires that one critically engage with the self to reconceive one's experiences. The critical engagement may provide one with the knowledge to understand the internalized gendered expectations in one's self, which may vary depending on contexts and cultures. However, paradoxically, women's "self-affirmation" may require others' acceptance, confirmation, or care-for-others. In this way we are again entering into the complex relationship between self-care and care-for-others. Men must acknowledge the difficulty and complexity of self-care that women face. Criticizing the hierarchical status of self-care over care-for-others—while recognizing Foucault's concern for care-for-others—Wang (2004) argues that "to open up an enclosed internal horizon, the nurturance of her inner self and a certain sense of turning away from others in order to cultivate her own space become crucial" (p. 37): "a room of one's own" (Woolf, quoted in Wang, 2004, p. 37). Incorporating Bakhtin's notion of the relationship between self and other into the Foucauldian notion of self-care as a work of art, Wang urges women "to create a third space" (p. 46) in which new modes of existence and relationships may emerge without completely resorting to the traditionally gendered roles.
4. The "authentic voice" stands against the self-renunciation that Foucault has criticized. One's "authentic voice" in one's education symbolically expresses one's subjectivity and one's capacity to be sensitive, or receptive, to one's inner self, which more often than not is replaced by the institutional instillation of discipline, propaganda, ambition, and competitiveness that culminates in an emphasis on the cognitive aspects of learning at the expense of the emotional, maternal components.

REFERENCES

Alexander, H. (2013). Caring and agency: Noddings on happiness in education. *Educational Philosophy and Theory, 45*(5), 488–493. doi:10.1111/j.1469-5812.2012.00852.x

Anderson, A., & Valente, J. (2002). *Disciplinarity at the fin de siècle*. Princeton, NJ: Princeton University Press.

Ang, R. P., & Huan, V. S. (2006). Relationship between academic stress and suicidal ideation: Testing for depression as a mediator using multiple regression. *Child Psychiatry and Human Development, 37*(2), 133–143. doi:10.1007/s10578-006-0023-8

Aoki, T. T. (1981). Toward understanding curriculum: Talk through reciprocity of perspectives. In W. F. Pinar & R. L. Irwin (Eds.), *Curriculum in a new key: The collected works of Ted T. Aoki* (pp. 219–228). Mahwah, NJ: Lawrence Erlbaum Associates.

Aoki, T. T. (1992). Layered voices of teaching: The uncannily correct and the elusively true. In W. F. Pinar & R. L. Irwin (Eds.), *Curriculum in a new key: The collected works of Ted T. Aoki* (pp. 187–197). Mahwah, N.J.: Lawrence Erlbaum Associates.

Bakhtin, M. M. (1993). *Toward a philosophy of the act* (M. Holquist & V. Liapunov, Trans.). Austin: University of Texas Press.

Bergman, R. (2004). Caring for the ethical ideal: Nel Noddings on moral education. *Journal of Moral Education, 33*(2), 149–162. doi:10.1080/0305724042000215203

Bettelheim, B. (1987). *A good enough parent: A book on child-rearing*. New York: Random House.

Biesta, G. J. (2013). *The beautiful risk of education*. Boulder; London: Paradigm.

Block, A. A. (2009). *Ethics and teaching: A religious perspective on revitalizing education*. New York: Palgrave Macmillan.

Bourdieu, P. (1986). The forms of capital. In John Richardson (Ed.), *Handbook of theory and research for sociology of education* (pp. 241–258). New York: Greenwood Press.

Britzman, D. P. (1998). *Lost subjects, contested objects: Toward a psychoanalytic inquiry of learning*. New York: State University of New York Press.

Britzman, D. P. (2003). *After-education: Anna Freud, Melanie Klein, and psychoanalytic histories of learning*. New York: State University of New York Press.

Buber, M. (1964). Dialogue between Martin Buber and Carl Rogers. In M. Friedman (Ed.), *The worlds of existentialism* (pp. 166–184). Chicago: University of Chicago Press.

References

Buber, M. (1965). Education. In M. Buber (Ed.), *Between man and man* (pp. 83–103). New York: Macmillan.

Card, C. (1990). Caring and evil. *Hypatia, 5*(1), 101–108.

Chien, C., Davis, T., Slattery, P., Keeney-Kennicutt, W., & Hammer, J. (2013). Development of a virtual second life curriculum using *currere* model. *Educational Technology and Society, 16*(3), 204–219. Retrieved from http://www.ifets.info/journals/16_3/16.pdf

Cho, K.-H. (2013). What does the "Gaebyeok-Thought of Donghak" mean for philosophy of history? *The Korean Journal of Studies of Dong Hak, 27*, 63–91. Retrieved from http://kiss.kstudy.com.ezproxy.library.ubc.ca/journal/thesis_name.asp?tname=kiss2002&key=3143611

Chodorow, N. (1978). *The reproduction of mothering*. Berkeley: University of California Press.

Choi, J.-S. [SSNBC]. (2013, November 14). *To live as the master of my life* [Video file]. Retrieved from http://www.youtube.com/watch?v=_khfDbhitZw

Coleman, K., Depp, L., & O'Rourke, K. (2011). The educational theory of Nel Noddings. Retrieved from http://www.newfoundations.com/GALLERY/Noddings.html

Cooper, D. (1967). *Self and others*. New York: Pantheon.

Cumings, B. (1999). *Korea's place in the sun*. New York: W. W. Norton.

Davion, V. (1993). Autonomy, integrity, and care. *Social Theory and Practice, 19*(2), 161–182.

Derrida, J. (1992). *The other heading: Reflections on today's Europe* (P.-A. Brault & M. B. Naas, Trans.). Bloomington: Indiana University Press.

Dewey, J. (1916). *Democracy and education*. New York: Macmillan.

Dewey, J. (1963). *Experience and education*. New York: Macmillan.

Doll, W. E., Jr. (1972). A methodology of experience: An alternative to behavioral objectives. *Educational Theory, 22*(3), 309–324.

Doll, W. E., Jr. (1986). Prigogine: A new sense of order, a new curriculum. *Theory Into Practice, 25*, 10–16.

Doll, W. E., Jr. (1993). Curriculum possibilities in a "Post"- future. *Journal of Curriculum and Supervision, 8*(4), 277–292.

Dreyfus, H. L. (2004). Being and power: Heidegger and Foucault. Retrieved from http://socrates.berkeley.edu/~hdreyfus/html/paper_being.html

Dunning, S. N. (1985). Kierkegaard's systemic analysis of anxiety. In R. L. Perkins (Ed.), *International Kierkegaard commentary: The concept of anxiety*. Macon, GA: Mercer University Press.

Earle, W. (1972). *The autobiographical consciousness: A philosophical inquiry into existence*. Chicago: Quadrangle Books.

Educational Act Compilation Committee (2015). *Korean education act*. Seoul: Kyohak Publishing.

Foucault, M. (1980). The masked philosopher. In P. Rabinow (Ed.), *Ethics: Subjectivity and truth* (pp. 321–328). New York: The New Press.

Foucault, M. (1982a). Technologies of the self. In P. Rabinow (Ed.), *Ethics: Subjectivity and truth* (pp. 223–251). New York: The New Press.

Foucault, M. (1982b). The hermeneutic of the subject. In P. Rabinow (Ed.), *Ethics: Subjectivity and truth* (pp. 93–106). New York: The New Press.

Foucault, M. (1983). On the genealogy of ethics: An overview of work in progress. In P. Rabinow (Ed.), *Ethics: Subjectivity and truth* (pp. 253–280). New York: The New Press.

Foucault, M. (1984). The ethics of the concern for self as a practice of freedom. In P. Rabinow (Ed.), *Ethics: Subjectivity and truth* (pp. 289–301). New York: The New Press.

Foucault, M. (1986). *The care of the self* (R. Hurley, Trans.). New York: Vintage Books.

References

Foucault, M. (1997). Self writing. In P. Rabinow (Ed.), *Ethics: Subjectivity and truth* (pp. 207–221). New York: The New Press.

Freire, P. (1970). *Pedagogy of the oppressed.* New York: The Seabury Press.

Garrett, J. (2003). John Dewey's naturalistic pragmatism. Retrieved from http://people.wku.edu/jan.garrett/120/dewey.htm

Gibson, R. (1991). Curriculum criticism: Misconceived theory, ill-advised practice. In D. Hlynka & J. Belland (Eds.), *Paradigms regained: The uses of illuminative, semiotic, and post-modern criticism as modes of inquiry in educational technology* (pp. 190–210). Englewood Cliffs, NH: Educational Technology Publications.

Gilligan, C. J. (1982). *In a different voice.* Cambridge, MA: Harvard University Press.

Gordon, S., Benner, P., & Noddings, N. (1996). *Caregiving: Readings in knowledge, practice, ethics, and politics.* Philadelphia, PA: University of Pennsylvania Press.

Grant, G. P. (1966). *Philosophy in the mass age.* Toronto: Copp Clark Publishing.

Grumet, M. R. (1975, April). Existential and phenomenological foundations of *currere*: Self-report in curriculum inquiry. Paper presented at the annual meeting of the *American Educational Research Association*, Washington, D.C.

Grumet, M. R. (1981). Conception, contradiction and curriculum. *Journal of Curriculum Theorizing, 3*(1), 287–298.

Guitar, B. (2014). *Stuttering: An integrated approach to its nature and treatment* (4th ed.). Philadelphia: Wolters Kluwer Heath.

Hakbeol. (2015). In *Korean standard unabridged dictionary.* Seoul: National Institution of Korea. http://stdweb2.korean.go.kr/main.jsp

Halford, J. M. (1999). Longing for the sacred in schools: A conversation with Nel Noddings. *Educational Leadership, 56*(4), 28–32. Retrieved from http://www.ascd.org/publications/educational-leadership/dec98/vol56/num04/Longing-for-the-Sacred-in-Schools@-A-Conversation-with-Nel-Noddings.aspx

Hampden-Turner, C. (1971). *Radical man: The process of psycho-social development.* Garden City, NJ; New York: Anchor Books.

Hassan, T. (2008). An ethic of care critique. *Digital Repository: SUNY.* Retrieved from http://dspace.sunyconnect.suny.edu/bitstream/handle/1951/43954/

Heidegger, M. (1996). *Being and time: A translation of Sein und Zeit* (J. Stambaugh, Trans.). Albany: State University of New York Press.

Held, V. (1995). The meshing of care and justice. *Hypatia, 10*(2), 128–132.

Held, V. (2006). *The ethics of care: Personal, political and global.* Oxford; New York: Oxford University Press.

Hlebowitsh, P. S. (1992). Critical theory versus curriculum theory: Reconsidering the dialogue on Dewey. *Educational Theory, 42*(1), 69–82.

Hong, S. K. (2004). Killing Seoul University: The controversy of abolition of Seoul University. *Citizen and Lawyer,* 126, pp. 19–23.

Hong, W., & Youngs, P. (2008). Does high-stakes testing increase cultural capital among low-income and racial minority students? *Education Policy Analysis Archives, 16*(6), 1–21.

Hopcke, R. H. (1995). *Persona: Where sacred meets profane.* Boston: Shambhala.

Huh, K. (2010). Michel Foucault's technology of the self and Haewol's Hyang-A-Seol-Oui. *The Korean Journal of Studies of Dong Hak, 19,* 69–112.

Hume, D. (1997). *An enquiry concerning the principles of morals* (T. L. Beauchamp, Ed.). Oxford; New York: Oxford University Press.

Husserl, E. (1964). *The Paris lectures.* The Hague, Netherlands: Springer.

Ingram, C. (2004). *Passionate presence: Seven qualities of awakened awareness.* New York: Penguin.

Johnson, R. A. (1986). *Inner work: Using dreams and active imagination for personal growth.* New York: Harper & Row.

Johnson, W. (1944). The Indians have no word for it. *Quarterly Journal of Speech, 30*(3), 330–337.

Jung, T. H., & Lee, B. W. (2003). General perception of halbul ideology and policies to overcome hakbeol problems. Seoul: Korean Research Institute for Vocational Education & Training. Retrieved from http://library.krivet.re.kr/search/detail/CATTOT000000024011?mainLink=/search/tot&briefLink=/search/tot/result?q=이병욱_A_st=FRNT_A_cpp=5_A_os=_A_si=2_A_oi=DISP06

Juon, H. S., Nam, J. J., & Ensminger, M. E. (1994). Epidemiology of suicidal behavior among Korean adolescents. *The Journal of Child Psychology and Psychiatry, 35*(4), 663–676. doi:10.1111/j.1469-7610.1994.tb01212.x

Kandel, D. B., Raveis, V. H., & Davies, M. (1991). Suicidal ideation in adolescence : Depression, substance use, and other risk factors. *Journal of Youth and Adolescence, 20*(2), 289–309.

Kang, B. S. (2011, November 15). Test-focused system should be changed. *Different Voice: Headline Jeju.* Retrieved from http://www.headlinejeju.co.kr/news/articleView.html?idxno=131969

Keller, J. (1997). Autonomy, relationality, ethics and feminist. *Hypatia, 12*(2), 152–164.

Kierkegaard, S. (1941). *The sickness unto death* (W. Lowrie, Trans.). Princeton, NJ: Princeton University Press.

Kim, C. W. (2011). Nature and issues of national assessment of educational achievement: Focused on Korean language education. *Korean Language Education, 134*, 1–33.

Kim, S. B. (2004). *Hakbeol society.* Seoul: Jipmoondang.

Kim, S.-S. (2008). Symbolic violence and pre-modern academic clique Society. *Society and Philosophy, 16*, 131–160.

Kim, T. H. (2011, September 6). Koreans think that hakbeolism is the worst social discrimination. *Christianity Daily.* Retrieved from http://www.christianitydaily.com/view.htm?id=1246

Kim, Y. C. (2007). *Secrets of academic success of Korean students: Stories of hakwon.* Seoul: Brenz.

Kim, Y. C. (2010). Transnational curriculum studies : Reconceptualization discourse in South Korea. *Curriculum Inquiry, 40*, 531–554.

Kim, Y., & Yoon, S. (2009). A constitutional review on the official approval/certification system of textbooks in Korea: Focused on educational system and rights. *World Constitutional Law Review, 15*(2), 203–228.

Kockelmans, J. J. (1994). *Edmund Husserl's phenomenology.* West Lafayette, IN: Purdue University Press.

Korean Studies Promotion Service (2015). *The digital encyclopedia of the ethnic culture of Korea.* Seoul: Korean Studies Promotion Service. http://encykorea.aks.ac.kr/Contents/Index?dataType=0801

Kumar, A. (2011). *Understanding curriculum as meditative inquiry: A study of the ideas of Jiddu Krishnamurti and James Macdonald.* Vancouver: University of British Columbia.

Kumar, A. (2013). *Curriculum as meditative inquiry.* New York: Palgrave Macmillan.

Laing, R. D. (1960). *The divided self.* New York: Pantheon.

Lake, R. (Ed.). (2012). *Dear Nel.* New York; London: Teachers College Press.

Lampert, K. (2012). *Meritocratic education and social worthlessness.* New York: Palgrave Macmillan.

References

Lather, P. (2007). *Getting lost: Feminist efforts toward a double(d) science.* Albany: State University of New York Press.

Lee, C.-H. (2007). A sociological research on the phenomena of showing-off one's good academic clique. *Korean Journal of Sociology, 15*(2), 380–414.

Lee, J. K. (2003). *Korean credentials and hakbeolism: Origin and development.* Seoul: Jipmoondang.

Lee, N. H. (2008). The state examination system, its lights and shadows. *The Journal of Eastern Philosophy of Today, 18,* 117–136.

Lee, S. W., & Jang, Y. E. (2011). A study on the effect of adolescent's academic stress to suicidal ideation: Moderating effect of family cohesion. *Korean Journal of Youth Research, 18,* 111–136.

Lee, S.-Y. (2011). Reasons for living and their moderating effects on Korean adolescents' suicidal ideation. *Death Studies, 35,* 711–728. doi:10.1080/07481187.2011.553316

Lee, Y. (2003). Politics and theories in the history of curricular reform in South Korea. In W. F. Pinar (Ed.), *International Handbook of Curriculum Research* (pp. 541–552). Mahwah, N.J.; London: Lawrence Erlbaum Associates.

Leggo, C. (2011). A heartful pedagogy of care: A grandfather's perambulations. In J. A. Kentel (Ed.), *Educating the Young: The Ethics of Care* (pp. 61–84). New York: Peter Lang.

Logue, M., & Conradi, P. (2010). *The King's Speech: How one man saved the British monarchy.* London: Penguin Books.

Macdonald, J. B. (1981). Curriculum, consciousness and social change. In J. B. Macdonald (Ed.), *Theory as a prayerful act: The collected essays of James B Macdonald* (pp. 153–172). New York: Peter Lang.

Mayer, S. J. (2012). An awareness of relatedness. In R. Lake (Ed.), *Dear Nel* (pp. 13–15). New York; London: Teachers College Press.

McClellan, B. E. (1999). *Moral education in America: Schools and the shaping of character from colonial times to the present.* New York: Teachers College Press.

McLaren, P. (2007). The future of the past: Reflections on the present state of empire and pedagogy. In E. Malewski (Ed.), *Critical pedagogy: Where are we now?* (pp. 289–314). New York: Routledge.

Megill, A. (1985). *Prophets of extremity.* Berkeley: University of California Press.

Miller, A. (1984). *For your own good.* New York: Farrar, Straus and Giroux.

Miller, A. (1997). *Prisoners of childhood: The drama of the gifted child and the search for the true self.* New York: Basic Books.

Miller, J. L. (1990). *Creating spaces and finding voices: Teachers collaborating for empowerment.* New York: State University of New York Press.

Miller, J. L. (2005). *Sounds of silence breaking: Women, autobiography, curriculum* (Vol. 1). New York: Peter Lang.

Miller, J. L. (2010). Autobiographical theory. In C. Kridel (Ed.), *Encyclopedia of curriculum studies* (Vol. 1, pp. 61–65). Thousand Oaks, CA: Sage Publications.

Milliken, B. (2007). *The last dropout: Stop the epidemic!* New York: Hay House.

Milliken, B., & Meredith, C. (1968). *Tough love.* New York: FH Revell Company.

Nahm, I. S. (2011). Contradictions of Korean education based on academic success. *Theory of Society, 40,* 101–123.

Ng-A-Fook, N. (2005). A curriculum of mother-son plots on education's center stage. *Journal of Curriculum Theorizing, 21*(4), 43–59.

Nichols, C. L., & Berliner, D. C. (2007). *Collateral damage: How high-stakes testing corrupts America's schools.* Cambridge, MA: Harvard Education Press.

Noddings, N. (1984). *Caring: A feminine approach to ethics and moral education* (2nd ed.). Berkeley: University of California Press.
Noddings, N. (1988). An ethic of caring and its implications for instructional arrangements. *American Journal of Education, 96*(2), 215–230.
Noddings, N. (1990). Feminist fears in ethics. *Journal of Social Philosophy, 21*(2), 25–33.
Noddings, N. (1992). *The challenge to care in schools: An alternative approach to education.* New York: Teachers College Press.
Noddings, N. (1995). Care and moral education. In W. Kohli (Ed.), *Critical conversations in philosophy of education* (pp. 137–148). New York: Routledge. Retrieved from http://insidetheacademy.asu.edu/nel-noddings
Noddings, N. (1999). Caring. In W. F. Pinar (Ed.), *Contemporary curriculum discourses: Twenty years of JCT* (pp. 42–55). New York: Peter Lang.
Noddings, N. (2001a). Care and coercion in school reform. *Journal of Educational Change, 2*(1), 35–43.
Noddings, N. (2001b). The care tradition: Beyond "Add Women and Stir." *Theory into Practice, 40*(1), 29–34.
Noddings, N. (2002a). *Educating moral people.* New York; London: Teachers College Press.
Noddings, N. (2002b). *Starting at home: Caring and social policy.* Los Angeles; London: University of California Press.
Noddings, N. (2003). Foreword. In Barbara J. Thayer-Bacon (Ed.), *Relational "(e)pistemologies"* (pp. ix–x). New York: Peter Lang.
Noddings, N. (2005). *The challenge to care in schools* (2nd ed.). New York: Teachers College Press.
Noddings, N. (2006). *Critical lessons: What our schools should teach.* New York: Cambridge University Press.
Noddings, N. (2007). *When school reform goes wrong.* New York; London: Teachers College Press.
Noddings, N. (2008). A way of life. In L. J. Waks (Ed.), *Leaders in philosophy of education* (pp. 135–144). Rotterdam; Taipei: Sense Publishers.
Noddings, N. (2010a). Complexity in caring and empathy [Special issue]. *Abstracta* (V), 6–12.
Noddings, N. (2010b). *Inside the academy: An interview with National Academy of Education member Dr. Nel Noddings.* Retrieved from https://www.youtube.com/watch?feature=player_embedded&v=LljOHeoz_Pg
Noddings, N. (2010c). Moral education and caring. *Theory and Research in Education, 8*(2), 145–151. doi:10.1177/1477878510368617
Noddings, N. (2010d). *The maternal factor: Two paths to morality.* Berkeley, Los Angeles, and London: University of California Press.
Noddings, N. (2011). Schooling for democracy. *Democracy & Education, 19*(1), 1–6.
Noddings, N. (2012). The language of care ethics. *Knowledge Quest, 40*(4), 52–56.
Noddings, N., & Shore, P. J. (1984). *Intuition, love, and education.* New York; London: Teachers College Press.
Novak, B. (2012). The heart's truth: Seeing philosophy anew through the lens of care, and care anew through the lens of philosophy. In R. Lake (Ed.), *Dear Nel* (pp. 78–82). New York; London: Teachers College Press.
Oksala, J. (2007). *How to read Foucault.* London: Granta Books.
Organization for Economic Co-operation and Development [OECD]. (2014). *PISA 2012 results in focus: What 15-year-olds know and what they can do with what they know.* Paris: Organization for Economic Co-operation and Development.

Palmer, J. (2013). *The King's Speech*: A Jungian take. *Jung Journal: Culture & Psyche, 6*(2), 68–85. doi:10.1525/jung.2012.6.2.68.

Park, C. (1999). A comparative study of the concept of dread of Heidegger and Kierkegaard. *Journal of Time and Philosophy, 10*(1), 188–219.

Park, S. J. (2007). *Wonhyo: His life and thoughts*. Seoul: Hankukminhwasa.

Park, S. M., Jung, G. S., Kim, H. S., & Park, G. (2004). *A survey on Koreans' perceptions about discriminations of the society*. Seoul: Korean Women's Development Institute.

Phelan, A. M. (2005). A fall from (someone else's) certainty: Recovering practical wisdom in teacher education. *Canadian Journal of Education, 28*(3), 339–358.

Pinar, W. F. (1974). *Heightened consciousness, cultural revolution, and curriculum theory: The proceedings of the Rochester conference*. Berkeley: McCutchan Publishing Corporation.

Pinar, W. F. (1975a). Currere: Toward reconceptualization. In *Curriculum theorizing: The reconceptualists* (pp. 396–414). Berkeley: McCutchan Publishing.

Pinar, W. F. (1975b). *Curriculum theorizing: The reconceptualists*. Berkeley: McCutchan Publishing.

Pinar, W. F. (1975c). The method of *currere*. In *Autobiography, politics, and sexuality: Essays in curriculum theory 1972–1992* (pp. 19–27). New York: Peter Lang.

Pinar, W. F. (1975d). Sanity, madness, and the school. In *Curriculum theorizing: The reconceptualists* (pp. 359–383). Berkeley: McCutchan Publishing.

Pinar, W. F. (1976). The trial. In *Autobiography, politics, and sexuality: Essays in curriculum theory 1972–1992* (pp. 29–62). New York: Peter Lang.

Pinar, W. F. (1978). Notes on the curriculum field. In *Autobiography, politics, and sexuality: Essays in curriculum theory 1972–1992* (pp. 77–99). New York: Peter Lang.

Pinar, W. F. (1979). The abstract and the concrete in curriculum theorizing. In *Autobiography, politics, and sexuality: Essays in curriculum theory 1972–1992* (pp. 101–116). New York: Peter Lang.

Pinar, W. F. (1981). Understanding curriculum as gender text. In *Autobiography, politics, and sexuality: Essays in curriculum theory 1972–1992* (pp. 151–182). New York: Peter Lang.

Pinar, W. F. (1985). Autobiography and an architecture of self. In *Autobiography, politics, and sexuality: Essays in curriculum theory 1972–1992* (pp. 201–222). New York: Peter Lang.

Pinar, W. F. (1994). *Autobiography, politics, and sexuality: Essays in curriculum theory 1972–1992*. New York: Peter Lang.

Pinar, W. F. (1999). Caring: Gender consideration. In W. F. Pinar (Ed.), *Contemporary curriculum discourses: Twenty years of JCT* (pp. 56–60). New York: Peter Lang.

Pinar, W. F. (2004). *What is curriculum theory?* (1st ed.). Mahwah, NJ: Lawrence Erlbaum.

Pinar, W. F. (2005). Preface: What should be and what might be. In J. L. Miller (Ed.), *Sounds of silence breaking: Women, autobiography, curriculum* (pp. ix–xxx). New York: Peter Lang.

Pinar, W. F. (2006a). The problem with curriculum and pedagogy. In W. F. Pinar (Ed.), *The synoptic text today and other essays: Curriculum development after the reconceptualization* (pp. 109–120). New York: Peter Lang.

Pinar, W. F. (2006b). *The synoptic text today and other essays: Curriculum development after the reconceptualization*. New York: Peter Lang.

Pinar, W. F. (2009). *The worldliness of a cosmopolitan education*. New York; London: Routledge.

Pinar, W. F. (2011). *The character of curriculum studies: Bildung, currere, and the recurring question of the subject*. New York: Palgrave Macmillan.

Pinar, W. F. (2012). *What is curriculum theory?* (2nd ed.). New York; London: Routledge.

Pinar, W. F., & Grumet, M. R. (Eds.). (2006 [1976]). *Toward a poor curriculum*. New York: Educator's International Press.

Pinar, W. F., Reynolds, W. M., Slattery, P., & Taubman, P. M. (1995). *Understanding curriculum: An introduction to the study of historical and contemporary curriculum discourses*. New York: Peter Lang.

Rabinow, P. (1997). Introduction: The history of systems of thought. In P. Rabinow (Ed.), *Ethics: Subjectivity and truth* (pp. xi–xlii). New York: The New Press.

Rauch, A. (2000). *The hieroglyph of tradition: Freud, Benjamin, Gadamer, Novalis, Kant*. Madison, NJ: Fairleigh Dickinson University Press.

Reich, G. A. (2013). Imperfect models, imperfect conclusions: An exploratory study of multiple-choice tests and historical knowledge. *Journal of Social Studies Research*, *37*(1), pp. 1–14.

Rodriguez, A. J. (2005). Unraveling the allure of auto/biographies. In W.-M. Roth (Ed.), *Auto/biography and auto/ethnography: Praxis of research method*. Rotterdam: Sense Publications.

Ruddick, S. (1989). *Maternal thinking: Toward a politics of peace*. Boston: Beacon Press Books.

Schön, D. A. (1991). *The reflective practitioner: How professionals think in action*. London: Ashgate; Basic Books.

Seidler, D. (2010). The King's Speech: *Screenplay and introduction*. New York: Newmarket Press.

Seth, M. J. (2002). *Education fever: Society, politics, and the pursuit of schooling in South Korea*. Honolulu: University of Hawaii Press.

Shell, M. (2005). *Stutter*. Cambridge: Harvard University Press.

Son, J. H. (1993). *A study of the practices of colonial domination on schooling under the period of the third Chosun educational ordinance by Japanese imperialism*. 경북대학교 대학원. Daegu: Kyungbuk University.

Son, J. H. (2007). The politics of school test system in the Japanese imperialism. *The Journal of Educational Philosophy*, *31*, 21–44.

Spector, H. (2013). *The primacy of the ethical in a cosmopolitan education: Fukushima Daichi and other global risks* (Doctoral dissertation). University of British Columbia, Vancouver, British Columbia.

Stone, L. (2006). Drawing parts together: The philosophy of education of Nel Noddings. *Utbildning & Demokrati*, *15*(1), 13–32.

Swonger, M. (2006). Foucault and the hupomnemata: Self writing as an art of life. *Senior Honors Projects, Paper 18*. Retrieved from http://digitalcommons.uri.edu/cgi/viewcontent.cgi?article=1017&context=srhonorsprog

Szalavitz, M. (2006, January 29). The trouble with tough love. *The Washington Post*. Retrieved from http://www.washingtonpost.com/wp-dyn/content/article/2006/01/28/AR2006012800062.html

Tanner, D., & Tanner, L. N. (1995). *Curriculum development: Theory into practice* (3rd ed.). New York: Merrill.

Taubman, P. M. (2009). *Teaching by numbers*. New York: Routledge.

Taubman, P. M. (2012). *Disavowed knowledge*. New York: Routledge.

Wang, H. (2004). *The call from the stranger on a journey home*. New York: Peter Lang.

Wang, H. (2009). Introduction. In H. Wang & N. Olson (Eds.), *A journey to unlearn and learn in multicultural education* (pp. xi–xxi). New York: Peter Lang.

Wang, H. (2010). The temporality of currere, change, and teacher education. *Pedagogies: An International Journal*, *5*(4), 275–285. doi:10.1080/1554480X.2010.509469

Winnicott, D. W. (1960). The theory of the parent-infant relationship. *International Journal of Psychoanalysis*, *41*(6), 585–595.

Winnicott, D. W. (1982). *Playing and reality*. New York: Routledge.
Woolf, V. (1929). *A room of one's own*. New York: Harcourt Brace.
Wrathall, M. (2006). *How to read Heidegger*. New York: W.W. Norton.
Yairi, E. (1999). Epidemiologic factors and stuttering research. In N. B. Ratner & E. Charles Healey (Eds.), *Stuttering research and practice* (pp. 45–53). Mahwah, NJ: Lawrence Erlbaum.
Zimmerman, G., Liljeblad, S., Frank, A., & Cleeland, C. (1983). The Indians have many terms for it: Stuttering among the Bannock-Shoshoni. *Journal of Speech, Language, and Hearing Research, 26*(2), 315–318.

INDEX

abnormal 92–3
absence 19, 79, 83, 92
abstraction(s) 30, 59–60, 62, 123
abuse 48, 51, 62, 108
accountability iii, 77, 93, 97
achievement i, 14–16, 23, 60, 94, 132; economic 13; technological 22
action ii, 17, 36, 43, 48–9, 61, 73, 87, 104, 111, 114–15, 122, 124, 136; affective 112; compensatory 63; human 22; moral 60; political 78; prescribed 54; self-affirmative 97
active imagination 84–6, 99, 132
adolescent iii, 2, 66, 109, 132–3
advice 5, 28, 39, 81
aesthetics 72–3; existence 71, 79
affection 90, 108, 113, 117
affirmation 42; self 104, 124, 127
agape 117
agency 4, 22, 24, 35, 39, 41, 50, 51, 64, 82, 106–7, 123, 129
aggression 58, 108, 110
agony 86, 89
Alexander, H. 50, 129
Alice, M. 62, 65, 108, 111
alienated 40
allegorical(ly) 76, 79–80, 119, 123
aloneness 116
alternative xii–xiii, 14, 21, 71, 77, 130, 134
ambition 127
ambivalence 39, 112

analytic 28
ancient Rome 23
Anderson, A. 117, 129
androgynous 55
anew 58, 75–6, 121, 134
Ang, R. P. 2, 17, 129
anger 74, 83, 86–8
anomaly x, 7
anomaly's own good 89–90
antagonistic 58–9
anthem of our time 106
anticommunism 3, 13
antinomies 105
anti-psychiatry 43
anxiety ix, 6, 19, 27, 30, 35–6, 38–40, 64–5, 76, 130; dialectic x, 25, 39, 120; existential 113, 124; freedom 37; neurotic 112
Aoki, T. T. iv, 33–4, 108, 125, 129
apathy 71
Apology (Socrates) 69
Apple, M. 14
arbitrary 4–5, 20–1, 78, 121
architecture of self 26, 73, 75, 121, 135
arduous step ix, 4–5
arrest(ed) 3–5, 7, 19–20, 26–7, 32, 34–7, 40–2, 58, 76, 89, 119–20; ego 39; self ix, 31, 43, 44
arrogant 47, 122
art ii, 14, 45; listening 35; existence 72; life 136; work of i, 72, 77, 114, 112–3, 121, 125, 127

artless 3
ascesis 76
aspiration(s) iii, 7, 37, 39, 44–5, 90, 124
association xii, 6–7, 10, 28, 41, 50, 68, 78, 97, 102, 104, 116, 119, 125, 131
assumption 17–18, 42, 60, 74, 93, 94, 100, 118, 123; destructive 21; detrimental 61; fundamental 94; mythic 117; unwarranted 111
attachment 39, 108
attention 1, 15, 17, 20, 25, 27–8, 38, 42, 49–50, 52, 58, 61–2, 68–9, 71, 73, 82, 99–100, 109, 111, 123
attraction(ive) 71, 108
attunement 53–4, 66
authentic xii, 98, 104; being 80; collective subjectivity 11; conversation 34; persona 84, 124; self 31, 88, 120; self-knowledge 80; self–self relationship 6, 26, 77, 102, 121; voice 80–1, 96, 123–5
authoritarianism 78, 122; social 19–20
authority 34, 40, 65, 81, 110, 112–13, 124–5; self-referential 72; teacher 119; unwarranted 109
autism 76
autobiographical 26, 29, 32, 35, 42–3; consciousness 40, 120, 130; engagement 43; inquiry 6, 21, 74, 121; study x, xv, 42, 68, 73, 119; theory(ies) ix, 25–6, 41, 42, 130
autobiography i, 26, 29, 43, 75, 77, 125, 133, 135; architecture 73; ontological 32, 76
autonomy 17, 47–8, 59, 89–90, 94, 130, 132; individual 50; limited 50; relational 51; women's 50
awaken(ing) 4, 119, 131
awareness 40, 51, 55, 114, 115, 120; ability 4; human 43, 58, 65, 83–4, 121, 131, 133; self- 36; subjectivity 12, 28

Bakhtin, M. M. 103, 127, 129
beautiful 59; risk 18, 55, 118, 129
Begrebet angst 36
being-in-the-world 40, 54, 120
benevolence 49, 59, 69, 108
Benner, P. 61, 131
Bergman, R. 47, 129
Berliner, D. C. 23, 133
Bertie xii, 82–90, 96–101, 120, 123–4
Bettelheim, B. 108, 111, 129
Biesta, G. J. 18, 22, 54–5, 118, 129
binary 8
biological 45, 56–7

Block, A. A. 78, 122, 129
Bloom's taxonomy 14, 22
body 1, 83, 96
Bourdieu, P. 2, 129
bracketing 29, 53–4, 60, 66, 75
brain xi, 1, 95, 115
brave(ry) 78, 88, 92, 100, 122, 124
breakdown ix, 25, 30–6, 39–40, 42–3, 120
Britzman, D. P. xiii, 35–6, 104, 108, 111–13, 117, 124–6, 129
Bruner, J. 14, 22
Buber, M. 53, 63, 91, 129–30
bucket 18, 89, 110, 123
Buddhism 78
bureaucracy 18
business 83–4, 117
bygone 71

cacophony 108
calculative 35
calling 5, 117
calmness 114–16
camouflaged 3, 110
Canada xv, 33–4, 95
canonicity 117
capacity 20, 28, 40, 48, 54, 56, 63, 65, 81, 112, 121, 127
capitalism 11, 80
captain 127
Card, C. 58, 130
care-for-others i, x, xii, 6, 44, 47, 65, 68, 70–1, 81–3, 99–100, 102–4, 108, 110, 113–16, 119, 123–7
caring i, xi–xii, 6, 44, 47, 48–9, 51, 52, 54, 56–7, 61–7, 70, 95–6, 98, 99–102, 113–15, 122, 129, 130, 134, 135; about 53; balanced 59; characteristic(s) 52; coercive i, x, 45, 48, 59, 61, 64, 123, 125; ethical 50, 123; for 53; ideal 59; natural 60; pathological 50, 65; receptivity 59, 67, 93; reciprocal 82; relation(ship) 55, 61, 63–4, 66, 121–2
categorical imperatives 111
causation 18, 21
censor 4, 19
centralization 11, 13, 15
certainty(ies) 32, 36, 39–40, 135
change(d) 13, 20, 23, 32–3, 35, 42–3, 45, 52, 58, 77, 79, 100, 105–7, 109–10, 126, 132–4; consciousness 4–5, 20; curriculum ii, 15; curriculum theorizing 26; democratic 14; institutional 21; intellectual 40; internal 88;

psychological 45; relationship 125; social i; structural 126; structure(s) 5, 122
character(istics) 4, 19, 27, 32, 40–1, 49, 52, 54–6, 58, 96, 104, 107, 113, 116, 119, 133, 135; Chinese 23, 81; detrimental 99; hakbeolism i; Korean education 119; paradoxical 6; women 56
cheating 17, 23, 61
Chien, C. 26, 130
China 22, 33
Chinese 22–3, 41, 81
Chinju National University of Education xv, 110
Cho, K. H. 79, 130
Chodorow, N. 56, 67, 130
Choi, J. S. 76–7, 130
Choi, J. W. 79
Choi, S. H. xii, 68, 79
choice 34, 36, 40, 48, 58, 72, 75, 78, 103, 124, 136
Chonghaejin Marine 127
Chosun Dynasty 12, 22–3, 136
Christianity 69, 73, 74, 79, 132
chungeo 12
circumstance 8, 20, 28, 49, 51–2, 70, 74, 103, 124; external 117; oppressive 72; study ix, 25, 27, 29, 42
civil rights 117
clan 11, 21, 120
clarity 19, 114
class 10, 45, 56, 70, 87, 98
Cleeland, C. 92, 137
closed-system paradigm 22
coercion 48, 61–3, 114, 134
cognitive 20, 56, 66, 127
Coleman, K. 46, 130
colleague(s) 23, 33, 42, 117
collective 5, 13, 23; encounter 42; subjectivity 11–12, 21
collegiality 45, 66
commercialized 106
commitment 49, 60, 107, 117, 125
commodity 65
communication 33–4, 40, 55, 81, 115
community(ies) 11, 22, 47, 109
compassion xii
competency 117
competition i, 35, 58; aggressive 16, 120
complementary xii, 7, 103, 116, 1243
complexity 38, 52, 134; self-care 127; self–other relationship 82, 103, 126; theory(ists) ii, xiii

compliance x, 63, 94, 110–11, 124, 126
complicated 30, 38, 41, 43, 51, 66, 77, 106, 121; conversation 30, 67, 100
computer 23, 74, 94
conditioned 26, 31, 40, 58, 65, 71, 75, 120
conditioning 108; cultural 26; social 19–20
confess 32, 48, 79, 87, 110, 113
conformity 34, 42, 65, 125
Confucianism 78
confusion 3, 103, 116, 124
connection(s) 11, 18, 30, 70, 103–4, 117; personal 12; unnecessary 73, 104, 121, 125
Conradi, P. 91, 96–7, 98, 101, 133
consciousness 4–6, 21, 52, 76, 83, 88, 96, 99; active 103; autobiographical 40, 120, 130, 133; critical 24; heightened 135
constraints xii, 7, 20, 68, 108, 121
contemplation(ing) ii, 40, 74, 114
context(s) i, 6, 14, 53, 61, 67, 73–4, 109, 127; cultural 58; free 21
contextual 17
contextualize 6, 68, 119
contradiction(s) 56, 119, 131, 133
contradictory 108
contribution i, 6, 12, 16, 24, 27, 29, 42, 45–6, 82, 96, 122, 124
control 4, 13, 15, 54, 89, 97, 109–10, 114, 117, 123–4; curriculum 77; political 5, 19
conversation(s) 23, 29, 40–1, 85, 97, 110, 131; authentic 34; classroom 21; complicated 33, 67, 100; critical 134; curricular ii
Cooper, D. 28, 43, 89–90, 124, 130
corruption 17, 23, 61, 66, 127
courage(ous) 66, 78, 86–8, 109, 117, 122, 124–6
cramming 17
cram school 22
creative relationship xii, 6–7, 71–3
creatures 60, 89, 115
credentialism 9–10
credential(s) 2, 4, 11, 23, 87, 133
crisis 13, 56; national 13; Oedipal 56
critical ii, 13, 48; consciousness 24; conversation 134; engagement 127; pedagogy(ue) 105, 133; theory 131; thinking 50–1
criticism 11, 26, 41–2, 50, 56, 66, 74, 79, 89, 106, 131
crucial 15, 55, 104, 127

culmination 15, 17, 39
culpability i, 18, 77–8, 111, 121, 126
culprit 2
cultivate xiii, 4, 8, 48, 77, 104, 106–7, 116, 122, 125, 127
cultural(ly) xi, 2, 6–7, 9, 10, 16, 56–8, 61, 67, 95, 100, 102, 126; capital 131; conditioning 26; creation 106; cross i–iii; distance 35; malady 4; norm 13; politico 75; revolution 135
culture(s) ii, 3–4, 8, 17, 26, 33, 35, 42–4, 50, 73, 75, 79–80, 91–2, 112, 127, 135; Ancient Greek 71; familial 100; hakbeolism xi; Korean 76, 90, 110, 119, 126, 132; outer-directed 19, 31–2, 120; sub 47
curiosity 15, 19
currere ii, v, ix–xii, 6, 8, 14, 65, 75–6, 79, 97, 111, 113, 119–21, 130, 131, 135, 136; method of i, 5, 25–6, 25–44, 74; reciprocity 81
curricularist xiii
curriculum i–xi, xv–xvi, 14, 23, 26, 28, 29, 33, 46, 56, 58, 61, 77, 110, 118, 129–36; development 14, 18; inquiry 25; local 14; national 3–4; reform 15; scholars 14; studies 27–8, 44, 78, 99, 107; theorizing 26, 29, 35, 43; transformative 22; understanding 14–15
cynical 106
cynicism 105, 125–6

danger(ous) ix, 2–5, 40, 50, 71, 80
Dasein 54
Davies, M. 17, 132
Davis, T. 26, 130
dead 3
death 1, 8, 40, 82, 85, 89, 97, 132; education 110
decisive break 73–4, 121, 124
de-commodifies 26
deconstruction 55
deformation 26, 75
delay(ing) 110–11, 113, 124
deliberations 47, 52; ethical 47, 122
democracy 14, 43, 105, 130, 134
democratic 14, 20, 70, 117
denaturalizing 36, 72
dependency 24, 77, 110–11, 118, 125
Depp, L. 46, 130
Derrida, J. 36, 55, 130
Derridian 55
descriptive 29, 41, 60, 121

designing 27
desire 11, 26–7, 32, 37–8, 45, 48–9, 52, 63, 72, 79, 90, 96, 103, 108, 114, 116, 117
destruction 31
determinacy 105
determination 17; self 29, 40
determine 2, 9, 38–9, 105, 116
detrimental 36, 38, 61, 96, 99, 111
devastation xi, 132
devoid 107
Dewey, J. 21–2, 43, 52, 55, 60–1, 66–7, 130; society 46
diagnose 83, 92, 94–5
diagnosogenic 92
dialectic x, 4, 37, 40, 58; anxiety 39, 120; relationship 25, 41, 43, 54
dictatorship 11, 15, 117
difference(s) 14–16, 21, 33, 44, 53, 60–1, 67, 70, 100, 104
Different Voice, In a (Gilligan) 131
dilemma(s) 19, 40, 111
dirty work 3
disappointment 35, 114, 126
disastrous xi, 57–8, 107, 125
disavowed 40, 95, 99, 136
discernment x, 7, 113–16, 126
discipline(s) xii, 66–7, 99, 117, 127
disconfirmation x, 7, 89–94, 99, 123–5
discontent 12, 126
discontinuity 25
discovery 29–30, 80
discrimination 10–11, 15, 21, 70, 135
disguise 62, 108, 110–11
disillusion 112
disintegration 28, 43
dissatisfaction 90, 115
dissonance 49
dissymmetry 71
distance x, 7, 32–5, 75, 105–7, 113, 115–16, 125
distinctiveness 8, 100
distress 36, 114
dizziness of freedom 36, 106
Doll, Jr. W. E. xi, xv, 17, 22, 29, 35, 43, 61, 65, 121, 130
domination 4–5, 21, 58, 136
donghak 69–70, 78–9, 130
Donghak Peasant Revolution 95
dormant 3–4, 35
dread 36, 80, 135
dreams 99, 105, 112, 117, 132
Dreyfus, H. L. 71, 89, 130

drug-addicted 109
dualism 83
duality 53
Dunning, S. N. 39–40, 130
duration 22

Earle, W. 32, 76, 130
edifice 75, 121
education xiii, xv, xvi, 3, 4, 7–9, 13–16, 18, 20–2, 28, 34, 37, 39, 42, 44–6, 53, 55, 58–9, 61–2, 64, 66–7, 75–8, 80, 89, 95–7, 100, 108, 110–12, 116–18, 129; banking 17–18, 94, 117, 120–7; child-centered 67; fever 15, 90; Korean xi, 2, 3, 5–6, 13, 99, 119–20, 126; moral 91; progressive 14, 66–7, 94; shadow 22; system 23; teacher 94; traditional 61, 66–7; transformative 26
educational meritocracy 16
efficiency 3, 13–16
egalitarian(ism) 16, 119–20, 126
ego xiii, 5, 19, 31, 83–4, 112–13, 120; arrested 32, 39; damaged 40, 127; defense 111
egoism 70
egoistic 70
Eichmann, Adolf 126
Elizabeth 83–5, 97
elusive(ly) 52, 117, 129
emotion(al) xv, 30–1, 41, 49, 52, 56, 59, 62, 66, 104, 110, 116, 120, 122, 127
empty buckets 110
encounter(s) 18, 24, 34, 42, 47, 51–2, 54–5, 91, 112
endeavor(s) 5–6, 27, 31, 41, 81, 122, 124
engagement xii, 5–6, 41, 43, 65, 102, 105, 123, 126–7
engrossment 49
Ensminger, M. E. 2, 132
environment(al) 33, 47, 93–4, 109, 115–16
Epimeleia heautou 69
epistemological 56, 71, 76
epistemology 28, 33
equality 84
era 13, 50, 107
eros 117
Esterson, A. 89
estrangement 25, 33, 106, 125
ethical xii, 6, 8, 24, 64, 70, 123–4; act 63; commitment 125; decision 78, 127; dilemmas 111; ideal 57, 129; judgment 3, 120, 125; principle 59

ethicality 108, 113–14, 125–6
ethicists 58, 62
ethic of care i, x, 6–7, 44–5, 50, 57, 59–60, 65–6, 68, 112, 119, 121–3
ethic(s) 23, 50, 52, 54, 57, 81, 103, 105–7, 116, 121–2, 125–6, 129–30; of care x, xii, 7, 44–7, 51, 57–60, 63–8, 73, 79, 82, 102, 112, 119, 121–2; feminine 57; Foucault 72; genealogy 69, 71; intention 104; justice 44–5, 59, 67; Kantian 59, 79, 122; male 58; Noddings 98, 123; relational 52; sacrificial 106; traditional 47, 122; twofold 112
ethnicity 17, 21, 61
evaluation 19–20, 23, 51, 54, 92, 100
evils of civilization 91
exam(ination) 2, 13, 15, 17, 20, 23, 29, 32, 34, 64, 100, 119–20, 123, 133; entrance 4, 9–10, 30; hell 119
examinee 12, 56
examiner 12, 19
exclusive(ly) 3, 5, 19, 22, 27, 30, 66, 77, 89, 104, 106, 111; attention 20; social status 12; socialized 39
exclusiveness 21
exile 33, 74, 106, 125
existence xi, 6, 18, 21, 25, 28, 47, 54, 62, 66, 70, 72, 86, 90, 120, 130; aesthetics of 71, 79; art of 72; human 36, 50; modes of 127
existential 26, 43, 47, 52–5, 89, 131; angst 35, 40, 111–12; anxiety 113, 124; freedom 28, 36, 76; phenomenology 53; understanding 29
existentialism 28, 43, 51, 55, 59–60, 67, 129
existentialist(s) 29, 53
expectation(s) 58, 63, 91; externalized 127; social 93
experience(s) xv, 4, 5, 10, 19–21, 23, 25, 29–30, 33–4, 39–40, 42–3, 45, 52–6, 59, 62, 84, 91, 109–10, 112–13, 120–2, 124, 127, 130; of anxiety 36; Dewey 22; educational 4, 7, 11, 14, 21, 28, 40–1, 44, 64, 66, 75–6, 78; ends of 22; female 58, 63; feminine 56; human 56; inner 26; intimate 48; life 99; lived xi, 21, 27, 42, 55, 76, 80, 119, 121, 126; painful 31; self-evident 107; subjective 3; women's 57–8
explanation 3, 11, 52, 56–7, 99
external(ly) 3, 15, 18, 26–7, 61, 65; circumstances 117; external constraints xii;

external(ly) *(continued)*
  factors 19; force 64–5, 72, 90, 123; law 90; power 39; standard xi, 5, 77, 121–2; world 39
externalize 19, 127
extracurricular 117
extraordinary 46

failure 2, 18–19, 60, 65–6, 103, 111, 113–15, 120, 124; academic 17
fairness 119
faith 18, 39, 98, 100
fallacy 15, 18, 22
false 75, 82, 95; persona 88; relationship 75, 81, 83, 89, 116, 121; self 31
fantasy 8, 28, 37, 111
fascism 43
father 12, 40, 49, 57, 60, 79, 85–6, 89, 97, 113, 117, 120
fear xii, 2, 19, 26–7, 30, 32, 35–8, 40, 57, 64, 76, 87, 90, 97, 108, 110–13, 115, 117, 124 134
feeling xi, xii, 31–3, 36–9, 47–9, 51, 53, 56–7, 59–60, 62–3, 76, 97–8, 111, 113, 115, 124
feminine 55, 59–60, 122, 134; care 64, 123; ethics 57; experience 56; naturalism 47; perspective 45, 47
femininity 58
feminist(s) 44, 47, 58, 132–4
filter 19
fire 18
force(s) 3, 32, 58, 65, 75, 77–8, 90, 105, 108, 121, 122; external 72, 90; inner 19, 65, 95, 123; reproductive 125; neoliberal 126
forest 115
for one's own good 62, 65, 123, 133
Foucault, M. xii, 59, 68–9, 71–6, 78–82, 89–90, 102–8, 113, 116, 121–2, 127, 130–1, 134
fragment 25, 28, 29, 35, 86
fragmentary 74
Frank, A. 92, 137
free association 28, 97
freedom 6, 17, 36, 47, 64, 81, 90, 94, 108, 126, 130; anxiety of 37; dizziness of 36, 40; existential 28, 76; intellectual and political 78, 106, 117; students 112
free semester 117
Freire, P. 17, 131
friendship 84, 86, 96–7
from outer to inner 40–1, 120, 122

frustration(s) 29, 112–15, 124, 126
fulfillment 39
Fürsorge 53
future 20, 29–30, 41, 45, 51, 76, 78, 106, 109, 113, 122, 126, 130

Gabo Reform 12
garden 45, 115
Garrett, J. 52, 131
gaze 104
gender 17, 55–9, 61, 64, 67, 70, 123, 135; roles 50, 127
genealogy 69, 71, 130
Gibson, R. 42, 131
Gilligan, C. J. 44, 58–60, 131
goal 3–4, 16, 26, 29, 53, 61, 64–5, 67, 98, 109
God 69–70, 79, 100, 113
good enough 111–12, 129
goodness 57, 108
Gordon, S. 61, 131
Goryeo Dynasty 12, 22–3
government(al) 13, 15–16, 22, 26, 39, 75, 110, 117; colonial 13; Korean 14; military 13; surveillance 15
governmentality 120
governmentalization 20
gradations of realization 40
Grant, G. P. 38, 131
gravity 41
Greek 7; Ancient 69, 71, 73–4, 95, 117
grief xi
grounded theory 30
Grumet, M. R. 26, 28, 36–7, 41, 43, 56–7, 65, 97, 131, 135
guarantee 65, 104, 113–14, 124, 126
guilt 111, 127
Guitar, B. 93, 100, 131
gwageo 12–13, 22, 23
Gwang Jong 22

habit(ual) 31–2, 34, 41, 51, 82, 100
Haewol xii, 68–71, 73, 131
hakbeol 4, 8–12, 16–17, 21–3, 131–2
hakbeolism i, xi, xvi, 2, 4, 6, 9–13, 15–17, 19–23, 68, 76, 79, 95, 119–21, 126, 133
hakwon 22, 132
Halford, J. M. 46, 131
hamartia 2, 7, 20
Hammer, J. 26, 130
Hampden-Turner, C. 37, 131
Han River 22
hanul 69–70

happy 2, 51, 64, 103, 114
harmony 108
Hassan, T. 50, 131
heart xi, 1, 22, 90, 94–5, 127, 134
Heidegger, M. 2, 27, 29, 35–6, 53–5, 66, 89, 130–1, 135, 137
Held, V. 58–9, 131
helplessness 78, 122
here and now 70–1, 73
hermeneutic 29, 69, 81, 130
hesitation 32, 37
hierarchical 2, 9, 20, 119, 127
hierarchy 17
high school 1, 10, 34, 45, 94, 109–10, 126
history 3, 20, 26, 43, 45, 73, 75, 79, 80, 99, 100, 107, 130, 133, 136; Christianity 69, 71, 73; Korean 44, 110, 119–20, 126; life 28; personal 84
Hlebowitsh, P. S. 42, 131
homogeneity 21
homosexuality 21
Hong, S. K. 20, 131
Hong, W. 17, 131
Hopcke, R. H. 83, 131
hopeless 83
hope(s) xii–xiii, 8, 27, 29, 32–3, 37, 63, 83, 126; naïve 78

institution(al) xii, 8, 10, 23, 39, 46, 50, 59, 62, 95, 99, 127; change 20; cramming 17; educational 2, 9, 63, 66, 80, 117; mandate 3; social 54
institutionalization 79; students 99
institutionalized 13
instruction(al) 27, 36, 44, 58, 94, 134
instrumental 21, 53; rationalism 94; rationality 2, 18, 78, 122
instrumentalism 18, 61
intellectual(ly) i, 26, 30, 31, 41, 99, 104, 113; activities 75; banking education 18; change 40; courage 122; critique 3; development 28, 36; freedom 6, 17, 94, 106, 117; interest 7, 42, 126; rigor 107; significance 61; snob 45; trap 20, 77, 120; wisdom 21
intelligent heteronomy 51
interdiction 79
internality 22
internalization 5, 89, 100
internal(ized) 16, 22, 48, 89–90, 94–5, 119, 124; change 88; forces 65, 123; horizon 127; oppression 43
interpretation 8, 18, 26, 29–30, 53–4

interpretive 29
intersubjective 56
intervention 24
intra-psychic corollary 19–20
intrinsic motivation 61
inventiveness 64
invitation 5
ironically 11, 126
Irwin, R. L. 145
isolation 116

Jang, Y. E. 2, 17, 66, 133
Japan(ese) 11–13, 16, 136
Jefferson award 109
Johnson, R. A. 99, 132
Johnson, W. 91–3, 95, 100–1, 132
Joseph K. 18–19, 31
judgment 7–8, 21, 29–30, 54; ethical 3, 120, 125–6; moral 59; professional 18; suspending 106; suspension of 54
Jung, C. 27, 32, 82–3, 96–7
Jung, G. S. 11, 135
Jung, T. H. 17, 132
Jungian psychoanalysis 28, 99
justice xi, xiii, 47, 59–61, 122, 131; ethics of 6, 44–5, 60, 67; juvenile 109; universal principle 123
juxtapose 7, 30, 76, 79, 119–21

Kandel, D. B. 17, 132
Kang, B. S. 17, 132
Kant, I. 59–61, 69, 79, 122, 136
Kantian ethics xii, 47, 59–60, 79, 122
Keeney-Kennicutt, W. 26, 130
Keller, J. 50, 132
Kierkegaard, S. 27, 36, 38–9, 41, 130, 132
Kim, C. W. 17, 132
Kim, D. J. 14–15, 132
Kim, H. S. 4, 10, 11, 135
Kim, J. R. 77, 132
Kim, S. B. 10, 11, 16, 21, 23, 132
Kim, S. G 110, 132
Kim, S. S. 2, 13, 22, 132
Kim, T. H. 4, 10–11, 132
Kim, Y. 15, 23, 132
Kim, Y. C. xv, 15, 132
Kimchi 34
kindness 86, 108
King George VI xii, 5, 82, 99
knowledge 3, 5, 8–9, 17–18, 21, 23, 29, 39, 69, 101, 107, 120, 125, 127, 131, 134, 136; academic 116; mandated 17; self 58, 75, 80; specified 61; structure 22;

knowledge *(continued)*
    teacher 117; transmission 2, 14; tyranny 16, 20
known 4, 41
know thyself 64, 69, 75, 123
Kockelmans, J. J. 54, 132
Korea(n) xv–xvi, 2, 5, 7–23, 27, 29, 33–4, 40, 66, 77, 79, 90, 100, 106, 110, 117, 119, 123, 127, 130–6; adolescents 2, 66, 132–3; Buddhist tradition 33; citizen 22; culture 76, 90, 119; education xi–xiii, 2–3, 5–6, 9, 13, 59, 76–7, 99–100, 112, 119–20, 126; educators 2, 5, 126; Gallop 110; history 44, 110; schools 93; society 4, 10–11, 15, 20, 23, 70, 119; students 2, 14, 22, 132; war 3, 11, 13, 15–16, 22
Koryo University 16
Kumar, A. 40, 132
KWDI 11, 132

Laing, R. D. 28, 31, 43, 89–91, 108, 117, 125, 132
lament(ing) 1, 66, 79, 95, 107
Lampert, K. 16, 132
language 13, 23, 33, 42, 46, 50, 52, 57, 60, 66, 92, 104, 108, 132, 134, 137
Lather, P. 105, 133
learning xiii, xv, 3–4, 6–7, 15, 18, 21–22, 26, 36–7, 55, 66–7, 75, 99, 111–13, 117–19, 125, 127, 129; Eastern 79; joys of 61; preceding 117; Western 79
lebenswelt 27
Lee, B. W. 2, 17, 132
Lee, C. H. 11, 133
Lee, J. K. 9–10, 12–13, 23, 133
Lee, J. S. 127
Lee, N. H. 23, 133
Lee, S. J. xv
Lee, S. W. 2, 17, 66, 133
Lee, S. Y. 2, 133
Lee, Y. 8, 14–15, 133
legacy 22, 27, 58
Leggo, C. vi, xiii, 102, 113, 118, 133
liberated 39–40
liberating 4
liberation 4, 21, 37, 40
life 2, 4, 6, 10, 19, 22, 27–8, 30–1, 35, 42, 46, 51, 53, 62, 66, 68, 70, 72, 76–8, 81, 85–6, 89, 91, 99–100, 105–7, 112–15, 121, 130, 134–6; educational 39, 104; ethical 58; harshness 111; human 52; inner 8, 28; lived 62; modern 28; moral 59; one's own 78, 122; private 39, 44–5, 66, 74, 98; professional 98; public 83; school 45; second 26, 130; social 31; of social service 5; storm 114; unexamined 64, 123
lifestyle 79
Liljeblad, S. 92, 137
limitation(s) 21–2, 60, 92
linear 29–30, 40–1, 121
linkage 79, 107, 125
lived x, 1, 8, 88, 100, 117, 119; experience x, 5, 26–7, 42, 45, 55, 75–6, 80, 121, 126; life 62; present 30; sense of self 28, 75; world 20
lofty principle 59–60, 122
logos 74
Logue, L. xii, 83–8, 91, 96–8, 100–1, 123–4
Logue, M. 133
loneliness 31, 116
loser(s) 16
lottery system 20
love x, 7, 30, 35, 45, 59, 62, 81, 86, 89–91, 94, 104, 108–9, 111–13, 116–17, 124–5, 133; abusive 114; attentive 50; tough 108–9, 133, 136; whip of i, 90, 110, 125

Macdonald, J. B. 4–5, 16, 20–1, 27, 132–3
machinery 77
madness 31, 89–90, 94, 135
malaise 2
malleability 111
manipulation 17, 62, 108, 111
marketing 117
masculine 55, 58, 60, 67
masculinity 56, 58
materialism 70
maternal xii, 49, 66, 127, 134, 152
maturation 110–11
Mayer, S. J. 49, 133
McClellan, B. E. 14, 44, 47, 133
McLaren, P. 133
means to an end 14, 18
mechanistic 26
meditative 35; inquiry 40, 132; mode 104
medium 5, 41, 81, 122
Megill, A. 26, 75, 133
memory 1, 74, 83, 86
meritocracy 16, 17, 95
Merriam-Webster 108
migratory 26, 42

Miller, A. 65, 81–2, 108, 110–11, 133
Miller, J. L. 25–6, 32, 42–3, 62–3, 133, 135
Milliken, B. 109, 133
mind 21, 30, 33, 37, 54, 69–70, 82–3, 96, 99, 115
miracle(s) 13, 22, 115
misery 35, 40
misunderstanding 22, 30
mobilization 117
modernization 11, 22
modes of action 43
modes of study 41
monopoly 15–16
morality 49, 59, 107, 134
moral(ly) 46, 49, 51, 58, 131, 133; action 60; conduct 72; education 44, 91, 129, 133; excellence 107; life 59; masculine 67; principles 122; puzzlement 60, 123; rationalists 57; superior 58; theory 47, 122; value 60
mother i, xvi, 21, 45–6, 48–50, 56–8, 60, 63–4, 66, 86, 103, 111–12, 115, 120, 127, 130, 133
motivational shift 49
murder 63, 110; soul 111
mutual(ly) xii, 7, 41, 81, 105; relationship 41; sacrifice 65
mystical alchemy 42
mythic 21, 117

Nahm, I. S. 9, 133
Nam, J. J. 2, 132
narcissism 37
national 14; assessment 132; crisis 13; curriculum 3–4; solidarity 13
National Education Information System 23
nationalism 3, 13
nationality 21
Native Americans 92, 100
native race 91
naturalistic pragmatism 131
natural(ly) 36, 49, 56–7, 86, 113, 115; caring 48, 57, 60, 64, 123; inclination 57; instinct 56; naturalism 47
nature 19–20, 30, 40, 47, 65, 89, 93, 123, 126, 131, 132; arrest 43; our being 18; breakdown 32–3; curriculum theorizing 26; feminine care 64; hakwon 22; human existence 36, 50, 52, 55, 57, 60, 66; individual experience 28; Korean education 9

negative(ly) 15, 17–18, 38–9, 47, 75, 79, 95, 99
negotiation 63, 110
neoliberal 67, 78, 106, 121, 126
New Jersey 45
Ng-A-Fook, N. 25–6, 42, 133
Nichols, C. L. 23, 133
nihilism 37, 105, 125–6
nihilistic 106
nobility 11–12
Noddings, N. xii, 6, 23, 35, 41, 44–67, 79–82, 91, 98, 101, 103–4, 108, 117, 121, 123, 129–31, 134, 136
noncoincidence 7, 106–7, 125
nonfluency 93
nonlinear xiii
nonsensical 56
nonviolent 59
normal(ly) 48, 72, 90, 92–3, 97, 106, 110
Novak, B. 52–3, 55, 134
number(s) 2–3, 12, 77–8, 94, 106, 122, 136

obedience 59, 101
objectification(s) 4–5, 19, 24, 30, 32, 60–1, 63, 76, 121
objectify 56, 60–1, 98, 123
objectivity 37, 43, 59, 77
obligation 47–8, 50–1, 59, 70, 72
observation 23, 52, 77
obsession 3, 17, 116
OECD 2, 134
Oedipal crisis 56
Oksala, J. 72, 134
ontological(ly) 6, 18, 28, 41, 44, 47, 51, 66, 71, 76, 81, 98, 103, 124; autobiography 32; shift 120, 122
ontology 28, 47
open-ended 29, 36, 64–5
openness 39, 54–5, 67
open-system 22
opportunist 126
opportunity xv, 36, 41, 122, 126
oppression 5, 30, 35, 58, 62–3, 89–90, 123; internalized 43, 94; political 4–5, 21; psychological 3
optimistic 65
orality 82, 94, 123
organism 47, 51, 115
originality 66
origin(s) 10, 12, 22, 52
O'Rourke, K. 46, 130
outcome 18, 21, 94, 106, 117

outer-directed 8, 19, 27, 31–2, 35–7, 42, 76, 120

pain(ful) i, 1, 31, 34, 37, 39, 47, 49, 65, 86, 94–5, 97, 109, 115
Palmer, J. 83–8, 99, 135
paradox(es) 35, 37, 40, 65, 78, 105–6, 108, 120, 122
paradoxical(ly) 6, 25, 36, 39, 66, 79, 120, 127
paralyze 94, 105
parent(s) xii, 1–2, 20, 22–3, 37, 46, 50, 57, 61–2, 82, 86, 89–90, 92–5, 97–101, 103, 108–12, 117, 122, 125–6, 129, 136
Park, C. 36, 135
Park, G. 11, 135
Park, G. H. 117, 127
Park, J. H. 13, 15, 117
Park, S. J. 33, 135
Park, S. M. 11, 135
particularities 113
passive(ly) 35, 58, 114
passivity 67
past 4–5, 21, 28–30, 32, 51, 54, 62–3, 65, 76, 79, 87, 113, 133
pathological 48, 50, 65
patient(s) 83–4, 87, 95–8
patriarchal 67
Pavlov, I. P. 94
peace 114–16, 125, 136
peacefulness 36
pedagogical xvi, 42, 53, 80, 82; watchfulness 108, 125
pedagogy 29, 53, 113, 118, 131, 133, 135; poisonous 62, 64–5, 82, 123
perception(s) 11, 26, 33, 72, 132, 135
performance 4, 15, 94
persona 83–4, 88, 96, 98, 124
personal(ly) xi–xii, 1, 4, 12, 15, 20, 26, 31, 33–4, 36, 39, 40, 42, 45, 47, 50, 58, 64, 81, 83, 85–6, 108, 115, 122, 131, 132
pessimistic activism 71
Phelan, A. M. 3, 29, 31, 35, 118, 127, 135
phenomenological 26, 43, 52–3, 55, 75, 131; *epoché* 54; reduction 29, 54
phenomenology 28, 43, 53, 55, 67, 89, 132
philia 117
philosophical 6, 27–8, 44, 55, 72, 130

philosophy 22, 44–7, 52–3, 58–9, 66, 82, 95, 105, 110, 129, 131–6
physical 18–19, 21, 30, 33, 35, 46, 83, 85, 100, 108, 116, 120
Piaget, J. 14, 22
Pinar, W. F. xi, xii, xv, 3, 5, 8, 14, 17–21, 26–9, 31–5, 37–41, 43, 49, 52, 55–7, 60–1, 65–7, 71, 73–82, 89–91, 94, 96–7, 104–8, 117–25, 129, 133–6
planet 60, 107, 125
planning 27, 58
Plato 74
plebeians 11
poem xi, 1, 20–1, 91, 94, 123
poisonous 87; pedagogy 62, 64–5, 82, 123
political xii, 5–6, 9, 17, 23, 26, 76–7, 80, 99, 103, 114, 125, 131; arrest 19; conflict 127; control 19; courage 122; diversity 14; freedom 78, 106, 117; independence 122; oppression 3–5, 21; parties 12; structure 71, 73, 104–6; trap 4, 18, 20, 120; universalism 13
poor curriculum 26, 135
poor system 18
positivist 22
possibility 34, 36, 40–1, 52, 54–5, 61, 65–6, 71, 74–5, 94, 104, 116, 119, 121
power 12–13, 15, 33, 62, 76, 87, 91, 108, 116, 130; changes 126; external 39; relations 72; self-determination 40; self-disclosure 97–8; social 11
pragmatic 67; naturalism 47, 52
pragmatism 22, 47, 51, 55, 59, 67, 131; deconstructive 55
praxis 136; impossible 105
precondition 5
preconscious 27–8
predetermined 17, 22, 26
predicament(s) 49, 60, 123
preference(s) 4, 7, 91, 104, 114–16, 125
preordained goal 3
prerequisite 13–14, 29, 34, 54
prescriptive 41, 53, 60, 121
presence xvi, 19, 51, 53–5; passionate 115–16, 131
present xii, 4–5, 21, 27–31, 34, 40, 51, 55, 70–1, 73, 76, 79, 83, 86, 94, 133
pressure 1–2, 66, 112, 119
pride 2, 19
Prigogine 22, 130
primacy 5–6, 28, 32, 66–7, 69, 96, 104, 136

principle(s) 47–8, 54, 57, 59–60, 66, 71, 81, 95, 97, 102, 122–3, 131
prioritization 59
private 16, 38–9, 58, 83, 100, 116–17, 126; endeavor 5, 41, 81, 122; life 31, 39, 44–5, 66, 74, 84, 98; politics 106; study 75
problematic 19–21, 39, 81, 83
proclaiming 4, 109
proclamation of government 26, 75
productivity 3
professionalism 23
progressive 14, 22, 29–30, 45; education 66–7, 94; feminists 58
prohibition 79, 101
project xv, 5, 29–31, 35, 43, 49–50, 52, 58, 67, 75, 93, 105, 136
projection 52, 87
propaganda 66, 127
psyche 11, 88, 108, 135
psychiatrist 89, 109
psychiatry 28, 43, 98, 129, 132
psychic 5; events 111–13; intra 19–20
psychoanalysis 28–9, 67, 74, 136
psychoanalyst 62
psychoanalytic 28, 67, 104, 129; analysis 99; theory 96, 113
psychological(ly) xii, 2, 5–7, 11, 18–19, 26, 28, 31, 33, 35–6, 40, 45–57, 75–8, 95, 99, 108, 110, 113, 121–2; arrest 3, 32; change 45; constraints 20; consultation 39; process 85; schema 14; shift 41; stability 19; theories 27; trap 4–5
psychologist(s) 22, 100, 109
punishment 30, 34–5, 89–90, 110
pupil 21, 66

question(s) xiii, 14, 17, 19–23, 30–4, 36, 38, 42, 48–50, 61–2, 65, 68, 71, 73, 77, 79, 85–6, 94–6, 103–5, 107, 110–13, 116, 119–21, 126, 135; thorny 111

Rabinow, P. 71–2, 130–1, 136
race 17, 56, 91
raison d'être 14, 21–2
rationality 2–3, 18, 22, 59; instrumental 78–9
Rauch, A. 76, 136
Raveis, V. H. 17, 132
rebirth 37
reception 52
receptive 55, 60, 81, 97, 127

receptive-intuitive mode 53–4
reciprocity 6, 25, 27, 34, 37, 41–5, 59, 63–4, 81, 101, 129
reconceptualization 26, 132, 135
reconstruction 6, 25, 27, 30, 34, 40–1, 68, 79, 120, 126; of self 40
recursive 30, 41, 65, 121
reflection xiii, 3, 7, 30, 64, 66, 74, 84, 130, 133; self 28, 36, 43, 51, 65, 73, 97, 121, 123
reflective practitioner 3, 136
regressive 11, 29–30, 34–5
regulation(s) 15, 93, 127; auto 22
rehabilitate 5, 20, 107
Reich, G. A. 23, 136
reinforce(ment) 50, 78, 90, 121
relational xii, 47, 59, 63, 67, 81, 97, 122, 134; autonomy 51; ethic 52; selves 66
relationality 50, 67, 132
relationship(s) xiii, 7, 12, 20, 27, 31, 35, 37–8, 48, 50, 60, 66, 72, 74, 76, 78–9, 85–6, 92–3, 99–101, 103–4, 107, 109, 114, 116–17, 119–20, 122–5, 127, 129, 136; abusive 81; authentic 26, 80; caring 48, 52, 54–5, 61, 63, 66; creative xii, 71, 73; dialectical 25, 41, 43, 54, 120; dynamic 105; false 116; inauthentic 5, 75; I-Thou 53; light 114; mutual 41; parent–child 61; reciprocal 27, 63–4; self-other 6, 81–2, 96, 102; self-reflective 32; self–self 5–7, 72–3, 81, 83–4, 89, 98, 102, 120–1, 124; structural 105; teaching-learning 55
renewal 37
repression 3
reproduction 14, 78, 105, 122, 130; social 17
research 2, 15, 22, 27, 45, 60, 89, 93, 119, 126, 129, 131–4, 136–7; method(ologies) 14, 29; scientific 18
researcher 11, 27
resistance 30, 34–6, 38, 40, 72, 77, 96, 105, 110, 122, 125
responsibility 17–18, 22, 36, 40, 70
responsive(ness) 64, 70–1
reward(s) 3, 16, 50, 69, 94, 111, 117
Reynolds, W. M. 43, 136
risk 37, 40, 51, 63, 103, 109, 120, 124, 132; beautiful 18, 55, 118, 129; global 136
robots 18
Rodriguez, A. J. 42, 136

role(s) 3, 7, 26, 29, 41–2, 51–2, 56–7, 59, 65, 71, 87–8, 95–6, 101, 121, 127; administrative 13; gender 50; hakbeolism 15; social 39
room 30, 84–5, 87
Ruddick, S. 50, 136
rule(s) xii, 71, 84, 93, 105, 107, 109–10, 117, 124–5; constitutive 4; disciplinary 109; own 90, 98, 124; universal 59, 122

sacrifice 14, 23, 50, 52, 61, 65, 66, 69, 103, 106, 115, 124
sadist 89
salvation 79
sameness 60, 123
sanity 31, 89–90, 94, 135
scapegoating 3
scars 23
schizophrenic 90
Schön, D. A. 3, 136
schooling 94–5, 107, 125, 134, 136; American 89, 123
school(s) xi, 2–4, 8–10, 14, 17, 20, 22–3, 26, 28, 43, 45, 46, 54, 58, 75, 89, 92, 94–5, 100, 110, 112, 117, 119, 126, 131, 133–6; deforms 5; high 1, 10, 34, 46, 109; informal 15; Korean 93; middle 117; reforms 67
scientific 17, 22; curriculum 15; development 16; norms 89; research 18
screaming 1
second life 26, 130
secret(s) 22, 98, 101, 132
Seidler, D. 88, 96, 98, 136
selection system 13, 22, 24
self xi–xii, 7–8, 19, 26–8, 30–4, 36, 39–41, 43–4, 47, 51, 62–3, 68–4, 79, 82, 88, 90–1, 94–5, 98–100, 103–4, 106–8, 111, 114, 116, 125–6, 130–5; absorption 70; actualization 65, 81, 88; affirmation 104, 124, 127; affirmative 97; analysis 63; arrested 32, 34, 40, 43, 120; authentic 80; autobiography 43; awareness 36; care xii, 5–8, 44, 68, 69, 73, 76–8, 79, 81–2, 99, 102–4, 108–9, 113–14, 116, 119–22, 124, 125–7; conscious 36, 43, 65, 107, 121; cultivation 75, 82, 95; denial 50; determination 17, 40; development, xii; disclosure 73, 97–8; essentialized 106; estranged 91; formation 26, 75, 116; formative 97; forming 72; hatred 90; inner 32, 35, 57; knowledge 25, 58, 75, 80; liberated 39; love 108; mortification 106; motivation 110; negation 106; other relationship 6, 81, 82, 102; outer-directed 37; purification 79; realization 96, 124; referential 25, 72; reflection 28, 43, 51, 65, 73, 97, 121; reflective 43, 51; reflexive 40; relational 47; renunciation 74, 79–80, 103–4, 127; report 43; respect 78, 94, 108, 122; sacrifice 50, 69; searching 75; self relationship 5–7, 72–3, 77, 81–4, 89, 96–8, 102, 120–1, 124; study 38; transformatively 28; understanding 5–7, 21, 28, 31, 34, 39, 41, 44, 63–5, 68, 73–8, 80–1, 110, 119–20, 122–4
semantic environment 7, 91–5, 99–100, 124
Seneca 81, 102
sensitivity 4, 26, 35, 117
Seoul University 10, 16, 20, 131
sequence 103
servitude 50, 104
Seth, M. J. 90, 119, 136
Sewol ferry 127
sexuality 29, 43, 135
sexual orientation 17, 56, 61
shadow 23, 58, 83–4, 86, 88, 133; education 22; educators 117; eruption 87; work 84, 86–8, 97
shame 19, 30
Shell, M. 92–3, 100, 136
shortsighted 47, 122
signal(s) 32, 34–5, 46, 52
significant(ly) 11, 37, 43, 59, 97, 99, 110; others 5, 78, 86, 89–91, 94, 122–3
signifier 36
silence 100, 115–16, 133, 135
sincerity 66
Singapore 66
skeptical 114
skills 2–3, 14, 16–17, 20, 44, 61, 94
skin color 21
Skinner, B. F. 14, 94
Slattery, P. 26, 130, 136
smart phone 116
snob 45
social(ly) 2, 10, 12, 15–16, 19, 31, 37, 54, 56, 71, 73, 76–7, 91, 93, 116, 125–6, 130–4, 136; animals 52; authoritarianism 19–20; authority 11; capital 8–10; conditioning 20; constraints xii; construction 26; Darwinism 16, 95, 120; discrimination 11; engineering 61;

ideology 16; inequity 11; norms 63; power 11; problem 11; psychology 89, 113; relations 59, 82, 103, 127; reproduction 14, 17; role(s) 39; science 18; service 5, 82; status 2, 4, 9, 12, 13, 83, 119; stratification 16; structure(s) 5, 10–11, 16, 21, 68, 104–5; studies 23; submission 106
socialization 56–7, 72
societal 2–3, 8–9, 15, 17, 79
society 4, 9, 11, 16, 19, 22, 24, 43, 46–7, 62, 70, 72, 92, 103, 105, 116, 120, 125, 130, 132–3, 135–6; Ancient Greek 79; clan 11, 120; credential 9–10; democratic 117; hakbeol 11, 23; John Dewey 46; Korean 4, 10–11, 15, 20, 23, 70, 119; modern 59; stratified 2
sociologist 12–13
sociology 2, 129, 133
Socrates xii, 64, 68–70, 73, 123, 130
solicitude 49, 53
solidarity 13
solitude 7, 25, 27, 29, 41, 81, 122
son 12, 40, 49, 89
Son, J. H. 13, 17, 136
sorrow xi
soul(s) xi, 1, 21, 49, 68, 73, 90, 94, 110; caring 50; dispensary 95; murder 63, 111; practice 81; service 103
space(s) xiii, 33–4, 104, 107, 116, 123, 125–7, 133; third 75, 106, 127
Spector, H. 126, 136
speech(es) 7, 82–3, 85, 87–9, 91–3, 97–8, 100–1, 109, 123, 132, 137
spirituality 104
Ssanggi 22
stammer(ring) xii, 7, 83, 86, 88, 93–4, 96, 99–101
standardization 77, 93
standard(s) 8, 18, 22, 77, 92, 100, 111–12, 121, 131; creative 80; external xi, 5, 122; imposed 78, 122; own xii, 7, 68, 76–8, 121–2; standardized tests 9, 17, 23, 93, 117
Starbucks 34
starvation 116
stasis 5, 19, 33, 37, 41
status 6, 16, 86; hierarchical 9, 119, 127; infantilized 122; institutionalized 3; social 2, 4, 8–10, 12–13, 83, 119; subordinate 58; undervalued 106
status society 9
stereotype 127

Stone, L. 45–7, 52–3, 55, 122, 136
strategy 98
stratification 4, 10, 16, 70
stress 20, 93, 129, 133; academic 2, 66
structure(s) 5, 52, 54, 58, 78, 104; constraining 105, 120; economic 105; of education 4; of knowledge 14, 22; oppressive 7, 104–7, 112, 116, 121–2, 124–5; political 71, 73, 105–6; social 11, 16, 21, 68
struggle(s) xii, 12, 20, 31, 40, 71, 74, 84, 106, 113, 116, 123–4, 126
student(s) xii, xv, 1–4, 6, 14–24, 26, 28, 34, 40, 42, 44–6, 52–3, 60–4, 66–7, 77–8, 89–90, 92–5, 97–101, 110–13, 117–18, 120–1, 123–6, 131–2; freedom 106; graduate 31; institutionalization 99; international 33; Korean 14, 38
study(ing) xi–xii, xv, 2–3, 5–7, 11–12, 15, 17–20, 22–3, 25–31, 33, 35, 37–42, 60, 66, 68, 73–80, 90, 92, 95–7, 105–7, 110, 113, 116–17, 120–1, 125–6, 132–3, 135–6; autobiographical 68, 73, 119; unethical 100
stultitia 81, 102
stupidity 81, 102, 117
subjectivation 71, 73
subjective 25–6, 42, 54, 106, 125; disintegration 43; endeavor 6; experience 3; meaning 105; reconstruction 25, 27, 68, 120, 126
subjectivity(ies) xi–xii, 3–8, 11–14, 17, 19, 24–5, 27–8, 30, 33–5, 37–8, 40, 41–4, 56, 60, 64–8, 74–82, 90, 94, 105–7, 110, 119–20, 123, 126–7, 130–1, 136; arrested 31; collective 21; first-person 32, 121
subject(s) 14–15, 24, 34, 38, 43, 46, 52, 59, 64, 71–2, 77, 98, 105, 110, 117, 122, 129–30, 135; female 60; hermeneutic 69, 81; school 93; specialists 3, 18

theoretical xvi, 6, 27–8, 44, 58, 68
theorization 79, 120
therapeutic 73, 87, 95; treatment 62, 108
thinking 8, 13, 21, 45, 49–50, 53, 55–6, 60, 64, 66, 82, 95–6, 104–5, 113, 123; conformity 65; critical 48, 51; educational 51; identificatory 111–12; maternal 136; passionate 35; re(un) 65, 104, 125–6
third space 33–4, 75, 106, 125, 127

152 Index

Thorndike, E. 94
thought(s) 13, 17, 30, 32, 34, 37, 41, 52, 56, 69, 74, 76, 84, 88, 109, 111, 115–16, 135–6; contemporary 35; Haewol 68, 79
threefold 111
Tokyo University 16
tolerance 37, 113
tolerating 36, 112
totalitarian 62
tragedy 1–2, 7, 62, 127
transcendent function 86, 99
transformation xii, 54, 76, 88, 119
transformational 22
transformative(ly) 22; education 26; self 28
transformativity 22
transformatory 22
transform(ed) 11, 22, 33, 35, 54, 89, 98, 103, 112, 123, 127
translate(d) 21, 29, 46, 110, 117
translation 29, 131
trap(ped) xi, 6, 8, 19, 63, 90, 109; intellectual 18, 20, 77, 120; political 18, 20, 77, 120; psychological 4, 5; winner-loser 16
trauma(s) 8, 28, 85–6, 100
traumatized 45, 112
treatment 78, 84–5, 93, 95–6, 98, 101, 108–9, 131
"The Trial" (Pinar) 18–19, 27, 31
Trueit, D. xv, 29, 35
trust(ful) xii, 84, 114
Tyler, R. 14–15, 22, 27, 60–1
tyranny 16, 20, 44

umso 12
Umsorge 53
uncanny 91
uncertainty 20, 33, 36, 105
unchanging 5
uncomfortable 20, 33, 38, 106
unconditional 48
unconscious(ness) 3, 19, 27–8, 32, 85, 97, 99–100, 111
unconstitutional 15, 23
uncritical(ly) 37, 48
understanding 4, 5–7, 14–15, 21, 27–9, 31–41, 43, 44, 48, 55, 61, 63, 64–83, 96–7, 100, 106–8, 110–14, 116, 119–26, 129, 132, 135–6
undifferentiated 56
unethical 70, 100
unforeseeable 55, 66
unification 22

uniformity 60, 123, 126
uniqueness 42, 59–60, 90, 122, 124
United States 16, 27, 77, 106
universalism 13
university application 14
unlearn(ing) 7, 26, 64, 75–6, 82, 95, 121, 123, 136
unrealistic 126
unspecified 55
untrained surgeon 5
urbanization 22

Valente, J. 117, 129
venture 126
victim(s) 91, 119, 127
violence 58, 62, 90, 94, 100, 104, 112, 115, 132
vitality xi, 11, 40
vocational 34, 132
voice xii, xvi, 3–5, 30–2, 44, 58, 78, 82–3, 88, 94, 96–9, 123, 129, 131–3; authentic 80–1, 124, 127; inner 47, 81, 94–5, 104; stammering 7
voiceless 87

Wang, H. xii, 26, 33, 36, 75, 102–4, 106, 125, 127, 136
waste 23, 66, 88
weak 18, 55, 97, 122
weaken(ed) 11, 24, 83, 94, 117, 126
weakness 18
weapon(s) 62, 107–8
well-being 7
whip of love 110, 125
winner 16, 109
Winnicott, D. W. 111–12, 136–7
women 11, 45, 50, 56–60, 67, 70, 104, 127, 133, 135
Wonhyo 33, 135
Woolf, V. 104, 125, 127, 137
work(s) xii, xv, 2–10, 13, 16–17, 19–28, 30–2, 34–5, 37–3, 45–6, 53, 55–7, 65–7, 69, 71–5, 77–9, 81, 84–8, 96–7, 99, 101, 103–4, 106, 111–13, 115, 120–7, 129–30, 132; Art 72, 77, 104, 112–13, 121, 125; *currere* 5–6, 8, 25, 28, 412, 79, 111, 120
Wrathall, M. 54, 137

Yairi, E. 93, 137
Yonsei University 10, 16, 23
Yoon, S. 15, 23, 132
Youngs, P. 17, 131

Zimmerman, G. 92, 137